Fly Fishing AUSTIN

IMBRIFEX
BOOKS

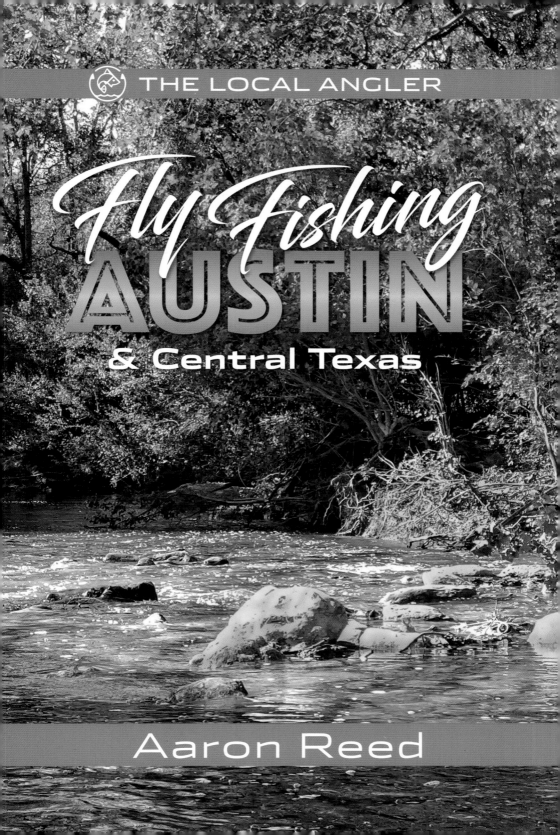

Fly Fishing AUSTIN
& Central Texas

Aaron Reed

IMBRIFEX BOOKS
8275 S. Eastern Avenue, Suite 200
Las Vegas, NV 89123
Imbrifex.com

Fly Fishing Austin & Central Texas

Editor: Victoria Adang
Cover and Book Designer: Sue Campbell Book Design
Maps: Chris Erichsen
Cover Photos: Erich Schlegel
All interior photos by the author except as noted on page 370

Library of Congress Cataloging-in-Publication Data

Names: Reed, Aaron, 1969- author.
Title: Fly Fishing Austin & Central Texas / Aaron Reed.
Description: First edition. | Las Vegas, NV : Imbrifex Books, 2020. | Series: The local angler |
    Includes index. | Summary: "It may be a "best-kept secret," but central Texas has some of the best
    fly fishing in America. With Texas native and fly fishing expert Aaron Reed as your guide, enjoy
    dozens of wades and paddles, all within easy reach of Austin. Discover secluded spring creeks
    braced by soaring limestone cliffs. Wade in broad pools dotted with lily pads and stands of water
    willow. Paddle deep, slow rivers. Easy-to-follow narrative, detailed maps, and gorgeous color
    photographs make it easy to "Go fishing now!" even if you have only a few hours to spare. There's
    something for every angler in central Texas. Visit the nation's southernmost trout fishery on the
    Canyon Lake tailwaters. Find seven species in a single day, including the native Guadalupe bass
    and the only cichlid native to the United States. "Fly Fishing Austin and Central Texas" is your
    passport to the challenges and rewards of angling in this unique and beautiful region"—Provided
    by publisher.
Identifiers: LCCN 2019036694 (print) | LCCN 2019036695 (ebook) | ISBN 9781945501241
    (paperback) | ISBN 9781945501258 (epub)
Subjects: LCSH: Fly fishing—Texas.
Classification: LCC SH456 .R435 2020 (print) | LCC SH456 (ebook) | DDC 799.12/409764--dc23
LC record available at https://lccn.loc.gov/2019036694
LC ebook record available at https://lccn.loc.gov/2019036695

First Edition: May 2020
Printed in the Republic of South Korea
IMBRIFEX® is registered trademark of Flattop Productions, Inc.
flyfishingaustin.thelocalangler.com | Imbrifex.com

Come & fish it!
Aaron

For my three sons:
Patrick, Conor, and Aidan.
Never stop exploring.

CONTENTS

Come & fish it!

Aaru

WHAT THIS BOOK IS ALL ABOUT

"I don't know exactly what fly fishing teaches us, but I think it's something we need to know."

—JOHN GIERACH, *Sex, Death, and Fly-Fishing*

NONE OF US IS BORN WITH A FLY ROD IN OUR HANDS. SOME lucky few acquire them along with first steps, or language, but the rest of us pick them up much later in life.

My own journey started with conventional gear on the Texas Gulf Coast, in neighborhood ponds, and on Texas Hill Country streams during summer vacations. Somewhere along the way, I became aware of the exotic subspecies of angler that favored ridiculously long and bendy rods. From there, it was a short leap to the conclusion that all that fancy twirling was just an elaborate Yankee way of showing off.

My godfather—an uncle who was a born waterman, lifelong angler, and onetime tackle shop owner—confirmed my suspicions. "Fly fishing ain't about catching fish," he told me. "It's about communing with the water column."

It turns out my uncle was right, though maybe not in exactly the way he meant. Fly fishing, for me, is certainly about catching fish, and I'm a little disappointed when I don't, but I can't recall a single day on the water that was time misspent.

There is so much else going on: the wildlife sneaking onto the scene, the temperamental moods of a stream, the changing of its bed since the last rain, that distinctive scent of hard water and sycamore and cypress, the never-ending quest to produce casts that appear effortless and graceful. Sometimes just the sounds of the water and birdsong and the absence of any other noise recharge my batteries.

I moved to the Austin area in 1995 and have been here ever since, with brief sojourns back to the coast, including a year chasing snook and redfish for money in deep South Texas and finding out firsthand just how hard professional fishing guides work. Reservist call-ups to three continents also took me away a couple of times. I kept returning to Austin, but for a long time I thought I'd eventually make my way back to Rockport, where I grew up and where redfish roam the flats.

The moving waters in the middle of the state won't let me go.

Each angler has his or her own reasons for fishing, or for fishing in a particular way. Yours may include family tradition, the thrill of the chase, a desire to experience nature as a participant, the determination to master an exacting discipline, or something else entirely.

My reasons include all of those, and my something else is a deep need for contemplative restoration.

I carry in my memory a series of snapshots, scenes dated 1996, 1998, 2003, 2005, 2008: a mass grave site near Srebrenica, burning houses, and a farmer's 9-year-old son, his leg severed by a land mine blast; an entire mountainside village splintered by a mudslide triggered by Hurricane Mitch; my divorce and a string of bad decisions that I barely escaped alive; a series of horrific child abuse and neglect cases from my time working at the Texas Department of Family and Protective Services; Hurricane Ike and the urgent search for survivors and then victims.

The author with a Guadalupe River stocker.

It could be that any one of those experiences, or the weight of all of them, has left me with an unquiet mind and a darkness that dogs me like a shadow. Or maybe I was born glum and anxious. Whatever the cause of my ailment, I have found fly fishing to be the perfect tonic. Sometimes it's the only effective treatment. So far as my wife knows, it's cheaper than therapy.

The Local Angle

When I first moved to Central Texas, I would throw my 6-weight at carp by way of practicing for monthly trips back to the coast. Eventually, I downsized my tackle and turned my attention to smaller and more reliably willing quarry. I discovered that a 12-inch Guadalupe bass on a 2- or 3-weight rod is every bit as much fun to trick as a broad-shouldered, 28-inch redfish on an 8-weight—and considerably less work. Now you couldn't peel me away from this land of limestone and clear, fast-running water for love or money.

Cory Sorel plays a winter bass on the South Gabe.

Fortunately, there is a lot of that water around here. Austin, that formerly weird town, is also geographically unique in that it straddles a major geologic fault. The eastern side of the metro area is firmly planted in Blackland Prairie, while the west side clings to the ridges and rimrock canyons of the Edwards Plateau. This rugged limestone formation merges with several uplifts to create the Texas Hill Country, a region of plateaus and prominences, some technically qualifying as small mountains. Beneath it, the Edwards and Trinity aquifers store and transport vast amounts of cool, filtered water that bubbles up in the most extraordinary places.

The dividing line between the Hill Country and the prairie follows the line of annual rainfall: less than 30 inches in the western region, rather more in the east. The dividing line also follows, almost exactly, the course of I-35 from just north of San Antonio all the way to Fort Worth. To the west of this north-south artery, you will find canyons and rangeland. To the east, you'll find farms laid across gently rolling hills. East of the interstate, roughly speaking, is the Deep South, and west is, well, "the West." Dallas is a southern city. Fort Worth is a western city.

Austin bridges both worlds and has its own unique culture colored by its famous music scene, half a dozen colleges and universities, a growing collection of craft breweries and distilleries, and, more recently, a dash of hipster sophistication courtesy of the latest wave of newcomers from both coasts. Hang out here long enough and you'll hear plenty of griping about that influx of coastal refugees, but the truth is, it's just the same as it ever was.

The Fly Fishing Community

Fly fishing has a long history in Austin. There have always been anglers here who traveled far and wide to stand in a river (or on the flats) and wave a stick, and in 1980, Texas's first fly shop—The Austin Angler—opened on South Congress Avenue. Ernest Hemingway's granddaughter Mina owned it for a while. It was a lovely little haven, situated in an historic building above a Mexican restaurant. The fly shop closed its doors in July 2004, but Manuel's is still going strong.

Today there is a world-class, dedicated fly fishing shop in Round Rock; an independent sporting goods store in southwest Austin with a robust fly fishing section; an Orvis store midtown; and three fly shops along the Guadalupe River between Canyon Lake and Gruene. Five of the state's nineteen fly fishing clubs meet between Waco and New Braunfels, and there are two more just west of the metro area in the Hill Country and one in San Antonio. (For a complete rundown of local shops, guides, and

Fly shops are much more than retailers; they also are cultural centers and social hubs for the local community.

clubs, see the **Appendices** page 351.)

So far as I can tell, two things contributed to the early interest in fly fishing around here: reasonable prox-imity to stellar flats fishing for redfish on the middle Texas Gulf Coast, and the establishment of the nation's southernmost year-round trout fish-ery in the tailwaters of Canyon Lake. An historic 2001 agreement between Guadalupe River Trout Unlimited and the Guadalupe–Blanco River Authority established minimum daily releases during the summer months during non-drought years.

With the local coldwater fishery already well-established, the more recent growth in fly fishing in Central

The warmwater stream fishing in Central Texas is, simply put, outstanding.

Texas is due to an increased appreciation for the quality of the warmwa-ter fisheries here. Unlike many western rivers, which may be salmonid monocultures, our streams boast half a dozen challenging (and increas-ingly esteemed) species of game fish, several of which are found nowhere else in the world in their native habitats.

Howler Brothers and YETI are headquartered in Austin and fre-quently host fly fishing-related events. Makers like Dustin Scott of Heart Wood Trade (his handcrafted landing nets earned him finalist honors in the *Garden & Gun* "Made in the South" awards in 2018), bamboo rod maker Craig Dunlavey of Williamannette Rod Co., Thomas and Megan Flemons of Diablo Paddlesports, and artists Edgar Diaz of Sight Line Provisions, Nathan Brown, and Alana Louise Lyons are all part of a homegrown fly fishing culture that, I am told by anglers from other places, is unlike any other in the country.

You can find a public fly-tying night somewhere in the area nearly every week of the year. Some weeks you'll have choices. One thing you won't find is a lot of competition or misdirection; maybe it's because we are still young as a fly fishing destination, but most folks around here are still Texas-friendly and happy to welcome newcomers to our waters. Between the fly shops, beer gardens, and streams, you'll probably meet at least a few friendly local anglers, some of them as quirky as Austin itself. If you are

There are a variety of waters to explore in and around Austin: everything from spring creeks to broad, meandering rivers.

new to the area and you post a query in the Texas Freshwater Fly Fishing group on Facebook, *someone* will offer to take you fishing. Guaranteed.

The Waters

There is so much good water around Austin, it was difficult to decide what to include in the book and what to *exclude*. In the end, I chose to focus on waters that are within roughly an hour's drive of the city (for a guide to some more westerly waters, see Kevin Hutchison's *Fly Fishing the Texas Hill Country*). I also opted to describe a variety of rivers and creeks that, taken together, provide experiences that a wide range of anglers can appreciate. In these pages you will find 104 legal access points on eighteen rivers, streams, and creeks, and forty-nine detailed route descriptions ("wades") on twelve of those streams. Whether it's an overlooked access point, an abundance of a particular species, an outstanding natural feature or view, or a bit of history to ponder, there is something of value here for everyone.

Most of these are smaller waters, suitable for walk/wade trips or a half-day paddle in a kayak or canoe. The Colorado River (and here I mean the *Texas* Colorado, not the one that has wild trout in its upper reaches and carved the Grand Canyon) is big water and is best paddled or floated. The San Marcos River is not especially large, but it's fast and deep and also is best floated. Most of the other streams are dealer's choice.

What I have *not* included are waters that require a motorized boat or a guide. Either will expand your opportunities, and hands down the best way to gain insider knowledge of a particular local water is to book a guide. A guide can also improve your fly fishing game. But the emphasis of this book is on DIY self-sufficiency because that's how I fish. In fact, it's how most Texas anglers fish.

Most of my fishing trips are pickup trips: I'll have half a day or even just a few hours to call my own, and I'll have a rough idea of which stream I want to explore, so I throw a rod and a box of flies in the Jeep and go. If I remember to put a bottle of water in my pack and make sure my phone is charged before I leave, I'm ahead of the game.

Of course, behind those spur-of-the-moment dashes to the water are two decades of experience fishing and exploring Central Texas, countless late nights poring over *The Roads of Texas* and maps on Google Earth, and a whole bunch of trips that ended in disappointment when I got to a crossing that looked good on paper (or, more often of late, the screen) but was impassable when I got there.

Going fishing around here is as simple as driving to the access point, parking, and getting in the water.

The point of this book is to provide a shortcut through all that stuff. If you are new to fly fishing or new to the Austin area, this book provides the information you need to get out there *right now.* Hopefully, veteran anglers will find some pleasant surprises, and everyone will use the book as a jumping-off point for their own explorations.

While I hope this guide is comprehensive, it is not exhaustive. Unavoidably, it also is subjective. These are some of *my* favorite waters: Some I discovered on my own, others are locally well-known, and still others were recommended by generous friends. Enterprising anglers no doubt will discover their own special places, some not listed here. Rivers also change. Some fish better one month or year than another. Everything I have presented in these pages is accurate at the time of publication, and I have concentrated on structures and features that I've seen year after year, but the next big rain could rearrange one or more streambeds.

How This Book Is Organized

While the choice of waters is not entirely arbitrary, the way they are pre-sented in this volume pretty much is. It seemed logical to organize des-tinations north to south, and upstream to downstream (notwithstanding the fact that most anglers prefer to wade upstream). Thus, you will find the northernmost spots at the beginning of the book, waters within the metro area in the middle, and the southern destinations in the final third.

Each chapter covers a particular body of water and includes several outings from different access points. Some routes can be combined for longer wades or paddles—just remember to reverse engineer landmarks and directions if traveling opposite from the direction I have described in the text.

You will find three maps in this book, plus an area map on the inside back cover. These maps are designed to orient you to the area and to each section (North, Central, South) of the book and note access points, detailed routes, fly shops, and hangouts; all 104 access points are shown on the area map on the inside rear cover. The numbers shown on the maps correspond with the forty-nine detailed route descriptions, which are called "wades" for this book. A "wade" could be done on foot, or in a kayak, or a canoe.

For convenience, the starting point for every fishing trip is downtown Austin. The iconic bronze statue of Stevie Ray Vaughan at Auditorium Shores on Lady Bird Lake (like many longtime residents, I still slip up and call it "Town Lake") is our zero point. All road mileage and drive times are calculated from that location, assuming the most direct route from the statue in usual traffic conditions. During rush hour, on holidays, or during music festivals, all bets are off; in those cases, your favorite mapping application will be your best guide.

You will see references in many chapters to farm-to-market (FM) and ranch-to-market (RM) roads, also referred to as "Farm Roads" and "Ranch Roads." These are paved, usually two-lane, secondary highways maintained by the state. Established in 1949 as a way for agricultural workers to get their products to market, the network now spans more than 50,000 miles. Some of the roads have been engulfed by growing urban areas but retain their rural designations. Generally, these highways are designated Ranch Roads west of US 281 and Farm Roads east of US 281. There are exceptions, and Farm Roads and Ranch Roads never share a number. In real life, a Farm Road or Ranch Road will be marked by a square sign with the shape of Texas and the road number; on the overview maps in this book, these routes (and county roads and park roads) are marked by a circle with the number.

Access points are identified by latitude and longitude coordinates, which can be plugged into Google Maps or another navigation app. The coordinates are usually pinned to the parking location; there may be a bit of a hike from the parking lot to the access point. Street addresses are also provided; these are more approximate than the coordinates but are helpful when trying to navigate unfamiliar roads.

Coordinates are also given for some of the most important river features, such as park boundaries, dangerous dams, and bald eagle nests. You might want to plug them into your phone before you set out.

Four icons identify the types of fishing available from each access point.

 Wade   Bank   Paddle   Handicapped Access

In the trip descriptions these are ordered according to what I view as the most suitable means of fishing the water; for example, if wade fishing makes the most sense but the reach can be paddled with some work, you'll see the wading icon first, and the paddling icon second. Where there is reasonably good access for anglers with mobility challenges, I have noted that, but the locations probably are not ADA-compliant.

Difficulty ratings. Ratings, ranging from "Easy" through "Difficult," are subjective; they take into account such things as how much scrambling you have to do to get up or down a riverbank, how far you have to walk to the water, and how secure the footing is in the stream. For paddles, portages and drags add to the difficulty rating.

Distances and directions. General distance references to features such as the origin of a stream or its confluence with another river, or to that town over yonder, are given in miles as the mockingbird flies. Road miles will almost certainly be greater, and never fewer. Drive times are averages and will vary with traffic conditions.

All river distances are calculated from the given access point in the direction of the suggested wade (or paddle). The "river miles" noted follow the twists and turns of a given stream but do not include backtracking, side trips up backwaters or tributaries, or all of the zigs and zags required to cast to every promising bit of water.

References to "river right" and "river left" follow the convention used

This reach of Brushy Creek is gorgeous and full of fish.

by rafters and kayakers and mean the right or left bank in the direction of stream flow, i.e., **as you are looking downstream**. Because I often prefer to wade and fish upstream, you may have to reverse engineer some of the references. Where appropriate, I refer to "your left" or "your right" and the "north bank" and "south bank," just to be clear.

Music. What would an Austin fishing book be without music? The "Listening To" note in each chapter offers a title from my "Fly Fishing Austin" playlist, a collection of songs I listen to when I'm headed to the river. You can hear some of these artists on a weeknight in Austin for less than $20 (pro tip: for local, live music, weeknights rule). Look for the "Fly Fishing Austin" playlist on Google Music, Pandora, Spotify, and iTunes, or build your own!

Hangouts. Fly fishing often enough is a solitary pursuit; at the very least, it's one in which you expect to have a decent buffer zone between you and the next guy or gal on the water. The mechanics of a cast pretty much demand it. But anglers of every stripe also like to get together when the fishing is done and talk about the ones they caught, the ones they lost, and the ones they missed. Sometimes this happens in person. Often it happens on social media. But reliving the day over a cold, freshly drawn pint (or a bottle of Topo Chico) will enhance the conversation.

I emphatically am *not* recommending that anyone spend a long day on the water and then an equally long evening in a bar before driving home. That would be stupid. And irresponsible. And possibly criminal. I *am* suggesting that if you want to check out the state of local craft brewing, and you are wearing damp shorts and flip-flops and your hands smell a little funny, these are great places to sit for a spell and reflect on your day with a cold beverage or a hot meal. Just be smart about it; taxis, rideshares, and designated drivers are available throughout the metro area.

At the end of the day, the most important thing is to have fun. Really, please enjoy yourself. If you're not walking out of a stream with a smile on your face, or feeling at least a little more at peace with yourself and the world around you, you're not doing it right.

Keep practicing. You'll get there.

 Something to Love, Jason Isbell and the 400 Unit

First Things

Chapter 1

The Lowdown on Fly Fishing

IF IT'S NOT CLEAR ALREADY, LET ME JUST SAY IT: I THINK *everyone* should have the opportunity to take a walk with a fly rod, and the sooner and the more often, the better. If you have been at it a while, you already know why and you also can probably safely skip ahead a few pages to one of those streams you've always wondered about but haven't had a chance to wade yet.

If you are just getting into the sport, or if you've been away for a while and need a refresher, or if you are new to warmwater fly fishing in general or Central Texas in particular, then this and the following two chapters are for you.

When to Fish Central Texas Waters

I sometimes pretend I am a gentleman of leisure. The fact is, I have a full-time job as a merchant mariner, and I am away from home half the year. Along with my shipmates, I pack fifty-four 40-hour workweeks into my 183 days on the tugboat and try not to think about what that means for my hourly rate of pay. The flip side is that I don't bring work home with me ever, and six months of my year are dedicated to family and fishing. It's sort of like being retired a week at a time, every other week. Or like having only half as much of a life as everyone else. I'm still trying to work out which one it is.

The point is, I fish when I can: when the moon is full and when it is new, when it is warm and when it is cool, when it is sunny and when it is overcast. It helps that most of our warmwater species aren't waiting on a particular hatch to ring the dinner bell. I had a terrific hour-long fishing session between rain bands during a tropical storm in 2017. I've had some spectacular days in the depths of winter, and I have experienced explosive topwater action in the middle of a bright summer day.

> "I believe that the solution to any problem—work, love, money, whatever—is to go fishing, and the worse the problem, the longer the trip should be. And I'm also certain that on the day I become a truly sublime fly-fisher, all my failings will be overshadowed and all my demons will swim under rocks and stay there until I go away."
>
> JOHN GIERACH, *Standing in a River Waving a Stick*

Common sense suggests that in the dog days of summer, fish might be more active in the mornings and evenings; conversely, during the cooler months, a warm, sunny afternoon might bring fish out from underneath the banks and up from the deepest pools.

From sometime in November through March or so, the largemouth bass bite slows down (this has at least a little to do with the introduction of Florida bass; our native, northern largemouths will eat in water temperatures all the way down into the 40s), but you can still find and catch some lunkers. You'll just have to work a little harder for them. Guadalupe bass eat well enough all year long, and most local anglers agree they catch bigger fish during the cooler months; the current world record Guad was caught on a fly on February 1, 2014.

Late fall through early spring, many fly fishers here switch their focus to trout on the Guadalupe River, and from late February through most of March, the white bass run above area reservoirs is the star attraction. By the time the sand bass have returned to the lakes, all of the other fish are becoming active again. Sunfish and carp are always around and willing to eat, though they, too, slow down during the colder months.

The point is, you can almost always find a willing dance partner for the end of your fly line. Just go fishing. Whenever you can. Don't let perfect be the enemy of good enough. Just go. Nine out of ten doctors who fly fish agree: it's good for you!

Barring thunderstorms or heavy, prolonged rainfall, a little precipitation is no excuse not to get on the water. The fish are already wet.

Ethical Angling

I'm all for anyone fishing any old way that is legal and ethical and respects the resource—both the fish and the environments they live in. My choice these days is to fish with flies and to practice catch and release on 99 percent of my freshwater outings, but I realize that each angler's journey is unique and we all grow into the sport in our own way. I find that *my* occasional feelings of self-righteous indignation interfere more with my enjoyment of the experience than does *your* occasional decision to lip a bass (or lay it on the grass) for a photo op. That said, I'll encourage you, nicely, I hope, not to do that.

Although it is not required on any of our warmwater streams, I tie my flies on barbless hooks and crush the barbs on the hooks of purchased flies. Before that was my practice, I inadvertently killed more than one fish that took a fly just a bit too deep. It made me feel lousy. It's also easier to get barbless hooks out of clothing, ears, eyebrows, and the back of your neck.

In my opinion, ethical use of the waters in Central Texas includes abiding by the following guidelines:

- **Fish legally.** Get a license (fees support all sorts of great programs that benefit fisheries and anglers). Most sporting goods shops, big-box retailers, and many convenience stores sell licenses. You can even order yours online (your receipt will serve as proof until the license arrives) at: tpwd.texas.gov/business/licenses/online_sales/

- **Respect private property.** Most streamside land in Texas is in the hands of private landowners. See the **Texas River Law** chapter for how to navigate that. *Do not trespass!*

- **Practice catch and release.** But if you do keep the occasional fish (on larger waters only, please), be sure to observe size and bag limits. If special regulations are in place on any of the waters listed in this book, I have mentioned them.

- **Treat fish well.** Play your fish quickly and minimize handling out of the water. Use a rubber net or wet your hands before touching

I have caught and released this particular bass more than once, in successive months.

the animal. If you do briefly lift the fish out of the water for a photo, support the weight of its body with your hands, displaying it horizontally. Holding a large bass vertically by the lower jaw stretches tendons and ligaments the fish needs to effectively capture prey; several studies suggest that many large bass that have been "lipped" die weeks or months later.

- **Leave no trace.** In fact, consider carrying a mesh bag to pack other, less considerate folks' trash out with you. What about going number two? Solid waste, whether human or animal, can have significant negative impacts on rivers. Because most lands around public waters in Texas are privately owned, it's often difficult to find a secluded spot at the recommended 200 feet from the water. You may, however, be able to find a streamside tree or bush for some privacy and then pack out your own poop. Consider carrying a "Biffy Bag," "Restop Wilderness Containment Pouch," or similar waste disposal system in your pack. "Dude Wipes" are a terrific, biodegradable option for cleanup. All are available online.

A celebratory beverage at the end of a day of fishing is sometimes welcome; just be sure to pack out your empties.

- **Be considerate of other anglers.** You won't run into a crowd on most of these waters, but if someone is fishing (or even observing or resting) a pool or a reach ahead of you, wait or quietly go well around. Always ask before entering water near another angler, and whatever you do, stay out of his or her backcast. With a little coordination, two or more anglers can productively fish a stream by "leapfrogging" or alternating reaches. If you park at a crossing that could be waded either upstream or down, consider leaving a note on your dashboard indicating which way you went and what time you left.

- **Don't feed the wildlife.** Streams are natural wildlife corridors, especially in urban and suburban settings. Fish the waters in this book often enough, and you'll encounter all sorts of critters. Most are not inclined to eat *you,* but many would be happy to take a handout if you're offering. Please don't feed them. It's against the law in all state parks and many cities, and when a wild animal loses its fear of humans, it rarely ends well for either the animal or for people.

Safety Considerations

It's always a good idea to let someone know where you are going and when you plan to be back … just in case. Keep an eye on the weather, particularly thunderstorm activity in the spring and summer, because a heavy, localized downpour can lead to a quick rise on some of our creeks and rivers; flash floods kill the inadequately warned, inattentive, and slow most years in Central Texas. If there is heavy rainfall anywhere in the vicinity, especially upstream from you, it's a good idea to call it a day. Carry plenty of water, or a water filter like the Katadyn BeFree system. The Texas sun can be brutal in the summer and you'll want to stay hydrated.

Many anglers choose to wear lightweight, breathable long-sleeve shirts, even in the summer, to guard against the sun.

A basic first aid kit can keep you on the water after a mishap. It should include a combination tool (pliers and heavy-duty wire cutter) to remove errant hooks; some alcohol, iodine, betadine or another sanitizing agent to treat cuts and scrapes; a topical antibiotic; and a small assortment of waterproof bandages. I also carry a SAM splint in my first aid kit. It's easy enough to put together your own supplies and store them in a resealable plastic freezer bag.

What the Heck Does That Mean?

You can judge how rarified and important a pastime is by the amount of jargon that accompanies it, right? Just kidding. The truth is, fly fishing has a long history. It also made the leap across the Atlantic from Britain, where people have all sorts of funny names for things. And, also, it's probably fair to say that a bit of snobbery has been involved through the years.

Here are some of the fly fishing (and river) specific terms you may want to know if you are new to the sport or new to fishing moving water.

Fly rods (aka "fishing poles") are rated in **weights**, from the esoteric 000 on the light end to 14 for triple-digit big game fish. The smaller the number, the lighter (or smaller) the rod. Rod weights *should* correspond to the weight of the **fly line**, which will seem crazy thick and a little heavy to someone used to conventional gear (in fly fishing, the weight of the line, not the fly or lure, makes casting possible). There are standard weights, measured in grains, for the first 30 feet of fly line, published by the American Fly Fishing Tackle Association (AFFTA).

Rods come in many different **tapers**, or design profiles (wall thickness, material selection, and section diameter all play a role in creating a specific taper), which result in **actions** that generally can be categorized as **tip flex** (that is, only the tip section bends easily and does most of the work of casting the line), **progressive** (the bend becomes progressively deeper the more line one is casting), **parabolic** (the rod bends in the tip and the butt with a stiff mid-section), and so on.

When discussing tapers and actions, we also throw around words like "**fast**," "**medium-fast**," "**medium**," and "**slow**." This refers to the relative stiffness of the rod. A slow rod also can be described as "**soft**" (and an extremely soft rod may be described as "**noodly**").

Fly lines, in addition to being rated by weights, can be weight forward ("**WF**") (the head, or "bulgy" part of the line is up front, with a relatively short, tapered section leading to the, usually, welded loop) or double taper ("**DT**") (the thin front taper leads to a long, thick "belly." These lines can be reversed, end-for-end, to double the useful life). There are other types, including level lines and shooting heads, but they are not much used in this part of the country. Fly lines can be floating lines, sinking lines, sink-tip lines, or intermediate sinking lines. Put it all together, and you'll find a shorthand notation that looks like this: WF3F (a weight-forward, 3-weight, floating line), WF6S (a weight-forward, 6-weight, sinking line), or DT4F (a double taper, 4-weight, floating line). Finally, fly lines are designed in a multitude of profiles for different applications: compact, heavy heads and front short tapers for quick loading or punching through wind, long heads and front tapers for delicate presentation, and so on.

Fly lines are typically 90 or 100 feet long, sometimes shorter for lighter lines, and are connected to reels with **backing**, usually a brightly colored 20- or 30-pound test Dacron or braided line. The fly line is connected to the fly by the **leader**, commonly a 5- to 9-foot tapered nylon monofilament or fluorocarbon section of line. The leader tapers down

Living Waters Fly Fishing in Round Rock stocks something like 1,200 bins of flies. For most Central Texas streams, you'll do fine with just half a dozen patterns in a couple of sizes and colors.

Fish every day for a week straight, and the back of your vehicle may end up looking like mine: a combination landfiill, fly shop, and outfitter's closet.

to a thin **tippet** section, which can be extended or replaced by tying on new tippet material, purchased separately on small spools. Leaders and tippets are described by the diameter of the tippet section expressed as a number and the letter "X." The smaller the number, the larger the diameter and stronger the line. For instance, 0X tippet has a diameter of 0.011 inches and an approximate breaking strength of 15.5 pounds. At the other end of the spectrum, 8X tippet has a diameter of .003 inches and a breaking strength of 1.75 pounds. Leaders and tippets in the range of 2X through 4X are commonly used on warmwater streams in Central Texas.

Flies are described, in addition to a general type (dry, wet, nymph, streamer) or specific pattern (Parachute Adams, Bennett's Lunch Money, Hare's Ear), by hook size. These range from 2/0 ("two aught") on the larger end of the spectrum to size 28 or so on the positively tiny end. There are sizes both larger and smaller, but they have no application here. In fact, it's unlikely you would ever tie on a size 28 anything for Central Texas waters, and most useful flies here range from a big, 2/0 deer hair bug for largemouth bass down to a size 18 or 20 nymph dropper for trout on the Guadalupe River. The middle range of size 2 down to size 12 catches most fish.

River **terminology** that will be helpful to know while using this book includes the following: **reach** (a segment or stretch of water), **run** (a deeper channel of relatively fast water), and **riffle** (a shallow, usually rocky or graveled section of river, often involving a more significant drop in elevation). A **braided** stream is one in which multiple channels or riffles meander through rocks, gravel, or sand. I use the word "**seam**" to indicate both the edge between "**hard**" or fast water and "**slack**" or slow water, or an **eddy** (where water flows or rotates toward the bank or upstream), and also in a few instances to refer to cracks, fault lines, or corrugations in limestone streambeds. "Slack" also can refer to the lowest or highest point of a tidal cycle, when water is neither flooding nor ebbing; in these pages I use it to refer to the low point of the Lower Colorado River's inland tidal cycle. **Snags, laydowns,** and **tree falls** all refer to brush or logs in the water, and while there may be more or less depending upon the severity of the last flood, wood tends to accumulate in the same place, year after year. **Gravel** refers to small rocks, the sort that work their way into your Chacos; **cobbles** are larger stones, from baseball to basketball size, that make walking difficult in places; and **boulders** are rocks you have to go around or clamber over.

If you are unsure what something is called or what a particular piece of jargon or fly fishing slang means, ask the friendly folks at your local fly shop. They live to welcome new participants to the sport, and they won't make you feel silly for not knowing what you wouldn't have any reason to know before you ask. You'll be fluent in no time.

 With a Little Help from my Friends, Joe Cocker

Chapter 2

Gearing Up for Central Texas Waters

STOMP A CREEK OR WADE A RIVER AROUND AUSTIN AND YOU'LL be hard put to spot an angler who looks like he or she just stepped out of a fly fishing catalogue. Unless you happen to run into my buddy Jess (see cover). In this region, "business casual" means a shirt with a collar and "formal wear" means you probably have socks on. We're still a little redneck and a whole lot laid-back here.

If the latest gee-whiz waders and felt-soled boots and stream temperature gauges turn you on, gear up and have at it. No one is going to laugh you off the water. But for about nine months out of the year, you'll fish just fine in board shorts and strappy sandals (or old sneakers).

Rods and Reels

Opinions differ as to the optimal fly rod weight for our waters. Lots of locals opt for a middle range of 4- to 6-weight rods to cover all the bases. Anglers targeting big carp or big bass exclusively might want to go even heavier, up to 8-weight, but I think that's overkill. In my opinion, a 9-foot, 6-weight rod is as big as you need to go for Central Texas waters.

I like so-called ultralight rods—fishing relatively short 1- to 3-weight rods most of the time. I have three reasons. First, the vast majority of our fish are sunfish or bass under 4 pounds, and those fish are a lot more fun on an ultralight rod. Second, many of my favorite fishing spots are small waters, sometimes with significant vegetation along the banks or overhead, and a short, light rod is easier to manage in tight quarters. Third, as I slide into middle age, I'd much rather swing a light rod than a heavy one all day.

> "There he stands, draped in more equipment than a telephone lineman, trying to outwit an organism with a brain no bigger than a breadcrumb, and getting licked in the process."
>
> PAUL O'NEIL, "IN PRAISE OF TROUT—AND ALSO ME," *Greatest Fishing Stories Ever Told*

There is an argument that ultralight fly rods kill fish. I disagree. I spend no more time playing a fish on a 3-weight than on a 6-weight, and there is ample evidence that lighter gear can shorten the fight as slower, lighter rods protect the tippet and the angler can play the fish more confidently.

If I had to recommend one outfit, it would be a 7- or 7.5-foot, medium or medium-fast 3-weight lined with a weight-forward floating line on a click-and-pawl reel with a palmable rim. This is the sweet spot for me—a rod with enough backbone to handle fish up to 5 or 6 pounds, light enough to swing all day, short enough to negotiate a brushy small stream, and tons of fun for the 6- to 14-inch fish that are most prevalent on any stream.

Here are the exceptions: you'll want a longer (8- to 9-foot) rod, probably a 5- or 6-weight, for the Canyon Lake tailwater trout fishery, where you may do a lot of mending between fighting big fish in current. You'll want at least that, and more likely a 7- or 8-weight rod for the stripers in the same water. A 6-weight is also a good choice if you are targeting large carp, and for throwing a sink-tip line and big streamers on the Colorado River in the winter, or size 2/0 deer hair bugs in the summer.

If you are picking up your very first rod, visit a fly shop and have the employees there walk you through the options. Line weight and rod length are the variables we talk about most often, but material (fiberglass versus graphite, or carbon) is something else to think about. Lawn cast a couple to get a feel for what works best for you. We have several terrific local fly shops in Central Texas (see the **Appendices** for listings), and their employees will encourage you to handle and cast various rods and will give you honest, expert advice on how best to get started.

Cost has long been a barrier to everyday folks who would otherwise give fly fishing a try, and it shouldn't be. There's no such thing as the "perfect" fly rod, and you'll lose a lot of valuable experience and even more precious enjoyment if you wait to afford the high-price models. Many really, really good rods are available at lower price points these days. Some that get labeled as "introductory" or "budget" rods are so capable you may never give them up completely as you grow in the sport.

ECHO, Redington, and Texas-based Temple Fork Outfitters (TFO) all manufacture high-quality graphite and fiberglass fly rods that are priced to be affordable. These manufacturers also offer generous, no-fault warranties: break a section, and you can usually get it replaced for $35 or less. Big-box retailer Cabela's offers a terrific deal on a slow, full-flexing fiberglass fly rod, the CGR ("Classic Glass Rod");

its price has dropped by nearly 50 percent in recent years to around $70, and it is often on sale for less.

Bottom line: you can cobble together a very capable and respectable rod-and-reel combination for less than $250; in fact, if you shop carefully, you can probably get that price tag down to the $150 range.

Once you have gotten your feet wet and figured out a few things—what waters you love best, the species you want to pursue, and what casting style works for you—that's the time to narrow down the choices and add a pricier rod to the quiver if you are so inclined. You can also start branching out, adding appropriate rods for other waters or species.

Scott, Sage, Orvis, G. Loomis, R.L. Winston, Thomas & Thomas, and others make beautiful, very capable rods that are a joy to fish and to own. I'm partial to small-batch, handcrafted fiberglass rods from C. Barclay Fly Rod Co. in North Carolina. They suit my fishing style and waters and make me happy just looking at them. Kabuto Rods, Graywolf Fly Rods, Steffen Brothers Fly Rods,

Don't forget about used gear. You can find a lively Texas fly fishing gear marketplace on Facebook, and Craigslist usually has some relevant ads in Austin. eBay is a great place to find budget-friendly rods and reels, especially if you are looking for vintage tackle. One of my favorite heavier rods is a two-piece, 7.5-foot, 6-weight fiberglass model manufactured by Browning in 1976. The Fiberglass Fly Rodders Forum (fiberglassflyrodders.com) has a wealth of information about current and vintage glass rods.

Livingston Rod Co., Leiderman Rods, and CF Burkheimer Fly Rod Company also craft beautiful custom or semi-custom rods. When you're

Local fly shops stock a wide variety of rods and other equipment. The pros there can help you narrow it all down to something that fits your intended fishing and budget.

A trio of anglers gear up for a misty morning on the Lampasas.

There is a lot of good gear available these days for less than stratospheric prices. Neither of these outfits cost more than $150 total.

ready to shell out more money for an heirloom-quality fly rod, consider supporting one of these small businesses and the innovative craftsmen behind them.

You'll probably find that fly rods tend to reproduce when you are not paying attention—or, more accurately, when your significant other is looking the other way. This is a good thing; just roll with it.

Note that, as you add rods for different species or scenarios, it's a good idea to do so in two-weight increments. There's not a whole lot of difference between a fast carbon 6-weight and a fast carbon 5-weight, but you'll notice when you step down to a 4-weight or switch from graphite to glass. Whether you start even (2, 4, 6, 8, and so on) or odd (1, 3, 5, 7 …) is largely a matter of personal preference.

Reels reproduce at a slower rate, mostly because one reel can serve several rods. Most reels can accommodate up to three line weights and extra spools are available for, usually, about half the price of the entire reel.

For most of our species, including bass, reels mostly serve as line holders. A simple click-and-pawl reel with an exposed rim (to make it easier to "palm" the spool, the traditional method of adding drag pressure) will suffice for just about any freshwater species other than carp or striped bass; the Orvis Battenkill series and the Redington ZERO come to mind. For carp and stripers, a good disc drag is added insurance; options are nearly endless.

Lines, Leaders, and Flies

Folks choosing to fish with ultralight rods will be limited almost by default to floating lines, either weight-forward tapers (most commonly) or double tapers. Floating lines are also appropriate for heavier rods on all of our shallow streams. Add split shot, a tungsten twist, or a heavier fly if you need to dredge the deeps. On the winter Colorado River and in the San Marcos and Guadalupe Rivers, a sink-tip or intermediate sinking line may be useful in some scenarios.

Don't be afraid to experiment with line weights; you can often go one weight up or (less frequently) down from the recommended weight printed on the rod. The rated weights of some rods and lines long ago departed from the American Fly Fishing Trade Association (AFFTA)

Events like Pig Farm Ink's Iron Fly, the LoCo Trash Bash, and weekly fly tying nights bring the Central Texas angling community together.

Edgar Diaz, the author, and Davin Topel are all—in one way or another—contributors to a vibrant local fly fishing makers' community.

standards, making matching a line to a rod something of a guessing game. The pros at your local fly shop can tell you what lines work well with which rods.

Because I fish mostly shorter rods, I opt for either 6-foot or 7.5-foot leaders. Fluorocarbon sometimes makes all the difference in some of our ultra-clear waters, and barbless hooks size 6 to 14 will cover most any situation—unless you are stalking big bass. In that case, tie on a deer hair popper, slider, or a large baitfish pattern up to 2/0; you'll want that 6-weight to throw the bigger bugs.

Most of our warmwater species are highly opportunistic feeders and eat a varied diet. Most days, your success won't depend on matching your fly to the insect hatch (and we do have hatches, notably of hexagenias, blue-winged olives [BWOs], tricos, slate drakes, and caddis, among others, and sunfish and Guadalupe bass do rise to them—as do trout on the Guadalupe River). For more on flies, see the chapter **A Central Texas Fly Box**.

Other Gear You May Want

I wade (and paddle) with a sling pack or day pack, a couple of bottles of water (or a bottle and a water filter), a rubber landing net, sunscreen, insect repellent, a mesh trash bag, and my cell phone. A hemostat (a surgical clamp) comes in handy when a sunfish unaccountably gets the whole fly inside its tiny mouth. Nippers are useful for trimming knots.

Sometime in November, after a couple of cold fronts have dropped the air and water temps, I'll start wearing breathable chest waders. I'll put them away again in early March. The Canyon Lake tailwaters are an exception to this rule, and anglers will benefit from waders year-round there (see the **Guadalupe River** chapter, page 307).

There are some terrific paddling opportunities in Central Texas, and one of the nation's pioneering kayak-fishing shops, Austin Canoe & Kayak (ACK), has several stores in the area. Liveries, particularly on the Colorado River, the San Marcos River, and the Guadalupe River, provide rentals and shuttles at reasonable rates; some anglers have started relying on Uber or other rideshare services for shuttles.

Paddle what you have or can easily get (at normal flows, the local streams are beginner-friendly). If you are considering purchasing your own boat, think about a roto-molded polyethylene sit-on-top kayak in the 12-foot range, long enough to track well on open, big-water reaches or in the wind, nimble enough to negotiate tight turns, and tough enough to withstand lots of contact with limestone.

Some manufacturers advertise models that are stable enough to stand and cast in. Generally there is a trade-off here: stand to spot and cast but struggle a little more with the paddling, or learn to cast from a sitting position from a faster boat that tracks better. Local manufacturer Diablo Paddlesports is an exception, and their boats are a favorite among Central Texas anglers; they paddle reasonably well (both as traditional kayaks and as stand-up paddleboards) and provide great stability for sight casting.

A 14- to 16-foot canoe works well for two, well-coordinated anglers if you are fishing with a buddy, and a two-wheel caddy will make the carry to and from water's edge easier, especially if you are fishing solo. Paddlecraft are exempt from registration in Texas, but *Texas law requires all paddlers to carry a personal flotation device when paddling and to display an all-around white light if paddling at night or in reduced visibility.*

In my day job as a professional mariner, and in a previous career as a spokesman for the Texas Parks & Wildlife Department (TPWD)—one

Veteran angler Charlie Goodrich of Pinedale, Wyoming, long ago figured out that Converse All-Stars a size larger than normal make fine wading boots. For slick bottoms, he slips surgical booties over the shoes.

year I got to talk about fifty-four boating fatalities over a twelve-month period—I've noticed something interesting and pertinent: life jackets work best when you wear them.

The Bottom Line

If you are coming to fly fishing from the conventional gear world, fly rods are—in one sense—just another tool. Everything you have learned about fish and fishing so far will help you. And yet, fly fishing is different. More than any other form of angling, it is a journey that, if not in itself a philosophy, has an awful lot of philosophy in it.

It also has, as Lefty Kreh pithily said, "more B.S. than a Kansas City feedlot."

For example, you thought that round, orange thing was a "bobber," didn't you? C'mon, admit it. Well, I'll have you know it is *not* a bobber. In the fly fishing world it's a "strike indicator" or just an "indicator." But really it's just a bobber. Like that.

Shrug off that nonsense. Be patient with yourself as you ease (or jump) into the sport. Find some guys or gals who have been at it a while. More than likely, they'll be happy to help you out.

 We Welcome You Home, Possessed by Paul James

Chapter 3

A Central Texas Fly Box

THERE IS A REASON TROUT ANGLERS CARRY DOZENS OF patterns and sometimes hundreds of flies on a single fishing trip: Trout can be picky. And while some fish on some streams will readily take impressionistic flies (a size 14 Parachute Adams mimics a range of mayflies, for instance), on many streams fish will selectively sip only the current hatch. And they may be keyed in on just one form of that hatch, say, nymphs or spinners. It's the reason many trout anglers learn a bit of Latin and become pretty good streamside entomologists.

We don't roll like that in Central Texas. In fact, I would argue that—even if we never give a thought to patterns that imitate various caddis or mayfly species—we still carry more flies than we need for our warmwater species. I know I do. Our fish aren't all that discriminating.

I'm pretty sure we could get by with just four or five patterns in a

> "The natural exuberance of fly tiers explains why there are so many patterns to choose from, including those brainstorms a guide friend calls 'three-beer flies.'"
>
> JOHN GIERACH, *All Fishermen Are Liars*

couple of sizes and colors: something that imitates a damsel or dragon-fly nymph; something that imitates a baitfish; something that imitates a crawfish; and something that floats and makes a commotion on the surface (depending on what species you are targeting, this could be anything from a size 14 ant or beetle to a 2/0 deer hair bug).

When I am putting together a box for a Central Texas stream, I always include at least some of the flies below, tied by locals and friends.

The Blanchard's cricket frog is a favorite prey of fish in Central Texas streams.

A Warmwater Nymph and a Tiny Amphibian

Umpqua Signature Tyer Josh Smitherman is an inventive local tyer whose patterns are available nationally as well as in local shops. When he's not out fishing, you can find him behind the counter at Living Waters Fly Fishing in Round Rock.

Draggin' Nymph

Josh developed the Draggin' Nymph after watching a creek entomology presentation by the Texas Parks & Wildlife Department (TPWD). Dragonfly nymphs are ubiquitous in Central Texas and a primary food source for most warmwater species, but especially Guadalupe bass. This fly also has been tested successfully on trout in the Canyon Lake tailwater. Josh wanted a pattern that was a bit meatier than others he had seen and also moved well in the water.

Hook: C450BL (size 10–14)
Thread: UTC 70 Denier (*Light Olive*)
Abdomen: Senyo's Laser Dub (*Light Olive*)
Abdomen Barring: Sharpie (*Brown*)
Thorax: SLF Dubbing (*Sculpin Olive*)
Eyes: Small beadchain (*Black*)
Wing: Whiting Farms Wet Fly Hen Saddle (*Grizzly Dark Olive*)
Legs: Flex Floss (*Brown Olive*)

Mini Dahlberg Diver

Another fly from Josh, this downsized version of the classic deer hair diver mimics the Blanchard's cricket frogs that throng area streams nine months of the year.

Hook: Gamakatsu B10S (size 6–12)
Thread: GSP 100 Denier
Tail: Whiting Farms Chickabou or Wet Fly Hen Saddle
Flash: Ice Dub
Body: Deer Hair

The Most Productive Carp Fly

Chase Smith is another talented Austin-area fly tyer who supplies local fly shops and individual customers through Instagram @fishchaseflies and online at fishchaseflies.com. If you visit Chase's site, be sure to check out his D.A.M. carp fly, an articulated bug that lands softly and has some crazy good motion in the water.

Scarpian

Chase invented his Scarpian pattern as a headstand-type carp fly that falls hook-up. The Scarpian was responsible for first-place wins in both the 2017 and 2018 esCARPment carp tournament, and it also has tricked big river bass and other species (including the largest catfish I've ever caught on fly).

Hook: Allen Barbless carp hook size 8
Thread: 140 denier Veevus Power Thread
Tail: Rabbit Fur
Foam wrap: 2 mm foam spiral wrapped
Legs: Brown w/orange flake crazy legs
Body: Soft hackle feather
Eyes: 4mm beadchain

Crawfish are a major prey item in Central Texas streams.

Skittles and Crawdads

Orvis fly designer Brandon Bailes isn't local, but he has lots of friends in Central Texas, and the streams he fishes in Alabama are pretty good stand-ins for small Central Texas rivers. If you didn't know better, you'd think the Coosa and Warrior bass he catches there are Guads. Brandon sells direct to the public through Panther Branch Bugs; find him on Instagram @panther_branch_bugs.

Petite Popper

It's not often you find a deer hair bug sized for 3-weight creek rods; Brandon ties 'em and jokingly refers to the colorful, popping, sliding, gurgling flies as "fish Skittles." They work equally well on bass and sunfish. Noted artist Nate Karnes likes the micro-bugs so much he used them as inspiration for a decal and t-shirt available through Remedy Provisions.

Hook: Gamakatsu B10s (size 8)
Body: Select deer belly hair
Eyes: 4mm 3d eyes
Legs: Fine round rubber
Tail: Laser Dub, Ice Wing Fiber, Craft Fur
Cement: Raidzap Flex UV on belly and face

Hatchling Craw

The big crawfish grab our attention, but area creeks are full of smaller crustaceans. This downsized, realistic crawfish pattern is terrific for all of our warmwater species, but especially Guadalupe bass and Rio Grande cichlids. For a larger, heavier crawfish pattern, check out Brandon's Fetal Craw.

Hook: Gamakatsu B10s (size 10)
Weight/Keel: Small brass dumbbell eyes
Claws: Trimmed pine squirrel zonker
Rib: 5x tippet
Underbody: Frankenfly Nymph Dub
Backshell: MFC Skinny Skin
Antennae: MFC Barred Fine Round rubber

A Creature, a Streamer, and an Impressionistic Craw

Umpqua Signature Tyer Chris Johnson owns Living Waters Fly Fishing in Round Rock. His patterns are thoroughly tested on area rivers, including Brushy Creek.

Johnson's Creek Leech

Chris designed this pattern to fill a major void in his bass box. He needed a "creature" pattern that had an insane amount of movement during the retrieve and continued to move when at rest. The rabbit zonker strip pulses like natural fur should, the marabou underwing breathes even when at rest, but the real kicker is the rubber legs. The "Perfect Rubber" legs from Hedron Inc. (the maker of Flashabou) actually float.

Hook: Gamakatsu B10S Size 4–8

Thread: 95 or 140 Denier, Black or Olive

Eyes: Painted Lead Dumbbell to match hook size

Tail/Rear Legs: Perfect Rubber in Olive and Smoke (floating legs)

Body: SLF Dubbing, Hellgrammite

Wing/Back: Frost Tip Rabbit Zonker, Olive/Black

Underwing: Whiting Spey Soft Hackle in Grizzly Olive

Legs: Same as tail/rear legs

Johnson's MardiCraw

The small MardiCraw crawfish pattern moves like crazy thanks to the use of Australian Possum and rubber legs, yet when at rest it still looks enough like the genuine article to be devoured without question. The fly is an easy tie, and you can take risks with the pattern, thanks to the lack of emotional investment at the tying bench. The MardiCraw has caught everything from Rio Grande cichlids to Rio Grande cutthroat and is a staple in local fly boxes.

Hook: TMC 403BLJ, Sizes 8–16

Thread: 70 or 95 Denier, Burnt Orange

Bead: MFC Tungsten Slotted, Red

Tail: Australian Possum Back/Rump Fur, Burnt Orange

Legs: Nymph Sili Legs, Pumpkin Barred

Body: Australian Possum Body Fur, Burnt Orange— Spun in a dubbing loop and trimmed flush on bottom

Johnson's Brushy Creek Streamer (Jigged)

This little baitfish pattern is one of Chris's first patterns. The Brushy Creek
Streamer was created primarily to tempt bass in low and clear water
conditions. It works fine for that; it has also caught sunfish, cichlids,
drum, bass, trout, and catfish and has even been sucked up by a few
carp. Originally, the fly was tied with a simple bead head on a light wire,
2X long hook, but Chris now prefers fishing it on a 60-degree jig hook
with a small tungsten bead. This allows the fly to be fished deeper without
as many hang-ups. This little streamer does a fantastic job of imitating
black tail shiners and other small baitfish species.

Hook: TMC 403BLJ, Sizes 8–14
Thread: 74 Denier, Black
Bead: Tungsten Slotted, Gold
Belly: Polar Blend, Brite White
Flash: Lite Brite, Shimmering Chartreuse
Wing: Craft Fur, Olive

A Foam Popper

Wes McNew is a local tyer whose meticulously crafted takes on popular patterns are thoroughly tested in Onion Creek, literally in his backyard, as well as other area streams. Be sure to check out his "micro" version of Blaine Chocklett's Game Changer, too. Find his flies in shops throughout Texas, on Instagram @onioncreekflyco, and at his website: **onioncreekflycompany.com**

Double Barrel Frog

Wes was looking for an alternative to stacking deer hair, a quick tie that could be crafted in a few different colors to match forage, and threw the double barrel frog together from materials he had on hand. His first field test yielded largemouth bass, longear sunfish, and redbreast sunfish. The fly scales up to a size 2 or down to a size 8.

Hook: Flymen Fishing Co size 6 popper hook
Thread: Danville 140 thread (black or chartreuse)
Body: Flymen Double Barrel Popper Head (small) in chartreuse
Rear Legs: Cohen's Creatures frog legs (size mini/1-inch)
Tail: Olive Finesse Chenille (medium)
Front Legs: Grizzly Flutter Legs (insect green)
Colors: Olive and black marker (color the frog legs olive and add black spots)
Cement: Gel super glue

Three Indispensable Flies

Matt Bennett is a full-time commercial tyer, as well as an Umpqua Signature Tyer, and a fixture of the Austin fly fishing scene. You can find Matt's flies in shops throughout the country, or order from him directly at **flygeek.net**.

Bennett's Carp-It Bomb

The Carp-It Bomb may have been designed with carp in mind, but if I had to fish just one fly on a Central Texas stream, this would be it. I've caught carp on it, sure, but also lots of Guadalupe and largemouth bass, white bass, sunfish, Rios, channel cats, freshwater drum, and even a spotted gar. Part of the fly's appeal is that it can pass for a large damsel nymph or a small crawfish, thus covering two out of the four major food groups.

Hook: Ahrex HR430 or Gamakatsu B10S or Ahrex NS122 for more general applications Sizes 4–10

Thread: Veevus Power Thread 140 (Olive)

Eyes: Bead Chain Eyes (Black, Large/Medium)

Tail and Wing: Marabou (Olive Brown)

Legs: Hareline Grizzly Flutter Legs (Root Beer)

Body: Dubbing Loop of Pat Cohen's Carp Dub (Olive Bar)

Overwing: Marabou and a clump of Carp Dub

Bennett's Rio Getter

The Rio Getter is similar to the Carp-It Bomb, just a lot smaller. Designed to appeal to picky Texas cichlids, it works equally well on sunfish, bass, and—in larger sizes—carp.

Hook: Gamakatsu B10S size 8–14
Eyes: Small Brass Eyes, Black
Thread: Veevus 10/0 Thread, Olive
Tail/Wing: Grizzly Marabou, Chickabou Brown
Dubbing: Whitlock SLF Dubbing, Nearnuff Sculpin Olive
Rib: Ultra Wire, Chartreuse, Small
Legs: Hareline Grizzly micro legs, root beer
UV Resin: Loon, flow fluorescent UV resin

Bennett's Lunch Money

The Lunch Money and its smaller sibling, the Brunch Money, are go-to streamers for bass and trout. This fly has a profile that closely matches the bite-sized sunfish that bass chase with abandon in our clear streams, and the materials give it excellent motion in the water. Try stripping it slow to give it a fluttering, "wounded" motion.

Hook: Gamakatsu B10S
Bead: Painted Lead Eyes-Medium
Thread: Fire Orange 140 UTC Ultra Thread
Tail: Barred Rabbit Strips
Rubber Legs: Hareline Sili Legs
Head: Senyo's Laser Dub

The Popper and a Damsel Nymph

Jeff Hoelter ties commercially for Living Waters Fly Fishing and is a pillar of the Central Texas fly fishing community. You may run into Jeff attending an Austin Fly Fishers or San Gabriel Fly Fishers event, teaching tying at the fly shop, or volunteering as a TPWD angler education instructor. With Jim Gray, Jeff is responsible for the development of an iconic Central Texas pattern, the Llanolope. You can find versions of that fly just about everywhere.

Llanolope

Based on Capt. Scott Sparrow's VIP, the Llanolope was developed specifically for the popular Llano River, a Hill Country stream just outside the scope of this volume. The Llanolope most closely mimics a large hopper, but it also could be taken for just about any critter making a commotion on the surface. It seems to be irresistible to Guadalupe bass and gets eaten by just about everything else, too. Many local anglers start a Central Texas stream session with this high-floating fly, and if the fish aren't looking up, add a dropper.

Hook: Gamakatsu B10S Stinger hook size 4–6

Thread: Ultra Thread 210 or GSP 130

Tail: Elk or deer body hair

Body: Antelope or deer hair

Head: River Road foam cylinders; 5/16 for size 6, 3/8 for size 4

Eyes: 5 or 6mm doll eyes or Fish Skull Living Eyes

Creek Damsel

There are dozens of damsel nymph patterns out there, but this take on one of the most important food sources for Central Texas fish, with its slim profile and soft hackle collar, is especially effective.

Hook: Gamakatsu B10S, Size 12 or 14

Eyes: Black bead chain, small or x-small

Rib: Ultra Wire, gold, small

Tail and Body: Marabou, damsel nymph olive (uv)

Hackle: Hungarian Partridge or Brahma Hen Saddle

Head: Dubbing, damsel olive

 Sixth Street Dam, Jeff Troutman

Let's Talk about Catch and Release

Here's a fundamental and perhaps shocking truth: The only truly ethical anglers are the men and women fishing to feed themselves or their families. That's right; the "meat haulers" have us beat.

Many fly fishers sport a sense of moral superiority that balloons apace with the number of fish released relatively unharmed. Barbless hooks, smooth rubber landing nets, campaigns to *#KeepEmWet*, and so on speak to a pretty large (and, happily, growing) constituency of catch-and-release anglers who like to think they are being ethical and respecting "the resource."

I've thought about this. A lot. My conclusion—and yours may differ—is that, as my grandfather used to say, "That's a bunch of hooey."

Let me explain.

Fly fishing is essentially a highly ritualized, symbolic imitation of something a lot of people in a lot of places around the world must do to survive. Collectively, we are the plump housecat playing with a mouse or a lizard on the front porch. Like the cat, we are "torturing" living creatures for the fun of it, not because we need the protein.

If we revere fish so much, the ethical action would be to not fish at all. After all, the fish is just trying to make a living, and the experience of being caught does nothing positive for the animal and—even when an angler takes extraordinary care and sends positive vibes to the fish—poses some risk of injury or infection.

Having caught the same redfish twice within the same hour, and knowing that redfish eat crabs and shrimp and pinfish and root around in oyster reefs—that is, they get poked in the mouth plenty—I presume that some species aren't terribly bothered by the experience of being caught on a hook. Others might be.

I'll admit right now that I'm not morally upright enough to stop fishing for sport. I hope I never will be.

Fisheries biologists have demonstrated, through controlled experiments, that with proper handling (using barbless hooks, handling fish only with wet hands or not at all, keeping the fish in the water as much as possible, supporting the fish's body if lifting it out of the water), "latent mortality"—fish that die days or weeks after being caught—can be reduced to less than one in ten for many species.

So I'm on board with catch and release. I practice it on all but a few occasions each year, limiting those to the white bass run and the occasional saltwater trip. And I'll be honest: My adherence to catch and release has more to do with being too lazy to clean a mess of fish, or find new, productive water, than with any notion of ethics.

It wasn't always this way; my fishing career started in the 1970s with all-night bait sessions and coolers full of speckled and sand trout. Some mornings my dad and I would still be cleaning fish as the sun came up. For a long time, I thought, "Man, we really like to fish!" It was only much later, as an adult, that I realized our family was poor back then and needed the meat.

I suspect that a lot of fly fishers started their journeys in similar (if less extreme) places. The more strident and less forgiving we are when talking to the "catch and grease" crowd, or those whose fish-handling methods are less refined than our own, the more we reinforce the unfortunate idea that fly fishing is an elitist pursuit. We then risk alienating anglers who someday may want to join our ranks.

Having said all that, if you are not fishing for food, I propose that rather than frame our desire to release fish back into the waters from which we took as some high-minded, pure, and ethical decision, we instead think (and talk) about it in practical terms.

A large fish of most any species from a small stream represents superior genetics (and wiliness and no small amount of luck) and should be allowed to contribute to future generations for as long as possible. Take a big bass out of a small stream or pool, and it could be years before you see another like it there.

To paraphrase Lee Wulff, most fish are too valuable to be caught just once.

Part 2

Northern Waters

Chapter 4

Lampasas River

Easy wading in a scenic rural setting; good populations of bass, carp, channel catfish, and freshwater drum; some huge and aggressive green sunfish; genetically pure Guadalupe bass in some sections; big enough to fish with a group of friends.
Access points: 6

THE LAMPASAS RIVER IS ONE OF SEVERAL MAJOR TRIBUTARIES of the mighty Brazos River that we will visit in these pages. The upper sections of the river lie just outside my self-imposed, roughly 60-mile radius from Auditorium Shores in downtown Austin, but it's still an easy hour-and-a-half drive. I keep coming back to it for a couple of reasons: It's a beautiful and diverse fishery, and the river is almost entirely passed over by all but a handful of dedicated local anglers and consequently receives very little fishing pressure.

The stream rises about 16 miles west of Hamilton and flows mostly southeast more than 100 river miles to its confluence with the Leon River, where—along with the San Gabriel—it becomes the Little River. Fed by springs and creeks, the Lampasas is clear but slow over the course of its upper and middle reaches, with a much more gradual drop than streams originating farther south in the Edwards Plateau. That low gradient means that fine silt and sediment from the surrounding sandy loam-and-clay agricultural lands can remain suspended for long minutes or even hours when a pool is disturbed. A school of carp or catfish, a herd of feral hogs, or a wading fisherman can muddy one pool while the pools above and below remain crystal clear.

> "Our tradition is that of the first man who sneaked away to the creek when the tribe did not really need fish."
>
> RODERICK L. HAIG-BROWN,
> *A River Never Sleeps*

The river likely takes its name from the town of *Lampazos de Naranjo* in the Mexican state of Nuevo León and was known to Spanish explorers at least as early as 1721. Or it may be named for a plant similar to the "elephant ears," or lampazos, for which the Mexican town is named. Our local "elephant ears" are actually taro, an Asian transplant that has naturalized in Texas and grows profusely along the river.

Wherever the name comes from, a community dating to the 1850s adopted it and quickly became a center for area ranchers and other settlers. Later in the nineteenth century, tourists flocked to the mineral springs that rise here. Today, Lampasas is a bustling town of about 8,000 souls. It's a terrific base for exploring the area's rivers.

There is one impoundment on the river, Stillhouse Hollow Lake, well downstream about 5 miles southwest of Belton, and many road crossings along the upper and middle reaches. We will take a close look at two sections of stream that offer good access and reliable fishing.

FM 1690 Near Adamsville
31.242261, -98.117366
2801 FM 1690, Lampasas, TX 76550
83.4 road miles, 1:25 drive time
Difficulty: Easy to Moderate

A FRIEND TURNED ME ON TO THIS REACH OF RIVER A COUPLE OF years ago, and it quickly became a favorite. I have run into other anglers there just once: a couple of good old boys who had been catfishing with gear, scrambling up the bank after an encounter with a herd of wild hogs. I continued on and had a lovely day on the unpeopled stream. Most of my favorite fishing spots give at least the illusion of rural seclusion. This section of the upper Lampasas truly is in the boonies.

On one trip I was perplexed by the sound of large projectiles crashing into the river behind me. I couldn't imagine who would be hiding just over the high bank, or why they would be throwing things at me, and I was getting a little worried. Then I realized that what I was hearing, but wasn't quite quick enough to see, was a bur oak shedding its golf ball-sized acorns into the river. It's that kind of lonesome out here.

What You Will Find

From the parking area alongside FM 1690, a well-defined trail disappears around the steel traffic barrier and continues under the bottom- *Native green sunfish, some reaching near state-record size, are common on the upper Lampasas.* land canopy and beneath the bridge before plunging down the bank on the upstream side. Some kind soul—his name rhymes with Chris Leslie— has installed a heavy-duty strap-and-rope climbing aid here. You won't need it unless the path or your shoes are wet, and then you'll quietly murmur, "Thanks, Chris!"

The portion of the pool beneath the bridge is a jumble of cobbles and boulders, but the water is knee-deep or less during normal flows. Whether fishing upstream or downstream, you can head straight across here and then proceed on the far bank if you wish; this far bank is tech- nically the south bank of the river, though it lies more westerly here.

1 Remote, No Pressure (Wading Upstream from the Bridge)

Let's head upstream first, starting with the pool that ends beneath the bridge. This pool is wadeable river left (your right as you head upstream) or may be fished from the limestone boulders on the other side. The deepest section of the pool lies against these rocks, which pro- vide fish-sheltering overhangs. There are big bass, channel cats, and carp in this pool, as well as bluegill, longear, and green sunfish. A pretty, low falls marks the top of the pool; from there it's a stroll across a corrugated limestone-and-gravel sill.

The next pool is a long one, and deep. Approach with care and probe the tail of the pool; the limestone sill here is deeply undercut and holds fish. Continuing upstream, wade the shallows in the sand and gravel along the south bank. The deeper channel river left (your right), with its heavy vegetation and steep bank, looks like the sure bet, but bass also cruise the drop-off just ahead of you. Bass here don't go far when spooked, and once they realize they're not being pursued by a predator, they seem happy to stop and consider whatever fly you drop in front of them.

One afternoon, I watched a series of slashing rises below an overhanging sycamore on that north bank, thinking I was seeing a bass feeding on drifting damselflies. It wasn't until I hooked up and brought the fish to hand that I realized it was a slab of a green sunfish, just an inch shy of the state fly fishing record. There are a lot of big greens in the river. They are aggressive feeders and a ton of fun on a light rod.

Native longear sunfish compete for the opportunity to have their photos taken on the Lampasas.

At the head of this pool, the river bends due west. Wade the deeper water up the middle and then cross over to the gravel bank river left before the stream curves back to the northwest. There's a jumble of boulders—a very fishy spot—on the far bank, river right. From here it's about 750 feet upstream over a corrugated limestone-and-gravel bottom to the next sill. During normal flows the water is knee- to thigh-deep; wade straight up the middle or to the right as you head upstream.

It's more of the same until, about 300 yards beyond the riffle that marks the top of the previous pool, you'll see a stand of flood-ravaged sycamores river right. There are a couple of nice, deep holes below the trees. Above this spot, the river shallows again, and you'll find the braided channel against the west bank. The slightly deeper pools in the sweeping channel bend here hold large numbers of longear sunfish. For some reason, the longears here retain their jewellike spawning colors much later in the year than the same species in waters farther south.

At the end of the bend, you may have to wade across the channel several times to follow the shifting gravel bars. Make your way to a spot on the east side (river left) so you can cast to the deeper water below the undercut bank river right. This is prime largemouth habitat and a great place to throw hair bugs, mice, big hoppers, or crawfish patterns.

Just ahead is a large gravel bar on the east side, where the neighboring farmer stores his canoe. As the gravel bank peters out, at about 1.25 miles from the FM 1690 bridge, you will see a beautiful, deep pocket across the river and a thigh- to waist-deep pool upstream. Catch some bass and turn around for the trek back.

2 Catfish Water (Wading Downstream from the Bridge)

The walk downstream from the FM 1690 bridge is mostly on gravel bars river right. A series of pretty, green pools with deep water along the far bank feature plenty of jumbled limestone boulders and sunken logs for cover. You are likely to pick up a bushel of rough cockleburs in your shoelaces and clothing, but otherwise it's an easy hike.

At about the 350-yard mark, you'll want to cross the river at a riffle and proceed along the north bank, river left. Eventually you will run out of gravel and find yourself wading in shin-deep water. This is a good stretch for sunfish and the occasional smaller bass.

At a bit more than 0.3 miles, **School Creek** enters river right. A short hike up that streambed will bring you to School Creek Falls, which are spectacular after a good rain. The large, circular pool below the falls holds a variety of fish year-round, but they are wary. You can also access School Creek by parking at the southwest corner of the **FM 2527 bridge** (31.23618, -98.11897) and hiking downstream to the Lampasas River.

Matt Bennett casts to a bass below School Creek Falls

Skirt the falls by following a dirt trail around the huge, fallen table rock river left. The Lampasas is 500 feet downstream.

Back on the Lampasas, make your way downstream over gravel bars to the left bank and the long pool that begins a little over half a mile below the FM 1690 bridge. The pool offers overhanging vegetation river left and jumbled boulders river right. Wade along the north bank or down the middle until it is about thigh-deep, at which point you will want to edge back to your left and hop up on the limestone shelf that continues downstream the length of the pool.

This is an extraordinary stretch of water—the pool stretches the length of about two football fields—and you could spend half a day here. There are ledges in shin- to knee-deep water along both banks, and they get wider the farther downstream you go. At the same time, the channel between them gets deeper—neck-deep toward the bottom of the pool. The ledges are deeply undercut and provide shelter for dozens, perhaps

Left: Most Central Texas fly anglers don't consider catfish unworthy quarry. We do get annoyed, though, when one steals a fly meant for a bass or a carp.

Below: Sturdy footwear, a sling pack, landing net, and a bottle of water are about all you need to fish the upper Lampasas.

hundreds, of channel catfish, freshwater drum, and big bass. The drum and bass follow foraging cats, waiting for them to kick up a meal.

None of the fish are studying the surface here, though you might pick up a loitering bass on a popper or hopper. A better bet is to fish deep— Woolly Buggers, crawfish patterns, and damsel nymphs seem to work well. If the school of fish moves away, be patient; they'll be back shortly. As the main channel begins to shallow again toward the tail of the pool, switch back to a light streamer or surface fly for bass and big sunnies.

Continue wading river left; there's another, smaller pool ahead with an undercut limestone ledge along the south bank. At 0.8 miles from the bridge, the river makes a gentle S bend and starts to move away from FM 2527, the road running alongside the right bank. A huge, silvered tree lies stranded atop the gravel bank at the bend; just beyond it, shallow water dotted with fish-sheltering boulders stretches toward the next curve of the stream. About a mile downstream from the bridge, you'll see a pool with spring seeps over jumbled boulders river left. There are bass, carp, and cats in this pool, and it's worth spending some time here. Plus, it's just downright beautiful water.

Below this last pool, a small waterfall spans the river. This is a great place to call it a day and begin the walk back upstream. There is good water below, as the river turns almost due south, but the next easy access point, at the **FM 580 crossing** (31.17184, -98.07101, park on the northeast side of the bridge), is 5.5 miles downstream. Still, you might want to check it out on the way home, because just below the FM 580 bridge, another long and broad pool, easily wadeable in thigh-deep water, narrows to a deep tail with undercut ledges. It offers the same assemblage of catfish, drum, and bass as similar pools upstream. From FM 580, it's another 4.8 river miles to the **FM 2313 crossing** (31.11895, -98.05533, excellent parking on the northeast side), where the mix of bass species begins to tilt significantly away from largemouth to Guadalupe.

From downtown, take US 183/183A (tolls on the US 183A section) north about 70 miles to Lampasas. On the north side of town, where US 183 jinks west, continue north on US 281 (the two highway numbers share the road through town) for 10 miles to Farm Road 1690 on the right. Follow FM 1690 3.75 miles and cross the Lampasas River. You will see a dirt track paralleling the road on your left. Park near the barrier close to the bridge.

Old Maxdale Bridge, Killeen
30.98992, -97.82894
28909 FM 2670, Killeen, TX 76549
62 road miles, 1:01 drive time
Difficulty: Easy

THIS STRETCH OF RIVER, ABOUT 3 MILES CENTERED ON THE historic bridge, is hands down my all-around favorite in Central Texas. The mixed schools of carp, spotted gar, redhorse suckers, gaspergou (freshwater drum), white bass, Guadalupe bass, and largemouth bass are one reason. The clear water that allows me to watch them is another. It's also the best stream in the area to fish with friends—lots of friends. The broad riverbed and easy-walking gravel bars easily accommodate up to half a dozen anglers at once.

What You Will Find
A very rough trail between the blacktop of the old road where you'll park and where the creek enters the Lampasas just upstream of the bridge.

Below: The view upstream from the Old Maxdale Bridge at normal low summer flows.

There is also a lot of poison ivy here. A better bet is to walk across the old bridge and follow the well-worn dirt trail down to the south bank on the downstream side of the bridge. There is a distressing amount of trash, along with graffiti tags and occult symbols. The bridge is allegedly a hot spot for paranormal activity; I say kids in the country both are inventive and have a lot of time on their hands.

A broad gravel bar in the streambed sometimes shows evidence of campfires, anglers, and picnickers. The river channel is shallow and runs along the north bank. About 800 feet below the bridge, the gravel bar comes to an end. A long pool stretching the better part of a quarter mile lies just upstream from the bridge. It is most often walk-through water. Let's head that direction first.

3 Integrated Schools (Wading Upstream from Old Maxdale Bridge)

Walk through the first long pool river right (your left as you head upstream) about 0.3 miles until you come to the new Maxdale Road bridge. Just above this span, which does not offer access to the river, you'll find a gorgeous, deep pool along the same bank.

A limestone ledge runs diagonally across the river and makes a fine casting platform. It also provides shelter for some hungry Guadalupe bass. Heavy vegetation and a giant submerged log river right provide good cover for largemouth bass and green sunfish. Look for carp, catfish, and drum in the deepest section of the pool and in the eddy at the head.

Cross the river where the limestone ledge meets the gravel shoal on the north bank. This is a great vantage point from which to survey the upper end of the pool. Sadly, some local bow fishers use it the same way, and if you see evidence that they have recently been there (carp and gar carcasses, beer and soda cans), keep walking. Bow fishing for nongame species is still legal in Texas, though waste of game and littering are not.

Cross the river again through the short riffle at the head of the pool. A tall sand-and-gravel dune river right affords a bird's-eye view of the next pool, which has a table-like limestone shelf jutting from the far bank just under the surface during normal flows. A persistent stand of coontail moss grows along the south bank, and sizeable largemouth bass are often waiting to ambush prey from its cover.

Past this pool, you'll cross the stream twice through two shallow and relatively unproductive pools. This is about as far as most conventional anglers and bow fishers care to trek; everything ahead of you is fly fishing water.

There are some stunningly beautiful pools an easy walk upstream from the bridge. Here, Danny Paschall of Houston casts to a Guadalupe bass holding against the far bank.

About 0.6 miles above the put-in, a 900-foot-long pool beckons. Head straight up the middle over sand and gravel, casting to the vegetated north bank and to the brush piles along the south bank. At typical flows, you'll get wet to mid-thigh.

Walk softly and edge toward the gravel bar below the south bank. You'll want to stop here a spell, unlimber your pack, crack a cold beer, and study the water. Spotted gar roll on the surface in the deeper water along the far bank, and there may be a couple of carp eating their way across the shallow, sandy bottom near the gravel bar. There will almost certainly be a dozen or so big fish lazily finning in and out of the shadows cast by overhanging elm and pecan trees on the north bank. Largemouth and Guadalupe bass, the occasional white bass, freshwater drum, and channel catfish track the carp, hoping they will scare up something edible.

A size 10 or 12 damsel nymph in black or olive, or a size 6 through 10 crawfish imitation, looks like something edible.

There's a lot going on here, and it's easy to spend an hour or two in this one spot. Stand in the shin-deep water just off the gravel bar long enough and the carp might nose right past your legs. Wait until they are headed away before casting; these fish are notoriously spooky in the clear, shallow water.

If you can tear yourself away (often I can't, and I end my wade here), there is more good stuff ahead. From the upstream end of the gravel bar, head straight up the middle of the upper segment of the pool, paying particular attention to the undercut bank on your left. The very top of this pool, at 0.9 miles, features a pretty run shaded by large pecan trees. It is a great place to pick up a couple of Guadalupe bass and green sunfish. Looking upstream, the valley frames a prominent hill, and the north bank transitions from gravel and rich topsoil to jumbled limestone blocks. It's a beautiful vista.

Cross the river again at the riffle and walk the gravel bar river right to a shallow bend at the 1-mile mark. Logs and brush accumulate here, and the force of the water over years has deeply undercut the bank river left. Some mammalian creature (probably a beaver—there are plenty of gnawed branches lying about) once made its home here and may still be in residence. Sunfish and Guadalupe bass are thick in the eddies at the bottom of the riffle and among the jumbled branches.

Continue upstream until you see a creek (Sycamore Branch) entering from the north. Here, at 1.1 miles, an undercut bank beneath trees river right holds Guadalupe bass, and a rock garden river left is home to some ferocious sunnies. The boulders on the north bank are a great place to take a break and enjoy the view.

Alana Lyons finds a willing dance partner beneath the trees.

As you continue upstream, edge left to get a good view of a head-deep, aqua pool below the north bank at 1.25 miles. Carp, redhorse suckers, and freshwater drum circulate in the eddy, waiting for something tasty to wash down to them. Again, a damsel nymph pattern looks pretty tasty, if you are one of those fish. So does a Pat's Rubber Legs stonefly nymph imitation.

Soon the river makes a sweeping turn upstream to the southeast. The channel is beautiful here, clear and narrow with jumbles of boulders in the middle and along the north bank, which is now solid limestone. At the end of the gravel bar river right, a large, sandy backwater usually hosts one or two feeding carp. Cross here and continue on the broad gravel along the north bank. At mile 1.4 you'll reach a deep pool with a jumble of large trees in the water; it's a terrific place to throw a larger baitfish, mouse, or deer hair slider for bass.

Usually that's enough for me, and I turn around here, but this beautiful, secluded gravel bar would also make a terrific camping spot.

Jaguars, Gators, and Boars

The Lampasas River marks the western limit of the natural range of the American alligator, and a few of the reptiles can still be found lurking in deeper pools upstream from Stillhouse Hollow Lake. In 2015, two Killeen men shot and killed an eleven-footer that was hooked on a catfish line. The men were rattled, but game wardens didn't buy the story that they'd shot the gator in self-defense and so charged them with misdemeanors.

Hunting and habitat loss threatened alligators with extinction in the 1950s, and by 1967 they were considered an endangered species nationwide. By 1985 numbers had rebounded so well that the species was delisted. There are approximately five million American alligators in the wild today, spread across the southeastern United States, including the eastern and southern parts of Texas.

Alligators can reach lengths of 8 feet or more in about fifteen years and continue growing until age 25 or 30. Some live so long they could collect Social Security if otherwise eligible. Only a few, perhaps five from an average thirty-eight-egg clutch, will survive to maturity. Fully one-third don't hatch, instead becoming snacks for raccoons or, increasingly, feral hogs.

Domesticated pigs were introduced to the Americas by Spanish explorers and colonists. If the first pigs arrived at a mission in Texas on a Tuesday afternoon in 1731, the first feral hogs were rooting around in a river bottom by that weekend. Smart, adaptable, prolific, and omnivorous, their success was assured even before Texas hunters imported Eurasian wild hogs, or "Russian boars," in the 1930s. The Russian hogs freely interbreed with the feral domestic species.

These are not the jolly pink porkers your grandmother raised on the farm. Swine in the wild revert to the hairy, heavily muscled, tusked versions seen in Stone Age cave paintings in just a couple of generations, which for pigs can be only a few years. The average size of an adult feral hog is 150 to 200 pounds, but animals four times that size have been recorded.

The population of wild pigs in Texas today is estimated to be 1.5 million and growing fast. These animals are seldom aggressive, but unprovoked attacks by large, solitary males have been documented. There are four recorded fatalities in Texas; three were by animals wounded by hunters. Given the choice, a wild pig will nearly always attempt to flee.

So will big cats. That's what "the Goldthwaite jaguar" was doing on the night of September 3, 1903, when it was cornered and shot out of a tree by a group of men who were likely looking to kill the much more common mountain lion, or cougar, when they went "tiger hunting." The 6-and-a-half-foot-long, 140-pound cat was killed three miles south of Center City, roughly twenty-five miles from our Lampasas River access point at FM 1690. Since male jaguars can range over more than fifty square miles, and love water, it's not unlikely that when we wade the Lampasas, we are walking in the ghost prints of that very cat.

Sadly, the killing of the Goldthwaite jaguar signaled last call in Texas for the world's third-largest "big cat." Jaguars were common, if never especially numerous, in the central and southwestern portions of the state as late as the 1850s, but habitat loss and conflicts with ranchers led to their disappearance from the scene by 1948. That was the year a jaguar was killed along Santa Gertrudis Creek on the storied King Ranch south of Corpus Christi.

Today, there are an estimated fifteen thousand of the big cats in Central and South America. Mexico is thought to have about five hundred remaining jaguars, including some in a pocket of habitat just seventy-five miles south of Texas's Rio Grande Valley. Like the remnant populations of ocelots and jaguarundis—Texas's other tropical wildcats—jaguars don't recognize political borders and historically have crossed back and forth over the Rio Grande. It's not impossible that they could return, as a few individuals have in Arizona, but it grows increasingly unlikely as South Texas's population continues to increase and suitable habitat becomes ever more fragmented. Wildlife biologists are in widespread agreement that the construction of a border wall to thwart human immigration would probably spell the end of all three tropical cat species in Texas.

4 **Friends Territory** (Wading Downstream from the Old Maxdale Bridge)
The stream runs faster here than it does closer to Lampasas, but it runs clear over a mostly gravel bottom. The first, broad pool is shallow but offers some decent water river right, along the south bank, which is shaded by cottonwoods, elms, and pecan trees. Wade down the middle of the river here, in knee-deep water, until you come to the next gravel bar, river right, at 0.3 miles. Your best shots along this stretch will be against the bank river left, where the water is a bit deeper and sunken logs and boulders hold fish.

As the gravel bar disappears, cross diagonally to the north bank of the river from which, at about 0.4 miles, you will be able to cast to a deep pool beneath large trees and heavy vegetation river right. This is another "everything pool," with bass, catfish, freshwater drum, carp, sunfish, and even white bass present year-round. This pool alone is worth the drive north. The current runs fairly fast through the pool, even at low to normal flows; be sure to cast far enough upstream that your fly has time to get down to the fish, which are typically patrolling the deeper water here.

At the tail of this pool, cross a pretty riffle to walk river right. You may notice some metal fence posts driven into the gravel bar here, with purple blazes warning that you are on or near posted private property. This is a questionable warning, at best; the fixed, permanent bank—not the gravel bar—is the legal boundary of public waters in Texas (see the **Texas River Law** chapter).

Walking along the edge of the bar, you will soon come to another deep run with dozens of boulders scattered throughout the water, mostly along the north bank. This run, at about 0.5 miles, is a great place to toss a mouse, hopper, popper, or small streamer for Guadalupe bass and big green sunnies.

At about 0.7 miles, as you run out of gravel on the south bank, wade across the shallow stream to proceed downriver river left. The deep water along the south bank flows beneath overhanging trees; this is a great spot for spotted gar and carp. At just short of a mile below the bridge, a large gravel shoal—an island, really—bisects the river. If you were inclined to camp, this would be a good (and legal) place to do that.

A deep, curving run river left is worth some time, especially if there is timber caught in the bend, but the portion of the river that follows the south bank also is interesting, with good bass and sunfish action beneath the willows in the bend just before the two channels come back together.

Cory Sorel reaches while trying to place a fly directly in the path of a foraging carp.

Below the confluence, a tall limestone bluff rises river right. Swing a soft-hackle wet fly or nymph through the riffle for feisty little Guadalupe bass. Wade down the center of the stream through scattered boulders and then edge toward the north bank to fish a deeper hole at 1.2 miles. There are some carp in this section of the river, as well as bass, catfish, and drum.

Below the long, rocky run, at 1.3 miles, the river bends south below a high dirt bank river left. A submerged limestone ledge runs down the middle of this bend and provides cover for some hefty largemouth bass. Cast against the far bank for Guads and sunnies.

A dirt track leads down to the gravel bar river right here. You will see picnic tables and a portable restroom under the trees on the bluff. Tempting! But this is private property—a neighborhood park owned and maintained by the River Ridge Ranch Property Owners' Association. Don't use it without permission.

Cross the shallow pool at the bottom of the bend to the gravel bar river left. If you'd like to catch your first redhorse sucker, this is a great place to find them feeding in the shallows. They have the profile, and most of the speed, of a bonefish.

Just below this pool, at mile 1.6 river left, a gravel bar separates a backwater from a riffle that empties into a deep pool with jumbled limestone along the north bank. The eddy in the backwater, together with some downed trees caught in the bend, are home to some huge common carp and at least two grass carp that surely weigh more than 40 pounds.

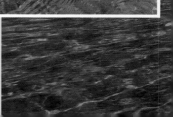

Largemouth bass are plentiful and willing on the reach of the Lampasas centered on the Old Maxdale Bridge.

  These fish will eat while cruising the edge of the current here. Try dead drifting a damsel nymph over the drop-off or placing a backstabber or crawfish imitation on the sandy bottom in the backwater. The fish will run for the brush pile; a 5- or 6-weight rod with some backbone may be needed to turn them. The remainder of this pool can be fished productively from the gravel bar river right and is home to some river bass in the 5- to 6-pound class.

  This pool is my usual turnaround point on the downstream stretch, but it's possible to continue on through productive, wadeable water to the **TX 195 crossing** (30.973171, -97.777378), about 4.8 miles from the historic Maxdale Bridge. If you choose to make a one-way wade or to

shuttle, park off TX 195 on the northeast side. A paved turnout there will leave your vehicle in clear view of passing traffic, which is more secure than parking beneath the bridge on the southwest side.

 From downtown, take I-35 north through Georgetown to Exit 266 and pick up TX 195, a fast, four-lane road headed north. After about 27 miles, less than a mile beyond the Lampasas River bridge and just before the Ding Dong Café on your right, cross the southbound lanes to go left (west) on FM 2670, which roughly parallels the river. Set your trip odometer as you make the turn. In about 3.6 miles, a single-lane blacktop on your left will lead to an abandoned iron truss bridge over the river. If you follow FM 2670 over the river on the new, fenced-every-which-way bridge, you've gone too far.

Take the old road down to the galvanized barrier and park in the old roadway.

 Out Here in the Middle, James McMurtry

⭐ Storm's Drive-In Hamburgers

stormsrestaurants.com
Open 6:30 a.m.–10 p.m., Sun.–Thurs., till 11 p.m. Fri.–Sat.

Storm's Drive-In in Lampasas has been in business since 1950, when it was the Dairy Cue (the old neon sign still graces the front of the restaurant). A drive-in fronting US 183/281 right in the middle of town, it features outdoor seating under a covered pavilion. The restaurant grinds its own hamburger on site, and the fries are fresh cut. Elvis was a frequent visitor when he was a soldier stationed at nearby Fort Hood more than half a century ago; folks say he would roll up in his Cadillac and order a strawberry shake with his meal. Storm's doesn't serve alcohol, but a frosted Coke can really hit the spot after a long day on the river.

Salado Creek

Ease of access, local history, gargantuan redbreast sunfish, feisty spotted bass. Access points: 3

Salado Creek rises in northwestern Williamson County about 5 miles west of the small town of Jarrell. It flows northeast for a little more than 21 miles before joining the Lampasas River 6 miles northeast of the village of Salado.

This charming little community is the antithesis of the sprawl around Temple, Belton, and Killeen, whose businesses are oriented toward young soldiers stationed at nearby Fort Hood, the third largest military installation in the world by population. Salado's small-town charm and quiet neighborhoods attract many Army officers and senior NCOs who choose to raise their families here or later retire in the area.

Access along the upper reaches of Salado Creek is difficult to nonexistent, with the few public road crossings fenced to the bridge abutments. Some sections of the creek are suitable for short paddle trips during normal flows, but you'll need to portage and drag your boat a bit.

Numerous springs in the vicinity of Salado provide adequate water for anglers year-round. Those springs also proved attractive to early settlers. The creek once supported nine mills along an eight-mile stretch, producing everything from carded wool to cornmeal, flour, and lumber. Beginning in the 1840s, Texas ranchers drove more than five million head of longhorn cattle through here along the Shawnee and Chisholm Trails, which crossed Salado Creek just east of the interstate, where Main Street spans the creek today. They were headed for railheads in Kansas, and they earned a place in Texas cowboy legend that is memorialized in more than two dozen films.

Stagecoach travelers on the Austin-to-Dallas route stopped along the river, at an historic inn that has been restored. We will stop there too.

I-35 at the Stagecoach Inn, Salado
30.94413, -97.53913
416 S. Main St., Salado, TX 76571
59.5 road miles, 1:02 drive time
Difficulty: Easy to Moderate

THE I-35 ACCESS POINT ADJACENT TO THE STAGECOACH INN provides good wading access both upstream and downstream; it is also an excellent put-in for a short paddle downstream. We'll focus on the upstream section here and cover the area downstream of the interstate bridge in the next section, **Sherrill Park** (see page 83).

What You Will Find

Beneath the highway bridge—actually four recently installed spans—the bank is lined with moderately sized limestone riprap; the creek is knee- to thigh-deep over a firm gravel and cobble bottom. It is rarely crowded here, even on weekends, but you may meet some conventional anglers who have wandered up from the public park just downstream.

5 The Old Plantation (Wading Upstream from the Bridge)

Between the traffic roaring overhead and the swallows flitting to and from their mud nests under the bridges, this access point is hardly tranquil. But the fish don't seem to mind. Vegetation along the shallower north bank provides good fish-holding structure, as do several deeper holes just off the south bank, where you parked, and some large boulders in the streambed. Take a moment to look over the water before hopping in. Redhorse suckers cruise the gravel bars, and there are plenty of sun- fish and a few larger bass around the rocks.

From here, the wade is more or less in a straight line up the creek for about half a mile. Just above the bridge, a spring enters from the antebellum Robertson Plantation river right (your left), and the cool, clear outflow is good for a few casts. As you continue upstream, the south bank is characterized by shallow gravel bars and large limestone outcroppings, while the north bank features heavy vegetation, including some truly epic pecan trees. Any dry fly or terrestrial plopped into the water just off the vegetated bank is likely to induce a strike, either from a sunfish or a lurking bass.

At approximately the half-mile mark, you will reach the first big karst formation, a heavily seamed limestone shelf that stretches across the stream. This looks like hard water, but some of the crevices are surprisingly deep and there are plenty of small sunfish here. If you have paddled upstream, this is where you'll beach your boat. *Take care traversing these karst formations.* They are knobby and twisted and often slippery. If you are going to sprain or break an ankle while wading around Austin, this is where it will happen.

The creek turns back toward the southwest here. Wade straight up through a sycamore-shrouded chute, or walk the gravel bank river left (your right). A huge dead tree river left marks a very productive pool above the chute.

About half a mile upstream from the Interstate, the creek narrows between thick groves of sycamore trees.

"Fishing provides time to think, and reason not to. If you have the virtue of patience, an hour or two of casting alone is plenty of time to review all you've learned about the grand themes of life. It's time enough to realize that every generalization stands opposed by a mosaic of exceptions, and that the biggest truths are few indeed."

CARL SAFINA, *The View from Lazy Point: A Natural Year in an Unnatural World*

The wade above I-35 is in a nearly straght line due west.

This pool is home to some nice bass along the undercut bank river right as well as a healthy population of colorful, aggressive longear sunfish. The stream above this point is broad and shallow with more karst formations.

The bronze statue of kissing giraffes behind the house on the north bank marks a good turnaround point, at approximately three-quarters of a mile from your vehicle.

Portages

If you are paddling downstream from I-35 to Sherrill Park, the next access point (1.13 river miles), your first portage will be in 500 feet at a low dam. You can go around on either side, but river right is better. You may have to get out and walk the next 500 feet or so, past the Salado Springs. Just below the springs, the stream becomes mostly floatable again. The cheese at the end is the extremely productive large pool at **Sherrill Park** (see next entry).

From downtown, From northbound I-35, take Exit 283 and continue on the frontage road. Just before the new frontage road bridge, behind the Stagecoach Inn, a single-lane blacktop road leads to the south bank of the creek below the highway. Park off the blacktop and lock your vehicle; the access point is not obvious to travelers speeding by on their way to Waco or Dallas, but it is upstream from a public park and might attract mischievous teenagers.

Sherrill Park, Salado
30.95186, -97.52477
South Ridge Rd., Salado, TX 76571
54.6 road miles, 0:55 drive time
Difficulty: Easy

SHERRILL PARK IS NOTHING MUCH TO LOOK AT, BUT THE POOL that backs up behind the low-water bridge here is well worth your time. Little more than an expanse of manicured grass and a few scattered picnic tables, the park provides water access as straightforward as any you'll find in this book, but getting to the park is a whole other story, so take a moment to plan your route. Your reward will be trophy redear sunfish on nymphs and spunky largemouth and spotted bass on terrestrials and poppers.

What You Will Find

A rough, paved lot sits beside the low-water crossing at the east end of the park. Well-kept homes overlook the area from the other side of Park Drive, and you're as likely to encounter a family having a picnic as fly fishers gearing up for a wade. You can enter the water pretty much anywhere there is a break in the elephant ears lining the bank or from the one-lane bridge itself. From time to time, "No Swimming" signs appear here. They are of dubious authority, and besides, wading is not swimming if you are doing it right.

The bottom here alternates between solid limestone and gravel bars, but the south side of the creek silts up significantly along the bank, which is one reason to choose a bridge entry. This is also your take-out if you're paddling down from I-35.

6 Sherrill Park (Wading, Paddling, or Bank Fishing at Sherrill Park)

As with the other access point on Salado Creek, anglers approaching the water at Sherrill Park would do well to probe the nearshore vegetation before hopping into the water. Elephant ears, spatterdock, and the muddy bottom near the bank conspire to create a happy place for fish.

Near the bridge, the north bank is heavily vegetated and provides good cover for fish, and the deeper trough along the stone wall a bit upstream can be productive for both bass and sunfish. Farther out in the pool, depths vary from waist-deep to shin-deep to *oh! there's a chest-deep hole!* On the submerged gravel banks themselves, clumps of American water willow often have washouts around their bases, and bass in the 2- to 3-pound range hang out there.

It's easy to spend an entire afternoon wading or kayaking this one pool—exploring every boulder, stand of aquatic vegetation, and washout. It's one of my favorite spots for explosive topwater action. It is about a quarter mile to the top of the pool, which narrows upstream, and an easy walk back through the park to your vehicle.

Left: This small but fesity bass, likely a Guadalupe x spotted bass hybrid, put a grin on Conor Reed's face.

Below: The short reach of shallow water below the dam at Sherrill Park is a great place to turn a kid loose In addition to fish in the potholes, frogs, turtles, and water snakes abound.

7 Mill Creek Golf Course (Wading or Paddling downstream from Sherrill Park)

Downstream of the bridge you will find one continuous braided riffle that continues for about 850 feet with shallow pools along both banks. There are small but willing fish in the deeper cuts and in the pools. The riffle ends in a knee- to thigh-deep pool created by a limestone ledge that crosses the stream in a northeasterly direction. The ledge is undercut and home to some particularly feisty bass that look like spotted bass or maybe Guadalupe x spotted bass hybrids. It's just a question of whether one will get to your fly before a sunfish.

Below the ledge another shallow riffle flows 375 feet to a second, nearly identical pool and ledge. Beyond this pool, the stream is shallow for long stretches. In theory, you could paddle or wade all the way down to **East Amity Road** (30.963306, -97.488692), 2.5 river miles downstream, but you would have to drag your boat at least half the time, and if wading, you'd have to figure out how to negotiate the last, neck-deep pool just before the take-out.

An added wrinkle is that the creek flows right through Mill Creek Golf Club here, and anyone seen standing in the river with a fly rod is likely to get a visit from a club employee who, while acknowledging that Salado Creek is public water, may attempt to dissuade you from continuing on. The only reason this should concern you is that Sherrill Park (where you left your vehicle), though mapped and signed as a public space, is actually owned by the golf club. Apparently, the club's strategy for maintaining the illusion of private waters for its residents and members is to attempt to corral members of the public in the area of

Above: There are nearly identical limestone ledges in knee- to thigh-deep water in the two long pools below Sherrill Park. The ledges provide excellent cover for both bass and sunfish.

Below: Green and redear sunfish are nearly guaranteed catches in the impoundment at Sherrill Park.

the park. Depending on your temperament, you will find this either a deterrent or a goad.

If you decide that discretion is the better part of valor, or if you've run out of daylight, pack up your gear and head back into town for some refreshment.

 Getting There

Once you have left Salado's diminutive downtown at the intersection of Main and Royal streets, there is no direct route to anywhere else on the south side of Salado Creek unless you paddle down from the I-35 bridge (see the preceding entry). The drive to Sherrill Park is a little circuitous.

From the Stagecoach Inn parking lot, cut through to Main Street, cross the creek, and drive north a little less than a mile to Salado Plaza Road. Take a right on Salado Plaza and then another right after a quarter mile onto Mill Creek Drive, which becomes Ridge Drive just before dipping to the creek, to recross the creek on the low bridge. The bridge is a single lane, and as elsewhere, the convention is for the nearest vehicle to proceed while cars on the other side of the bridge wait their turn. Parking is available in the rough, paved lot immediately past the bridge on your right.

From downtown, take I-35 north to Exit 286. Stay on the frontage road until you reach Salado Plaza Road and then follow the directions above.

 Fort Hood, Mike Doughty

 Chupacabra Craft Beer & Salado Lone Star Winery
chupacabratxcraftbeer.com
Opens at noon seven days a week

After fishing, head over to **Chupacabra Craft Beer & Salado Lone Star Winery** on Main Street to upload your photos and fortify yourself for the trip home. This modest tavern features a lineup of more than fifty Texas-brewed craft beers, free wi-fi, board games, and friendly staff. Out the back door and across the parking lot you will find Salado's own **Barrow Brewing Company** in the old feed store at 108 Royal Street. I'm partial to Barrow's Creek Don't Rise Lager at either location. Chupacabra is open late seven days a week; Barrow's taproom is open Thursday through Sunday, afternoons and evenings.

Chapter 6

San Gabriel River North Fork and Mainstem

Scenery and solitude in upper sections, spring run of white bass at Tejas Camp, ease of access and terrific fishing at San Gabriel Park, Rio Grande cichlids below the park. Access points: 11.

FROM THE UPPER LIMITS OF ITS TRIBUTARIES, THE SAN GABRIEL River stretches 120 river miles to its confluence with the Little River north of Rockdale and thence to the Brazos River. Named *Río de San Javier* by the Spanish explorer Domingo Ramón during his expedition of 1716, the river suffered a transcription error when Stephen F. Austin drew his map of 1829, mistakenly calling the stream the "San Javriel," which has evolved into the name used today.

As recently as the late nineteenth century, alligators were found well upstream in the river and its tributaries; a rather large specimen was caught and dragged by horse from Blue Hole in Georgetown in 1897. There have been recent gator sightings downstream, near Granger Lake, but today "the Gabe" is much better known for its fish: largemouth bass, common carp, freshwater drum, spotted gar, both channel and yellow catfish, and at least five species of sunfish. Texas specialties Guadalupe bass and Rio Grande cichlids approach the eastern limit of their ranges here.

The Gabe has three forks—North, South, and Middle—all small, spring-fed streams well suited to wading. The **South Fork**, a lovely stream, is described in **Chapter 7**. The short Middle Fork (we call it the "Missing Fork," it is so obscure), while quite beautiful and productive, is extraordinarily difficult to access and is not covered in this book.

> "The only way to be sure how a fishing trip will turn out is to not go, but the regret that can dog that decision is the kind that breaks spirits and ruins lives."
>
> JOHN GIERACH, *All Fishermen Are Liars*

The North Fork is a river interrupted, first by Lake Georgetown, a 1,300-acre impoundment managed by the U.S. Army Corps of Engineers (USACE), and then by several smaller dams downstream of the lake. The river becomes slower and siltier as it moves south and east, but you will find some very clear runs and pools all the way to the mainstem. At the confluence of the North and South Forks, at San Gabriel Park in Georgetown, an outstanding and popular wade less than a mile downstream can accommodate up to four anglers at a time. Below that, the river is best fished from a canoe or kayak.

North Fork, US 183, Liberty Hill
30.70043, -97.87758
3581–3485 US 183, Liberty Hill, TX 78642
34.3 road miles, 0:36 drive time
Difficulty: Easy

I STRUGGLED WITH WHETHER TO INCLUDE THIS REACH OF RIVER. On the one hand, it is drop-dead gorgeous, and the easy, 1.75-mile wade ends at a craft brewery. On the other hand, the three times I have fished it, I have had to really work for the fish here, especially in the pools closest to the bridge. Cast nets and trotlines may have something to do with the latter, or maybe I just hit some slow days. In the end I decided it's worth checking out at least once, just for the scenery. And the beer.

What You Will Find

On the southwest side of the bridge that spans the North Fork, a large gravel bank with some established trees provides good parking. The entire bank is used by visitors, but if you want to stay within the law, park close to the bridge. You will find a small pool and run immediately in front of the parking area; enter the water there.

8 **Brewery Reach** (Wading Upstream from the Bridge) The first pool upstream from the parking area is broad and shallow with few fish, though you may find a few larger specimens lurking beneath the under-

cut north bank (on your right as you head upstream).

The second pool, at about a quarter of a mile from the bridge, is a little better, particularly at the top where a spring enters on the south bank. From here, you will walk up a long, broad riffle: pretty, but not much going on fishwise. There is easy walking on a limestone shelf along the north bank. At 0.8 miles another spring cascades down the limestone river left (your right), and the river gets a bit deeper.

At 0.9 miles a narrow channel empties into a pool with some decent bass and sunfish. From here, the river becomes more interesting and more fishable. A spring-fed draw enters river right just shy of the 1-mile mark, and above it a lovely long pool features undercut limestone and overhang-

Top: The Brewery Reach of the North Gabe above US 183 is gorgeous.

Above: The track down to parking beneath the bridge is a bit of an adventure.

ing and standing brush upstream on the south bank. The north bank is equally magical, with a limestone shoulder and spring seeps slanting into a shallow, wooded corner.

At the head of this pool, at 1.1 miles, a deep, curving channel river right holds some terrific bass. It is best fished from the gravel bar above it—just watch your backcast between the sycamores. At the top of this run, a deep pool with limestone overhangs river right is best waded from

Kevin Olivier reaches for a fish on the far bank of the North Gabe above US 183.

the shallower north side. Don't neglect the water along the vegetation at the top of the pool river left.

At about 1.4 river miles, the stream gets shallow again and is best waded along the south bank. Small pools just above that and at 1.5 river miles are worth some time. I've seen some healthy spotted gar cruising the deeper edges here. A final, bowl-shaped pool with heavy vegetation and sunken trees on the north bank and a high, limestone shoulder on the south bank begins at 1.6 river miles and ends at the trail up the south bank to the corner of **San Gabriel River Brewery**'s seven-acre property at 1.75 river miles. It's about 500 feet to the tasting room and parking lot (**sangabrielriverbrewery.com**). The brewers, brothers Joe and Patrick Peck, are happy for anglers to leave a vehicle in their gravel lot to shuttle back to the US 183 access point. They are often on the premises brewing even when the tasting room is not open; just call ahead or e-mail.

From downtown, take US 183 north to US 183A through Cedar Park and Leander and then back onto US 183 (US 183A is a toll road, but it beats all those lights on US 183). The turnoff is a long, rutted dirt track that begins opposite Cole Drive, about 3.25 miles north of the TX 29 crossing; it runs alongside northbound US 183 for about 400 yards before diving down the river bank and disappearing below the bridge. Cross under the bridge and park on the gravel on the west side.

North Fork, Tejas Camp
30.69583, -97.82797
4560 CR 258, Liberty Hill, TX 78642
35.6 road miles, 0:43 drive time
Difficulty: Easy

TEJAS CAMP (ALSO CALLED TEJAS PARK OR TEJAS CAMPGROUND on some maps) is a USACE campground located on the south side of the North Fork just below the CR 258 bridge, about 3 miles upstream from the open water of Lake Georgetown. It occupies an expansive, grassy site near the turnaround point of the 28-mile Good Water Loop, a hiking and bike trail that circles the reservoir.

Wildlife is plentiful on the public lands surrounding the 1,300-acre lake, and you are likely to see several species of wading birds as well as belted kingfishers, red-tailed hawks, diamondback water snakes (harmless) and diamondback rattlesnakes (not harmless) along the trail. White-tailed deer, foxes, skunks, armadillos, raccoons, and opossums also frequent the area.

Among anglers, Tejas Camp is best known as a hotspot for white (sand) bass during the annual spawning run, which usually peaks around the third week of March. It's also a popular family campground with twelve primitive campsites, picnic tables, grills, and plenty of space to run around.

What You Will Find

The campground has a spacious parking area that is open from 6 a.m. to 10 p.m. Park here and head down through the campground to the river. Alternatively, you could park in the pull-out at the north end of the CR 58 bridge (this is also the best launching spot for a kayak or canoe), but this area is less secure than the campground, which has a volunteer host. Plus, the campground has public composting toilets.

You'll likely meet a crowd of anglers near the campground on weekends during the white bass run, and swimmers, paddlers, and dog owners frequent the location on warm days throughout the year. The mood is always friendly, sometimes festive. The easiest entrance to the river is on the north side of the one-lane bridge. Just step over the steel cable on the west side; it's there to keep vehicles out of the river, not you.

You can fish the river either upstream and downstream—or both.

The North Gabe above Tejas Camp is Central Texas in a nutshell: gorgeous small water surrounded by a sere, rocky landscape—and wildflowers.

White Bass

White bass, or sand bass as they are sometimes called, are a "true" or temperate bass species closely related to striped bass. Stripers (and their hatchery-produced hybrids) are the only species you would likely confuse with sand bass, which are quite a bit smaller on average. White bass grow to 9 or 10 inches in the first year of their life, and males are sexually mature at that point. Females need another year and a length of 12 to 13 inches before they can reproduce.

White bass spend most of the year in the open waters of reservoirs chasing shad and other baitfish and eating emerging insects. In late winter, they congregate in the upper ends of lakes, and when some combination of temperature, stream flow, and daylight hours is just right, the males begin a mad dash upstream, followed in several weeks to a month by the larger ladies.

On the San Gabriel River, anglers will start seeing the males in the river above both Lake Georgetown and Granger Lake as early as mid-February, with the females making their way up anytime from the middle to the end of March. After the spawn, the fish will slowly make their way back down into the reservoirs, and they will be hungry!

White bass readily take small streamer patterns in white, chartreuse, pink, or some combination of those colors and are often found at the bottoms of pools or stacked up at a barrier to their further progress. You may have to fish deep to get them.

Because white bass are such prolific spawners and rarely live beyond five years, TPWD manages them with a statewide 12-inch minimum and twenty-five-fish daily bag limit. Game fighters, white bass also are excellent table fare; if you are going to keep some fish, these are the ones to take home and serve to the family.

9 Riffles and Wildflowers (Wading Upstream from Tejas Camp)
There is not a great deal of structure in the upstream water, and the fish, ever alert to the shadow of a great blue heron, can be spooky. Slow, deliberate movements, long casts, and soft presentations are key to catching them. Patience can reward you with redbreast and longear sunfish as well as largemouth and Guadalupe bass, some as big as 14 inches. In high flow years, the white bass will stack up in the first pool above the bridge.

If you don't see many fish in the shallow water here, take some time to poke around the gravel banks on the north side of the river and check out the flora. From spring through fall you'll find a diverse array of native wildflowers, including Maximilian sunflowers, coreopsis, and the startlingly deep purple Leavenworth's eryngo. At the water's edge, look for the delicate yellow blossoms of Mexican primrose-willow.

At 0.6 river miles, just upstream from a large cliff river right, Sowes Branch enters on the south bank. Above the branch, two pools hold small fish. The first is easily identified by a triangular limestone block in the middle of the river. The second, at approximately 0.9 river miles, is more productive at both the head and tail of the pool and at the margins of the boulders river right. This second pool, about a mile from County Road 258, is a good place to turn around and go back to explore the more productive downstream section, as the next 0.7-mile reach to **Ronald Regan Boulevard** (30.69776, -97.84944) is much the same as you have already experienced.

10 Goodwater Loop (Wading or Paddling Downstream from Tejas Camp) During the white bass run, water levels will dictate how far upstream the fish can travel. In most years, they are limited to the reach below the County Road 258 bridge, most often below one of several limestone sills that cross the river below the crossing. Because there are deeper pools here as the river slows and begins to fill Lake Georgetown, this reach is also better for bass and carp. The easiest access is on the northeast side of the CR 258 bridge; you can also enter at any of several locations along the Good Water Loop Trail on the south bank. Much of this stretch is floatable, but there will be some drags in the first quarter mile.

We'll take it from the bridge. There are fish here, on both sides of the bridge and in the deeper washouts beneath it, but they are harassed on a regular basis and are usually quite shy. From the water's edge, it's about 600 feet to a large, flat rock river right. There are fish around the base of the rock, and it's a nice vantage point for scouting the pool below. The pool, about 500 feet long, is bounded at the bottom by the first limestone sill. The sill might be underwater during normal and high flows; during low flows, a narrow channel cuts through the center and tumbles down a short riffle on the other side. A slough river right and boulders in the channel river left hold small fish, including Guadalupe bass.

Just beyond this riffle, at about the quarter-mile mark, the channel

Tejas Camp is most well-known among anglers as a white bass hotspot during the spring spawning run.

When flows are up, the Goodwater Loop reach at Tejas camp is a terrific paddle.

becomes braided before opening into the first really big and reasonably deep pool. Stop on the gravel bar in the center of the streambed and cast toward the backwater river left, below the high limestone-and-dirt north bank (a small subsurface spring adds to the flow here). There are some pretty good fish in this skinny water.

To fish the pool, you have three choices: climb up the bank river left (there's a dirt trail) and fish from above the pool; wade along the north bank, along its massive limestone outcropping; or follow the south bank, which starts out with a good gravel bottom but soon becomes uncomfortably silty. Deeper water and good structure (sunken logs and boulders) are just right of the center of the channel.

At 0.4 river miles, another limestone sill angles across the river to the northeast, stopping white bass headed upstream during low flows. The long pool below this sill has a bottom covered in fine silt, which affects the water clarity, but it is wadeable at normal to low flows; alternatively, walk along the limestone ledge on the south bank. This pool ends in a riffle at about 0.7 river miles, just past a majestic limestone cliff on the north bank. There is a refreshing seep spring here, where my youngest boy has been seen miming the motions of taking a shower while cooling off after a tough casting session.

Below this point, the river is still confined to its original channel, but it begins to take on more of the character of the coming impoundment at Lake Georgetown; you'll notice it mostly in the deeper water and steep banks on the south side. You may feel eyes on you, too—from hikers walking the Good Water Loop Trail, which parallels the river here on both sides about 150 feet from the water.

At about 1.25 river miles you'll encounter the final low-flow obstruction to the white bass run: the usually submerged low-water crossing locally known as Third Booty's Crossing or Box Crossing. Wade or walk the shoreline on the north side to get there (all the undeveloped land surrounding Lake Georgetown is public land, owned and managed by the federal government, so you are not trespassing).

If you are paddling downstream or exploring upstream by canoe or kayak, **Russell Park** (30.67226, -97.75468), on the north shore, is a fine place to put in or take out, but be sure to take some time to explore the more interesting south shore, with its hollows and standing timber.

From downtown, take US 183A north to RM 2243 in Cedar Park, go east 1.75 miles to Ronald Reagan Boulevard, take a left, and continue for about 7 miles to County Road 258. Alternately, take I-35 north to Exit 261 and then TX 29 west approximately 8.25 miles to Ronald Reagan Boulevard, take a right, and continue about 3.5 miles to the same spot. Turn right on CR 258. Tejas Camp is about 1.25 miles down the road, just south of the one-lane bridge over the North Fork.

North Fork, Chandler Park, Georgetown	
30.65334, -97.69754	
106 Spring Valley Rd., Georgetown, TX 78628	
32 road miles, 0:39 drive time	
Difficulty: Easy	

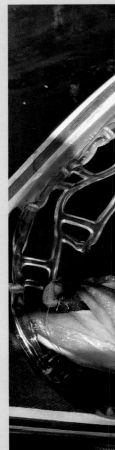

BELOW LAKE GEORGETOWN WE ENTER INTERESTING COUNTRY. Otters play in the river here, and coyotes roam the greenbelt corridor at night. We're going to skip over the stilling basin at Booty's Road Park immediately below Lake Georgetown, as well as the heavily silted and difficult-to-access reach of stream along the San Gabriel River Trail just below it, and head downstream a bit farther to Chandler Park, a pleasant little neighborhood green space that offers an easy paddling experience behind a small dam, with shots at big largemouth bass, spotted bass, monster redbreast sunfish, warmouth, and gaspergou.

What You Will Find

There is some limited bank fishing here, but a better plan is to launch a kayak or canoe (or belly boat) from the bank and explore the nearly half-mile-long impoundment that way. I like to put in at the gravel-bottomed creek inlet about 250 feet upstream from the dam. A two-wheeled dolly will be a big help getting your boat from the parking area to the water's edge.

11 Chandler Park (Paddling the Impoundment)

From the Chandler Park shoreline, head across the impoundment and fish up the north bank, targeting the weedy shoreline and areas below overhanging trees. Alternate between shorelines as structure presents itself (there are some floating docks, massive boulders, and sunken trees), but don't neglect the open water; submerged boulders and gravel bars in murky, waist- to head-deep water hold lurking bass.

The bottom of this reach, which fishes much more like a pond than a river, alternates between gravel, heavily moss-covered limestone, and sucking muck. The water becomes clearer and shallower the farther upstream you travel, and is easily wadeable from the top of the pool all the way to the **San Gabriel River Trail** crossing

Above right: The Chandler Impoundment. Below: This big bass was caught at Chandler Park.

(30.662813, -97.706521). If you choose to do that, anchor or stake-out your boat in shallow water as there is no legal place to beach it on the banks. As an alternative, you can walk in to the river at the trail crossing and wade down to the impoundment.

12 Mouth of the Middle Fork (Bank or Wade Fishing below the Dam)

After following sidewalks through the Oak Crest neighborhood, the San Gabriel River Trail rejoins the stream in Chandler Park. About 400 yards below the dam, its cement path arrives at a park bench and open meadow on the north side of the river opposite the point where the Middle Fork enters the stream.

The knee-deep pool at the confluence of the two forks is excellent for aggressive sunfish, especially on terrestrials and other dry flies; it can be fished from the bank or waded. At the tail of the pool, the river splits into two channels. Walk down either one, fishing pocket water in the faster channel along the north bank or fishing beneath towering pecan trees on the south bank. Where the channels come back together, two deeper pools, boulders, and logjams hold fun-sized bass.

The Middle Fork itself, while navigable by statute here, runs through the Georgetown Country Club, and it is difficult to portage the numerous impoundments through the golf course.

From downtown, take I-35 north to Exit 261, Williams Drive. Go west on Williams 0.36 miles to Rivery Boulevard and take a left. At the bottom of the hill, at the traffic light, turn right onto Country Club Road. Country Club Road will cross the river just below the dam at Chandler Park. Turn right on Spring Valley Road and pull into the parking area on the right.

Mainstem, San Gabriel Park, Georgetown
30.64740, -97.67207
Lower Park Rd., Georgetown, TX 78626
31.3 road miles, 0:37 drive time
Difficulty: Easy to Moderate

SAN GABRIEL PARK HAS BEEN A POPULAR GATHERING PLACE FOR locals since long before a large tree here was used for hanging murderers in the late nineteenth century. The city purchased the property and dedicated it as a park in 1933; today walking and running paths wind through the park beneath 200-year-old oaks (not knowing which one was used for executions, I side-eye every single one). Across Morrow Street, ball fields and a community center dominate the higher ground, and once a month the local Fly Fishers International-affiliated club, San Gabriel Fly Fishers, meets at the Scout Hut. Much of the older stone and cement work in the park, including the dam that forms the impoundment, was completed by the Works Progress Administration between 1935 and 1937.

What You Will Find

San Gabriel Park pretty much has it all. The North Fork and South Fork come together just above the low-water bridge at the top of the impoundment. Either fork can be waded upstream, as can the upstream third of the half-mile-long pool. It is also pretty easy to launch a kayak or canoe from the low-water bridge or from a ramp on the south side. Folks with limited mobility will find decent casting opportunities from the bulkheaded north bank or from the upper pedestrian bridge. Below the impoundment a locally legendary three-quarter-mile wade awaits.

 13 San Gabriel Park (Fishing the Impoundment)

Let's begin with a kayak tour of the impoundment. From the parking area, it's about 175 feet down to the water; a kayak dolly will be helpful. The shallows on either side of the bridge are good for common carp and small-mouth buffalo, especially very early in the day. Downstream of the low-water bridge, look for Rio Grande cichlids and assorted sun-fish beneath overhanging carrizo (giant cane) and other vegetation along the south bank. Two old, vault-like concrete structures cover springs in the river-bed along the same side of the stream. These make fine casting platforms, and there are fish around both, but beware the fire ant colonies on top.

San Gabriel Park is one spot on the Gabe you'll have near-guaranteed shots at Rio Grande cichlids.

Amanda Ashton, a South African by way of the UK, expertly presents a fly to longear sunfish bedded near the bank of the mainstem Gabe below San Gabriel Park.

As you continue downstream, probe the south bank beneath over-hanging trees and the edges of the coontail moss colonies river left. At about 750 feet, you will reach a large gravel bar; this marks a good turnaround if you are wading (you can find waist- to chest-deep water almost to the dam, but there are pockets that are more than head-deep and mucky silt along the south bank). If you're paddling, go around the gravel bar river right.

At about a quarter mile, a large spring enters from the north bank, and you'll see two more on the same side a bit downstream. Spring outlets, with their constant-temperature, highly oxygenated water, are always worth a few casts. River right, you'll see a deep woody pocket, a partial concrete weir, and a tall cliff face. A Masonic lodge sits atop the cliff. Sunken timber and the channels between the coontail moss colonies provide great structure for bass. You can find spotted gar throughout the impoundment, but this shaded water below the cliff is the only place I have actually caught one.

The rest of the impoundment is much the same, with increasingly heavy aquatic vegetation and silt buildup in front of the dam. There is

While the two big pools river left may hold larger fish, the channel river right is downright magical.

Left: Most of the Guady-looking bass below San Gabriel Park are naturally occurring Guadalupe x spotted bass hybrids.

some very deep water along the stone wall on the north bank. This is also where the Texas Parks & Wildlife Department (TPWD) stocks rainbow trout in the winter. A fair number find their way over the dam and can be pursued in the more natural stream setting downstream. The fish that aren't eaten by resident bass or herons, or harvested by anglers, may be found here as late as April, depending on the weather.

It's possible to portage the dam river right and continue downstream 21 river miles (with several portages) all the way to the canoe launch at **Granger Lake** (30.65307, -97.41277) or, more reasonably, 7.3 river miles to **Mankin's Crossing** (30.64584, -97.58418). For the first half mile below the dam there will be plenty of drags at normal flows, but the river becomes imminently floatable at river mile 0.56 below the dam with only a few places where you will need to get out and walk; one of those places is a broad limestone sill below Berry Creek.

 14 Katy Crossing (Wading to the Dam below the Park)

The first reach of the river below the dam at San Gabriel Park is shallow with a scoured limestone bottom; it is best waded straight down the middle. Deeper pools along the north bank hold fish, as does the gravel fan around the wastewater outflow on the south bank. Toward the end of this long run, at 0.25 river miles, a deeper pool river right often collects fish as does a smaller pool and rock garden river left. Either may hold Rios, in addition to sunfish and small bass. A very shallow riffle here continues as a deeper, heavily cobbled channel river left; it also splits into a pool river right.

Jess Alford ignores a light rain and casts from a boulder in the pool formed by the confluence of two channels of the Gabe.

If you go right, you'll find Rios, sunfish, and small bass in the pool. The problem is getting a fly to them. During the warm summer months, this pool tends to become heavily matted with filamentous green algae, or "pond snot," which makes casting difficult. Wade through the pool and you'll find a beautiful, tumbling riffle that ends in a larger pool with a muddy bottom and clumps of water willow and other vegetation. Approach slowly and fish for Rios, sunfish, and bass from the rocky south bank. Below this pool you'll see a crossover from the main channel (eddies and pocket water here hold fish) and then a long, shallow run down to the point where the north and south channels come back together. Don't neglect the shade beneath carrizo cane river left; Rios are plentiful here.

If you go left, to follow the deeper north channel at the split, go carefully. The large cobbles and faster current make for more difficult wading.

Target Rios beneath the trees on the north bank, and then continue past the crossover to several deep, slow pools with spotted and largemouth bass, sunfish, Rios, and spotted gar. Though there are reliable reports from several other spots along the river and its tributaries, this is the only place along the Gabe that I have ever seen a river otter. Fishing at dusk one evening, I watched the animal waddle out of the stream and up the bank behind the dense elephant ears river left.

The best wading in this section is along the graveled right side of the channel. Below the first big pool you will find a second one, very similar, and then a third, smaller pool just before the north and south channels come back together.

At the confluence of the two channels, pay particular attention to the point of the island in the center of the stream and to the jumble of boulders along the north bank. After carefully covering this water, wade across the main channel to the south bank and follow the limestone ledge down to the concrete weir downstream from the railroad bridge. There are bass to at least 8 pounds in this reach of river, both in the deep, main channel and around sunken logs and vegetation along the south bank.

The channel river left has more vegetation and cover, though not quite as much now as before the high water events of 2018 and 2019.

The channel river right is shallow, but holds Rios, hybrid Guadalupe bass, and sunfish along the bank and beneath ledges.

Fish local, drink local. Most Austin-area craft brews are available in local supermarkets and liquor stores, and with a long-awaited change to the law in 2019, consumers may purchase beer directly from brewers.

West of the railroad bridge, there is river access at **Katy Crossing Trail Park** (30.656225, -97.658162) on the north bank, but the bank is high and the trails down to the river are a bit sketchy. As of this writing, the City of Georgetown Parks and Recreation Department is in the planning stages of building a trail along the north bank connecting Katy Crossing Park to San Gabriel Park. When this project is completed, it will be easy enough to recross the river at the weir at 0.75 river miles and take the trail back to your vehicle.

 From downtown, take I-35 to Exit 260 (TX 29/West University Avenue) or Exit 261 (Williams Drive) and head west to South Austin Avenue. From University, turn left on South Austin and drive through the historic downtown square to East Morrow Street; from Williams Drive, turn right on South Austin, and then take a relatively quick left on East Morrow. After four blocks, bear right on Lower Park Road at Bob's Catfish-N-More if you want to fish the impoundment. If you'd rather wade downstream of the dam, continue on East Morrow through the park and use the parking area at the **San Gabriel Park pedestrian bridge** (30.65231, -97.66504) or continue under the **College Street vehicle bridge** (30.65303, -97.66382) to a small parking area there.

 Feelin' Good Again, Robert Earl Keen

⭐ Rentsch Brewery
rentschbrewery.com
Open Noon–10 p.m. Fri. and Sat., Noon–8 p.m. Sun., 4 p.m. –10 p.m. Wed. and Thurs., closed Mon. and Tues.

Rentsch Brewery opened in Georgetown in 2015 and offers a core lineup of four German-inspired beers and a rotating cast of seasonal specialties (the Red Poppy Red Ale is my favorite). The taproom is family-friendly with a laid-back vibe and stacks of board games on shelves against the wall. Outside, a spacious, oak-shaded biergarten invites some serious relaxation. There is often live music on weekends and a food truck in the parking lot. Rentsch, like the City of Georgetown itself, derives most of its energy from renewable sources. They like to say they make "wind-powered beer;" it's most definitely excellent beer.

Katy Crossing

Neighborhood and subdivision names have always been a source of wonder and amusement for me. Too often they seem, however unintentionally ironically, to memorialize the things a developer displaced or altered forever to build houses: trees, streams, springs, ranches, wildlife. Often they are laughably redundant: Woodforest, Bahia Bay, Glen Hollow. Sometimes they are just right, and even historically accurate.

You might think the newish neighborhood of Katy Crossing or the Katy Crossing Trail Park were named for the builder's cherished daughter, but you'd be wrong. Katy, in this case, was the familiar (and later quasi-official) shorthand for the Missouri-Kansas-Texas, or K-T, Railroad, and it did indeed cross the San Gabriel River where the park and subdivision now stand.

The successor to several late nineteenth-century attempts to connect Georgetown to a major north-south rail line farther east, the M-K-T began service on the Granger-Georgetown-Round Rock-Austin spur in 1903. Over the years, the trains served soldiers going to war in Europe, cattle going to market in Fort Worth, and Southwestern University students going home for the holidays. Passenger service was regular—and cheap—enough to facilitate date nights in downtown Austin.

By the late 1960s, the line was no longer profitable and service was discontinued. The tracks were pulled up, or mostly pulled up. Wading the braided channel of the mainstem of the San Gabriel River below San Gabriel Park, anglers can still find railroad spikes lying on the river bed and old track jutting from the bank. They are the last vestiges in this area of the once iconic Katy Flyer and Texas Streamliner, M-K-T's "Trains on the Plains."

Chapter 7

South Fork San Gabriel River

Clear free-flowing water, scenery, feeling of remoteness even in residential areas, dinosaur tracks, Guadalupe bass, Rio Grande cichlids. Access points: 7

THE SOUTH FORK OF THE SAN GABRIEL RIVER RISES IN BURNET County just east of Burnet approximately 42 miles northwest of downtown Austin. The stream runs 34 river miles south-southeast through rugged limestone formations to its confluence with the North Fork at San Gabriel Park in Georgetown, 27 miles north of downtown Austin.

The South Fork is a classic pool-and-drop stream to its confluence with the North Fork. Of the three forks of the Gabe, it is undoubtedly the prettiest and feels much more remote than it is all the way into Georgetown. Wading the South Gabe's famously clear waters over a limestone and gravel bottom, you would be forgiven for thinking you were many miles west in the heart of the Texas Hill Country.

As with many smaller Central Texas streams, the South Gabe's flow is seasonal, but there are scores of springs along the river, and the deeper pools remain fishable even during droughts. During normal flows, the South Fork is not suitable for canoeing and kayaking above its confluence with the North Fork unless you are okay with dragging your boat more than paddling it.

Local anglers worry about development. All along the river between Georgetown and Liberty Hill to the northwest and Leander to the southwest, sprawling ranches are being converted into equally sprawling housing subdivisions at an alarming pace. So far, most are set back far enough from the water to preserve the illusion of wildness, but the effects of additional acres of cement and asphalt, not to mention lawn fertilizers and pesticides, on water quality remain to be seen. For now, the fish are here and happy, and I'm thankful. My hope is that this lovely stream will reward anglers for years to come.

US Highway 183, Leander

30.61982, -97.86022

South Gabriel Dr. at Green Valley Dr.,
Leander, TX 78641

28.5 road miles, 0:30 drive time

Difficulty: Easy

WHEN I FIRST FISHED THIS STRETCH OF THE SOUTH FORK, I thought, "Okay, now *this* is the prettiest place around here!" My wife describes it as being something out of *The Lord of the Rings* or *Jurassic Park*, the former because there are dramatic cliffs and ledges and lush vegetation here (not to mention hobbits), the latter because a really big dinosaur left traces behind in the riverbed.

I'm kidding about the hobbits, but there *are* little people here—mostly youngsters on outings with their parents. They will probably stick to the trail on the south bank, which leads to the large, three-toed tracks of an early Cretaceous theropod: a great big, scary, bipedal carnivore. Paleontologists think it was an *Acrocanthosaurus*, a reptile similar in size and habits to *T. Rex* that roamed Texas and Oklahoma more than a hundred million years ago.

This part of the river is also well loved by local fly fishers, but there is plenty of water for everyone. The best fishing is upstream of the highway crossing, where just below the northbound bridge a long, shallow riffle begins.

What You Will Find

From the parking area, it is an easy 500-foot walk down to the river between the northbound and southbound highway bridges on either side of the fenced area. If you have four-wheel drive and are feeling adventurous, you can take the heavily rutted trail that loops below the fenced area right down to the river's edge. If you drive all the way down, be sure to pull off the trail so others can get by.

> "[I]n fishing I had always all my life brought the best of myself. My attention and carefulness, my willingness to risk, and my love. Patience."
>
> PETER HELLER, *The Dog Stars*

This is a terrific place to practice your "Leave No Trace" ethic. Between the passing vehicles and casual visitors, a disturbing amount of litter accumulates here. Bring a mesh bag or trash bag and pack some out, will ya?

15 Dinosaur Tracks (Wading Upstream from the Bridge)

This stretch of water can be fished before you get wet. The knee-to thigh-deep pool between the bridges is littered with boulders, and the fish—sunfish and small bass, mostly—act like they've never been disturbed.

About 1,000 feet upstream from this pool, above the old broken bridge, is the first really big pool. Formed behind a natural limestone ledge, the pool is 300 yards long and chest-deep at the tail. The ledges along the south bank hold fish, as does the vegetated shoreline on your right (river left). There are some big bass in here, as well as catfish. A wade in thigh- to waist-deep water straight up the middle, beginning just above the bottom of the pool, will allow you to fish both banks.

Above this pool, wade the shallow riffle or walk the limestone ledge along the south bank to the dinosaur tracks, at about 0.45 miles from the put-in. A dramatic limestone cliff looms 100 feet overhead along this bank. A few houses and some new construction peek out over the edge.

The thirteen tracks are big and well defined; one has a circle incised around it where a vandal tried to remove it. Depending on the stream flow, some or all of the tracks may be awash. The vagaries of erosion make it look like the animal strode out of the river channel and then vanished upstream into the south bank. There are other, less distinct tracks in the same sedimentary layer farther along this bank; look for the round footprints of sauropods and the three-toed tracks of smaller theropods.

Just above the tracks, another smaller pool with overhanging vegetation on the north bank can be productive. A little farther upstream along a long run, a silty slough river left holds fish, as does the shallow pool shaded by grapevine-draped trees where an intermittent stream enters from the south. Look for Rios here, at the 0.7-river-mile mark. Farther along, numerous springs seep from the limestone south bank. The run is shallow here, but the more heavily vegetated north bank holds fish in slightly deeper water.

Upstream, as the river emerges from a tunnel formed by overhanging trees, a large pool will become visible through the trees outside the river channel to your right. In short order you will arrive at a natural dam created by tree roots and rocks on the north bank. Clamber across and fish the long pool here, at river mile 0.8. The entire pool is wadeable and holds a nice mix of large sunfish, bass, channel cats, and carp. The outflow of a spring below the only visible house here, on the north side near the head of the pool, is good for a couple of sunnies and a bass.

The head of this pool is a good place to turn around and begin your trek back. Imagine that dinosaur, 35 feet long and 15 feet high, hot on your heels.

There are several access points upstream of US 183, notably the **Ranch Road 1869 crossing** (30.65991, -97.93843) just west of Liberty Hill. The next downstream access point is at **Ronald Reagan Boulevard** (30.61165, -97.81882), where the river can be waded upstream or downstream. Just 1.8 river miles below Ronald Reagan Boulevard, the 525-acre City of Georgetown **Garey Park** (30.61165, -97.81882) sprawls along the south bank of the river. The former ranch, donated to the city by Jack and Cammy Garey in 2004 and opened in the summer of 2018, includes seven miles of trails and two stocked fishing ponds.

The South Fork of the San Gabriel River, despite ongoing development, is still a beautiful river.

Tracks of a large therapod (thought to be Acrocanthosaurus) are currently exposed in a layer of limestone in the bed of the North Fork above US 183. They are believed to be between 125 and 100 million years old.

From downtown, take US 183/183A north through Cedar Park and Leander to the crossover just south of the bridge over the South Fork. If you want to avoid the tolls on US 183A, take TX 29 west from Ronald Reagan Boulevard or I-35, and then go south on US 183 over the bridge and left at the crossover. The crossover is signed as Green Valley Drive to the west and South Gabriel Drive to the east. Parking is in the sometimes muddy, unimproved lot north of the crossover, in front of the fenced area.

River Down Road, Georgetown
30.61761, -97.70785
522 River Down Rd., Georgetown, TX 78628
30.3 road miles, 0:33 drive time
Difficulty: Moderate

THE RIVER DOWN ROAD ACCESS POINT IS SOMETHING OF AN open secret, beloved of neighborhood families and local fly fishing guides but unknown to visitors and casual passers-by who haven't done some sleuthing. It's the only spot on the South Fork where I regularly run into other anglers, and that's because the trail ends at the first of several very fishy pools, possibly the best waters along the 9.6-mile reach between I-35 and Ronald Reagan Boulevard.

If you are fishing with a friend, bring two vehicles; leave one here, and wade upstream from **Wolf Ranch Town Center**, the next access point (see page 121).

What You Will Find

This access point is an undeveloped city park, and from the street it looks like nothing so much as a well-manicured, if narrow, residential lot. There may be a *#flybraryproject* here somewhere. The park actually spans thirty-six acres: all of the cleared area along the river you can see, and then some.

At the tree line, descend a rough but moderately easy dirt trail into a meadow filled with wildflowers (spring through fall, anyway). Across the meadow, a final pitch with a significant washout leads to the gravel-and-stone riverbank. The distance from the street to the river bank is about 750 feet, all downhill. As of this writing, some helpful soul had installed a knotted rope rail on trail right.

A large, round boulder in the river marks the trail entrance. Take time to orient yourself because the trail itself is virtually invisible from the river.

16 River Down (Wading Downstream from River Down Road)
The trail ends at the shallow tail of a pool dominated by a rock garden at its head. This is a popular play area for neighborhood families, and the fish in this pool can be skittish. Still, Guadalupe bass may be found at the edge of the hard water in the main channel here, and the many undercut boulders provide shelter for several species of sunfish.

A good strategy is to cross the river at the shallow tail of the pool and walk downstream through the small sycamore trees on the gravel bar river left, parallel to a long, hard-bottomed run. This run can be productive and is best fished up from the bottom.

The next pool downstream is a big one with a deep trough river right and a silty, vegetated bottom in shallower water beneath overhanging trees on the left; channel catfish cruise this bank. The shallow shoulders at the head of this pool can be productive. A small branch created by a hillside spring enters river right; if you probe the shelf below this opening, you might turn up some larger bass.

The next pool downstream begins in a rock garden below a dramatic cliff. Probe the south bank for bass and look for sunfish at the base of the rocks. Below the rock garden, the main channel of the river empties between two submerged boulders. At dusk, bass stack up in this chute waiting for something yummy to wash down.

This stretch of river is easily wadeable river left or by following the shifting gravel bars that snake through the pool. Deep water, some brush, and overhanging vegetation offer cover for large fish river right. This pool is also good for large redhorse suckers, if you can get them to eat. Long casts and realistic flies are the order of the day here as the water is exceptionally clear. If you haven't been

Getting there is half the fun, especially when the trail to the river leads through more than thirty acres of wildflowers.

For guys who are wet wading when they should have remembered their waders, Spidey-skills can prevent immersion to a shockingly uncomfortable level.

using a fluorocarbon leader, this might be a good time to swap out.

This pool tails out into a long, deep, hard-bottom run with a surprising number of fish along the bank river left and in deeper holes. To fish this run from the bottom, walk on the gravel bank river right and turn back when the dry footing peters out. A deep backwater on the south bank (possibly with a spring at the bottom), behind the gravel bank, is home to some decent bass and at least one trophy redear sunfish.

From here, legal bank access becomes limited, but it is possible to wade all the way down to the **Wolf Ranch Town Center** access point (see below), a total of about 1.3 river miles from the River Down Road entrance.

From downtown, on I-35, take Exit 260 to FM 2243 (Leander Road). Turn left, cross the interstate and continue west approximately 1.1 miles, and then take a right on River Ridge Drive. At the first stop sign, take a right on River Down Road and continue nearly to its intersection with Rim Rock Drive. You'll find yourself in a neighborhood of nice homes and friendly folks, many of whom will be out walking their dogs. Park on the street in front of the four large limestone blocks at the right-hand curb. The fish are down back.

Wolf Ranch Town Center, Georgetown
30.62789, -97.69278
1019 W. University Ave., Georgetown, TX
78628
29.6 road miles, 0:33 drive time
Difficulty: Easy to Moderate

WOLF RANCH TOWN CENTER IS A SPRAWLING RETAIL COMPLEX set hard against the southbound lanes of I-35. Despite its proximity to the hubbub of commerce, one corner of the shopping center provides terrific foot access to the South Gabe. It is a bit of a hike down to the river from the parking lot. A fit and determined angler could get a kayak down there (or back up), but there is really no need. This is a fine place to begin a one-way, upstream wade to **River Down Road**, see above, or to climb out after walking down from there.

What You Will Find

The parking lot ends at a well-tended box hedge; from there a paved trail leads downhill parallel to the highway. Hop over or walk around the chain barring vehicle access; pedestrians are welcome (oddly enough, this is another undeveloped city park). At the power substation, you will see a rough trail to your left; continue downhill on the trail or on the bridge apron to the water.

The river at the trail's end is a shallow run that broadens into a deeper pool beneath and just downstream of the bridge. Above this run and riffle, a broad, relatively shallow pool extends upstream approximately 650 feet.

17 Wolf Ranch (Wading Upstream from I-35)

Downstream, the seams along the south side of the river beneath the bridge hold fish, and the deep pool below the bridge is actually pretty wonderful. St. David's Georgetown Hospital looms on the bluff above, and large boulders, overhanging vegetation, and downed trees provide great cover for bass. Make sure your footwear is secure—there's some muck up against the bank. The usual sunfish suspects can be found here. The pool tails out into a braided riffle past St. David's. You could wade all the way down to **Blue Hole Park** (30.643151, -97.679865) or **San Gabriel Park** (see page 231) from here, but the best fishing is in the other direction.

A series of broad, relatively deep pools above the Wolf Ranch Town Center shopping center at Williams Drive and I-35 shelter bass, sunfish, and carp.

Wading upstream, it doesn't take long to get away from the noise of the interstate. In the first, broad pool—never more than thigh-deep—pay attention to the shady shallows river right (your left), the big boulder with a washout around the base there, and the grassy north bank on your right. Don't neglect the middle of the stream; a deeper washout below the next gravel bar often has a few good bass, though they'll see you coming from a long ways off if you're not stealthy. At the head of this pool are several truck-size boulders balanced in the river along the north bank, and fish hang out in the shadows and deeper pockets there.

A gravel bar along the south bank will take you up the next long riffle to a beautiful house on the left and a spring that enters on the opposite bank. Look for Rios along the north bank and sunfish along the rock wall in front of the house. Continue upstream to the next pool, at about 0.4 river miles, and fish from the tail river left or from the gravel bank river right.

The next big pool is at 0.5 river miles; it can be fished from the tail and from gravel bars extending into the pool. This pool is deep and clear and holds large bass, catfish, and some good-sized carp, especially in the slower water beneath overhanging trees on the south bank. In the warmer months, dense stands of coontail moss also provide good fish cover. To get around the pool or to the top, follow the gravel bars through waist- to chest-deep water or hug the cliff face on the north bank.

A short riffle leads to another similar pool at about 0.7 river miles. Again, fish from the foot of the pool and the gravel bar that meanders across it. Ford the pool in water that may be more than waist-deep diagonally toward the lawn on the south bank. The property owner has installed wooden steps down to the river here. They are not for us, and the large, loud resident dog lets you know it. He always stops at the water's edge—so far, anyway.

Continue upstream along the south bank to the tail of the last run in the **River Down Road** section, above.

 From downtown, take I-35 north to Exit 261 and loop around in the left lane to the southbound side. MoPac/Loop 1 and TX 130, both toll roads, are good options if you want to avoid the Austin-to-Round Rock traffic mess. There is an exit for TX 29 off TX 130 that will take you past Southwestern University, through a whole bunch of traffic lights, and across I-35, where you will turn left on the frontage road and then right into the shopping center.

 Heaven, Jeff Troutman

Mesquite Creek Outfitters

mesquitecreekoutfitters.com
Open 10 a.m.–10 p.m. Mon.–Sat., noon–6 p.m. Sun.

Mesquite Creek Outfitters, on Georgetown's historic square, somehow makes everyone feel comfortable.

Mesquite Creek Outfitters (MCO) on the historic Georgetown square features a revolving menu of sixteen Texas craft beers, twenty wines, and light pub fare. Free wi-fi and a staff heavily tilted toward accomplished fly fishers and tyers make this cozy, lodge-like venue a no-brainer for visiting anglers. This place, more than any other, is my "local." MCO hosts live music in the front and food trucks in the alley out back on weekends. The ever-changing selection of custom t-shirts (many with fishing-related art or slogans) and outdoor wear by Costa, Howler Brothers, Patagonia, and others is a constant temptation. One of the things I like best about this place is that it somehow manages to be equally welcoming to hipsters, outdoorsmen, families with young children, and veterans.

*Merrill Robinson and Cory Sorel test
the pool at trail's end at River Down.*

Part 3

Meet Your Quarry

Chapter 8

Know Your Central Texas Bass

"Is this a Guad?"

That's the question posted beneath fish photos on social media platforms just about every week.

The question is common because Guadalupe bass (*Micropterus treculii*) are found only in Central Texas, and they're beautiful, strikingly patterned fish. These riffle-loving bass evolved in the spring creeks of the Edwards Plateau and top out at around 18 inches. They punch well above their weight on 3X tippet. They sip bugs like trout and will pounce on a crawfish, baitfish, or mouse pattern like largemouth bass, and—oh, yeah—they live in our prettiest places. Guads are the official state fish of Texas, and they're just *cool*.

Turns out lots of folks agree with that assessment. An economic impact study conducted in 2016–2017 by the Texas Parks & Wildlife Department (TPWD) and Texas Tech University found that anglers generated $71 million fishing Hill Country streams over a 16-month period. More than 40 percent of those anglers were specifically targeting Guadalupe bass.

The angler posting the photo of a bass invariably will be rewarded with lots of opinions. Depending on the angle and quality of the photo (not to mention the angle and quality of the audience—both seem to deteriorate late at night), some of those opinions will be correct.

When I first began seriously targeting our scrappy, endemic bass, I wanted every blotchy fish I encountered to be a Guad. Over several years I read everything I could get my hands on about the species. I posted dozens of photos to iNaturalist, talked with biologists at TPWD, and even took specimens in to the University of Texas Biodiversity Center's Ichthyology Collection to be identified.

My identifications were wrong pretty often at the beginning. Then I batted about .500 for a while, and now I'm probably up to 80 or 90 percent certainty on most fish I see and … well, probably about the same for fish I actually handle.

In other words, I'm still no expert.

But sometimes neither are the experts. I've had two esteemed fisheries biologists give me well-reasoned and contrary opinions as to whether a particular specimen was in fact a Guadalupe bass. On the same day, with the fish in front of them.

Largemouths Are the Heavyweights

For a long time in Texas, largemouth bass (*M. salmoides*), fondly called "bucketmouths," have been the king of freshwater game fish, and certainly the best known of the black basses. Texas reservoirs built in the mid-twentieth century quickly came to national attention for the quality of the native largemouth fisheries that were established there. Those fisheries were (and continue to be) "enhanced"

Conor Reed shows off a beautiful largemouth bass.

A typical Central Texas small stream largemough bass. Note the deeply divided spiny and soft-rayed dorsal fins.

with introductions of Florida bass (*M. floridanus*) a fast-growing, non-native species that frequently exceeds 13 pounds.

Of course, nearly every landowner wanted trophy bass in his stock pond or estate lake, so Florida bass ended up there as well—and in neighboring rivers, where they freely hybridize with our native (northern) largemouth bass. The state has rewarded and expanded the propagation of the big, invasive fish through a program that encourages anglers to donate live trophy fish to a hatchery program that will return the lunkers' progeny to the waters from which they were captured.

Those Florida bass bring in big bucks. The Toyota Texas Bass Classic (now called the Toyota Bassmaster Texas Fest) tournament alone generated about $2 million in local economic activity in 2014, and year-round fishing on Lake Fork, where it was held, was worth about $27 million to Wood County that year.

But the Florida bass aren't doing the closely related native largemouths any favors, and they may have already sounded the death knell for another, little-studied native bass: the Nueces largemouth (*M. sal-moides nuecensis*), which once swam in the Rio Grande and (presumably) Nueces River basins in West Texas. Until recently, at least, it was still found in Dolan Creek, a tributary of the Devils River.

Then something happened: Either an invasive fish made its way around Dolan Falls in a flood, or—more likely—a well-meaning angler caught a couple of bass below the falls but released them above the falls. Now there are Florida bass genetics upstream. It's no surprise, really, since the Devils River is connected to Lake Amistad on the Rio Grande, and Lake Amistad is heavily stocked with Florida bass (more than half a million of them in 2017 alone).

It remains to be seen whether the Nueces bass will be lost to hybridization. Fortunately, largemouth bass haven't had much impact on the Guads. The two species do sometimes hybridize, but not often and not in most places.

The good news in answering the question "Is this a Guad?" is that there are some pretty obvious differences between largemouth and the closely related Florida bass on the one hand and all the other Texas basses on the other.

- If the jaw, when closed, extends past the back of the eye, it's a largemouth (unless it is very young fish).

- If there is a deep notch between the spiny dorsal fin and the soft-rayed dorsal fin, it's a largemouth.

- If the tongue is smooth (i.e., there is no "tooth patch"), it's probably a largemouth.

- If there are dark (black, olive, or golden) spots forming rows on the belly scales, it's NOT a largemouth.

You can also count the rays in the soft dorsal fin: largemouth bass will have thirteen or fourteen, spotted bass and Guadalupe bass will have twelve; smallmouth bass will have thirteen to fifteen. Or look at the scales on the cheek: Bucketmouths have nine to twelve, which (in comparison with other species) makes those scales look relatively large.

Smalljaws: The Gang of Three

Once we eliminate largemouth bass from the mix, that leaves only small-mouth bass (*M. dolomieu*, "smallies"), spotted bass (*M. punctulatus*, "spots"), and Guadalupe bass in our waters. *In none of these species does the closed jaw extend beyond the rear margin of the eye.*

Smallies are the problem child of black basses in Texas. First intro-duced into Hill Country streams in an effort to establish new sport fisheries in the 1950s, stockings of the hard-charging bass beloved of Midwestern and Northeastern anglers continued in Central Texas rivers through 1980 (they are still stocked in some reservoirs and in the Brazos River to this day). That's when state biologists realized that something unforeseen had happened: Smallmouth bass genetics were creeping into Guadalupe bass populations on the Blanco, Guadalupe, Medina, San Gabriel, and other streams where the non-native fish were stocked.

Oops.

For more than a quarter century now, fisheries scientists have been working to reverse that trend and prevent the possible extinction of our endemic species. They're taking a deep dive into bass genetics,

A Central Texas smallmouth bass. Note the overall brown or bronze color and vertical barring that extends onto the belly.

developing optimal hatchery and stocking strategies to overwhelm the invasive DNA, and working with landowners to restore and maintain suitable habitat for Guadalupe bass.

It's working. Late in 2017 TPWD declared a premier stretch of the South Llano River restored, with more than 98 percent of fish sampled showing up as pure Guadalupe bass.

In their namesake stream, there are pockets of pure-strain Guadalupes, but non-native smallies from stocked reservoirs continue to make their way upstream, in some years raising the hybridization rate to something like 70 percent. Success there will depend on working with landowners to manage barriers to movement (i.e., low-head dams). Some barriers may need to go; others may be beneficial in protecting pockets of genetic purity.

> "But a river shouldn't be all long, deep, slow pools. Bass can live there, but there are not nearly as many of them as if there were intermittent pools and ledges and rocks and ripples and so on."
>
> BERNARD "LEFTY" KREH, "INTERVIEW: LEFTY KREH ON A LIFETIME OF SMALLMOUTH BASS FISHING," *Midcurrent*

The San Gabriel River has much lower rates of smallmouth introgression, but recent research has suggested there may be a very broad area of natural hybridization between native spotted bass and Guadalupe bass, and even some fish with genetic contributions from all three species.

So how do you know if the small-jawed bass you're holding is an actual smallmouth?

- If the coloring tends toward a uniform dark brown or bronze and vertical barring extends from near the dorsal fins to near the belly, it's a smallie.

- If there is NO tooth patch on the tongue, it's a smallie; if there IS a tooth patch, it's a spot or a Guad or has one (or both) of those species lurking in the family tree.

Smallies also will have more than twelve soft dorsal rays (usually thirteen to fifteen), and a scale count of eleven to fourteen above the lateral line (all other species in Texas will come in at ten or fewer).

This black bass apears to be a spotted bass, with triangular or diamond-shaped blotches on the lateral line. Note the broadly connected dorsal fins.

The closed jaw of this bass does not extend past the rear margin of the eye. Definitely not a largemouth bass.

A distinct tooth patch is a hallmark of spotted and Guadalupe bass; smallies have smooth tongues.

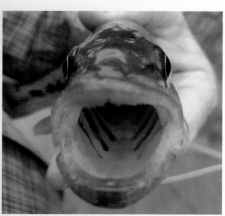

Rows of black, brown, or olive spots on the belly could be indicative of either a spotted bass or a Guadalupe bass.

Guadalupe Bass or Spotted Bass?

The real trouble comes in distinguishing native spots from Guads. The shallow dorsal notch, number of soft dorsal rays (twelve), tooth patch, and scale counts are the same in both species. Moreover, Guads are tricky as hell. In addition to the rare Guadalupe bass x largemouth bass hybrids, and the all-too-common Guadalupe bass x smallmouth crosses, Guads and spots hybridize readily, and pure-strain Guads will sometimes sneak around in the guise of their spotted cousins

It's enough to make an angler, never mind a biologist, throw up his hands in despair.

Dijar Lutz-Carrillo, a geneticist at TPWD's A. E. Wood Fish Hatchery, told me a story. It goes like this:

A world-record Guadalupe bass was caught from the Colorado River below Austin, and the district biologist wanted to verify that it was not a hybrid with the spotted bass. So the first thing we did was collect phenotypic Guadalupe bass and phenotypic spotted bass from the drainage and identify genetic differences that we could then use to evaluate the world-record fish. What we found was that the Guadalupe bass produced DNA sequences that looked like other Guadalupe bass, but spotted bass produced sequences that looked like Guadalupe bass, too—rather than spotted bass from elsewhere. In all the fish we looked at we never found a genetic spotted bass, but we did find hybrids (Guadalupe bass x spotted bass).

"Phenotypic," by the way, means the sample fish were chosen on the basis of how much they looked like known specimens of those species.

This opens up a whole new can of worms: How many fish that have entered the record books as spotted bass might, in fact, be Guads? And how many races, or even subspecies or species, of spotted bass might there be in Texas?

Maybe more than we think. Lately, new species of native, riverine black basses are being identified at a pretty brisk pace across the South and Southeast U.S.—the Guadalupe bass is just one of a group of (currently) nineteen similar fish that includes the warrior bass, the redeye bass, the shoal bass, the Choctaw bass, and so on. Fly fishers are now pursuing river bass "slams" much as they do cutthroat or native trout challenges in the Mountain West.

To compound the problem, Guadalupe bass, like many species of fish, are highly variable in pattern and color. This variability is partly due to environmental influences: Fish that spend time in more turbid water tend to be paler, for example, and fish in clear water more vividly patterned. This also is true more broadly and is one reason many people at first glance mistake strikingly blotched Hill Country largemouth bass for Guadalupe bass.

Geneticists also have discovered that Guads from different water-sheds (Guadalupe bass are native to the Brazos, Colorado, Guadalupe, and San Antonio river basins) are genetically distinct; not species-level distinct, but enough to exhibit structural differences and differences in appearance.

This handsome Brushy Creek fish has all the hallmarks of a genetically pure Guadalupe bass.

Whether it's environment or genetics or some interaction between the two, a Pedernales River Guad is likely to display a pale golden color and faint vertical barring while its Brushy Creek cousin is more likely to be a vivid brown and black with clear tiger stripes ... unless it comes from a turbid, lower reach of the stream, where it may be so pale as to defy easy identification from a photograph.

So if you ask a biologist about a fish caught in Texas, he or she will probably ask you right back, "Where did you catch it?"

That's because, short of genetic analysis, reliably separating the Guads from the spots is a challenge. Oh, some are clearly one or the other. Or appear to be. But geography is a clue for the in-betweens. Outside of stocked ponds and reservoirs, spotted bass are found primarily on the coastal plain and in East Texas. Guadalupe bass, on the other hand, are creatures of the Edwards Plateau and its spring-fed streams.

On the Colorado River, Guadalupe bass persist well below the Edwards Plateau, down to around the Bastrop area, which marks the beginning of the borderlands for Guads. By the time they get down toward LaGrange, they're entering foreign territory. In that transition zone you'll find both Guads and spots, as well as naturally occurring hybrids of the two species. On the San Gabriel River, that transition zone now appears to extend all the way up to Georgetown, on the edge of the Edwards Plateau.

This light-colored fish from Onion Creek is likely a Guadalupe bass.

What the biologists do know, from sampling, is that Guady-looking fish from **Lake Travis** are Guads (based on a sample size of 10). Guads from the **Lower Colorado** down to the Bastrop area are usually Guads. Guads from the **Pedernales** are always Guads, except in a few rare instances when they are Guadalupe x largemouth hybrids (sample size 100). Guads on **Brushy Creek** are, so far, almost always Guads. Guads on the **South Llano** are good to go, thanks to years of restoration work. On the mainstem **Llano River** a Guad is probably, but not certainly, a Guad; likewise on the little-fished **San Saba**.

If you're fishing out west on the **Nueces** or **Sabinal** Rivers, and you catch a smalljaw bass, it's a Guad. The species is not native to those rivers (but neither are spotted or smallmouth bass, and those species have not been stocked there) but was introduced to the Sabinal to establish a refuge population and to the Nueces to increase angling opportunity.

On the **San Gabriel**, if you are fishing below Lake Georgetown, it may look like a Guad, but it's almost certainly a naturally occurring Guadalupe x spotted bass hybrid—still a native fish. On the upper reaches of the **forks of the Gabe**, it's anybody's guess. Likewise, on the **Guadalupe**, **San Marcos**, **Lampasas**, **Medina**, and **San Antonio** rivers … on **Onion Creek** and **Cibolo Creek** and **Salado Creek** … who knows? There are fragmented populations of genetically pure Guadalupe bass on most of these streams. There also are reaches where most of the fish are heavily introgressed. Sampling and genetic analysis of specimens from many of these waters is ongoing, and biologists should have more to tell us over the next few years.

The best advice I can offer when it comes to identifying spotted bass—and it's the advice biologists gave me—is this:

- If the blotches along the side of your fish are triangular or diamond-shaped—especially if they merge into a nearly solid lateral stripe near the tail—it's a spotted bass.

- If the blotches don't extend much below the lateral line, it's probably a spotted bass.

But then again, it might be a Guad in spot's clothing.

A Singular Fish

So back to that fish our angler posted in the Facebook group. Here's the answer: If the closed jaw doesn't extend past the back of the eye, if the dorsal fins are broadly connected, if there is a tooth patch, if there are dark or golden dots arranged in rows on the belly scales, and if it was caught anywhere upstream of I-35 (or some miles east of the interstate on some streams)—then, congratulations! It's a Guad. Probably.

 The Five Pound Bass, Robert Earl Keen

Chapter 9

The Queen of Rivers (and Her Court)

SUBURBAN SALMON. MUD MARLIN. DITCH TARPON. SOME OF our off-handed, half-ironic nicknames for common carp reflect the ambivalence with which many anglers regard them. For many years carp were thought of (mostly mistakenly) as a threat to native species and a destroyer of aquatic habitat. American anglers have in the past decade or so begun to catch up to European anglers, who have long regarded carp as worthy sport fish.

People have been writing about carp at least since Aristotle penned his *Inquiries on Animals* in the fourth century B.C. Izaak Walton published *The Compleat Angler* in 1653, and he had nothing but admiration for *Cyprinus carpio*, calling the species "... the Queen of Rivers, a stately, a good, and a very subtil fish." A growing number of Central Texas (and, indeed, North American) fly fishers agree.

When carp were introduced to the U.S. (to replace native species depleted by market fishing and habitat loss) in the late 1870s, they were considered so valuable that their eggs were fenced and guarded.

In 1879, the U.S. Fish Commission (the predecessor to the U.S. Fish and Wildlife Service) included carp in its initial stockings in Texas

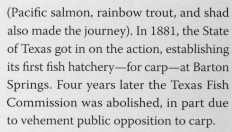

> "Whilst some anglers consider salmon to be the king of fish, or describe wild trout with elitist praise, the wild carp is an icon that forges a living connection between the past and the present."
>
> FENNEL HUDSON, *Wild Carp, Fennel's Journal No. 4*

(Pacific salmon, rainbow trout, and shad also made the journey). In 1881, the State of Texas got in on the action, establishing its first fish hatchery—for carp—at Barton Springs. Four years later the Texas Fish Commission was abolished, in part due to vehement public opposition to carp.

And so it has gone ever since, with carp by turns celebrated and vilified.

I am firmly and unapologetically in the celebratory camp for the following reasons: the by-now-naturalized carp (they've been in the Austin area far longer than Rio Grande cichlids, redbreast sunfish, or Florida bass) are nearly ubiquitous in Texas—most streams and reservoirs contain a healthy population; carp are (sometimes maddeningly) challenging to catch on the fly; and carp are tireless and savage fighters at the end of a line.

A Brief Life History of Carp

Common carp, not to be confused with the distantly related Asian carp or grass carp, are native to the rivers that flow into the Caspian, Aral, and Black seas where Europe meets Asia. When the federal government implemented large-scale importation of carp to the United States 150 years ago, it acquired fish from the Danube River basin in Europe. For that reason, the fish still are sometimes referred to locally as "German" carp, especially in the areas of Central Texas first settled by immigrants from that country.

Carp are deep-bodied, typically a golden yellow or olive dorsally, and can be easily identified among other sucker-like fishes by the pair of fleshy barbels at the corners of their mouths. They are long lived (in Texas warmwater environments, on average up to eleven years, and as much as five decades in protected waters) and fast growing (averaging 17.5 inches at the end of year one, and over 30 inches at the end of year four).

The current rod and reel record for Texas is a 43.75-pound fish from Austin's Lady Bird Lake, which is widely considered one of the world's best carp fisheries and draws a steady stream of international anglers to test its waters. Fish between 20 and 30 pounds are, well, common.

Carp are a highly adaptable species, and while they do sometimes root around on the bottom of streams and lakes, disturbing vegetation and increasing turbidity, they also tolerate brackish, low-dissolved oxygen and very turbid water—leading observers to blame them for the sometimes poor conditions in which they are found.

The adaptability of carp extends to its diet. Opportunistic feeders, they will consume whatever food items are most prevalent in a given water body or season. Fly fishers have to match a hatch that may include anything from terrestrial and aquatic insects (nymphs, emergers, or spinners) to freshwater mussels to crawfish to small fish to cottonwood seeds. A good hopper crop, or cottonwood seed dispersal, can lead to exciting dry fly action. In 2014 Orvis published a *Beginner's Guide to Carp Flies* that includes more than one hundred patterns.

Fishing for Carp

In Central Texas, we prefer to stalk carp in clear, spring-fed rivers and creeks where they forage on sandy flats, lurk in deeper pools, and cruise the seams and eddies of the current. Fishing for carp, Texas-style, is not unlike sight-casting to redfish, bones, or permit in saltwater.

Small carp, like this Pedernales River fish, can be tussled with safely on a 3- or 4-weight rod. Larger fish demand something in the 5 to 7-weight range.

Walton, in his chapter on carp, observed, "… that if you will Fish for a Carp, you must put on a very large measure of patience; especially to fish for a River Carp …"

Finding carp isn't hard; spotting one before it sees or hears you is a real challenge. Carp have massive lateral lines; they are, essentially, one big, vibration-sensing "ear." My friend Ryan Gold, who catches more than his share of suburban salmon, recommends "angel wading."

If you are lucky, you'll happen on a carp single-mindedly foraging with its tail in the air, much like a tailing redfish. A softly presented fly placed in the fish's path is probably the best bet for an eat. If you spook the fish, as often happens, either go find another one or have a seat and eat some lunch. By the time you're done, it may be back to grubbing and you can try again.

My friend John Henry Boatright, also an avid fly carper, sometimes picks a convenient cypress knee and sits in the shade, waiting for the carp to come to him.

The take itself may be an energetic turn and

Common carp are powerful fish and provide outstanding sport on a fly rod.

pounce, or even a chase, or—more often—a gentle slurp. That slurp is often followed by a spit. A carp may eject a morsel for several reasons, including to inspect what it just put in its mouth or to pick a particularly tasty bit out of a cloud of detritus in the water column. In any event, the key is to set the hook in the animal's tough, leathery mouth in that moment between the slurp and the spit. It helps if you can watch it happen.

If you are successful, hold on! Small fish up to about 6 or 7 pounds can be handled on well-made 3- and 4-weight rods, but if targeting larger carp specifically, you'll want something in the 6- to 8-weight range and a reel with a good drag.

> A school of foraging carp will almost always be trailed by opportunistic, predatory fish: largemouth and Guadalupe bass, freshwater drum, white bass, and sometimes even catfish, waiting to snap up something the carp have uncovered or spooked.

Related and Similar Species

Koi, the colorful, ornamental variety of carp that descend from the very closely related **Amur carp** (*Cyprinus rubrofuscus*), **leather carp**, and **mirror carp** (both forms of *C. carpio*) all occur in Central Texas and may be found, in small numbers, keeping company with the much more common wild-type carp. While mirrors result from a naturally occurring recessive mutation of common carp, koi were domesticated and deliberately bred for color, beginning in Japan in the early nineteenth century. Leather carp are believed by some to have been selectively bred to be scaleless (for easier transition to the refectory table) by medieval monks and are genetically distinct from other commons. Other cypriniformes (the order that includes carps and minnows) are not closely related to common carp but are sometimes encountered in Central Texas.

Despite possessing a face only a carp angler could love, common carp are beautiful in their own fashion, with regular rows of subtly shaded golden scales.

Grass carp, like this one at Pedernales Falls State Park, have escaped to a number of Central Texas streams.

Grass Carp

Native to China, grass carp (*Ctenopharyngodon idella*) were first introduced to this country by the U.S. Fish and Wildlife Service in 1963.
Escapees from various experiments have since resulted in established
populations throughout the Missouri and Mississippi river basins. In
Texas, the only verified, reproducing populations are in the Trinity River
basin and in waters connected to Lake Conroe in the Houston area.
Other Houston-area streams that are suspected to have reproducing
grass carp include Brays and Buffalo bayous and Clear Creek.

Since the early 1990s, the Texas Parks & Wildlife Department
(TPWD) has allowed the stocking of triploid (sterile) grass carp by permit to control aquatic vegetation in ponds and lakes. They do make their
way into area rivers, where they are likely to be the biggest fish you see
all day (grass carp can live more than thirty years and reach lengths of 4
feet). Grassers are a favorite quarry of urban fly fishers in the Houston
area, but are not much targeted in Central Texas.

Smallmouth Buffalo

Smallmouth buffalo (*Ictiobus bubalus*) is one of several closely related
species of large, deep-bodied fish found in Texas. Bigmouth buffalo and
black buffalo are largely confined to the Red River basin in North Texas,
while smallmouth buffalo range across the entire state, with the exception
of the Panhandle.

Smallmouth buffalo resemble common carp, but lack the distinctive
barbels at the mouth and can be flesh-colored, gray, or even black dorsally. They grow quite large, to lengths exceeding 36 inches and weights
of more than 80 pounds.

Buffalo are often caught by traditional "Euro" carp anglers fishing
over baited waters or with prepared baits, but for fly fishers are mostly
by-catch while targeting carp. Interestingly, smallmouth buffalo are the
number one species caught and marketed by freshwater commercial
fishermen in Texas.

Gray Redhorse

Gray redhorse suckers (*Moxostoma congestum*) might, at first glance,
be mistaken for smallish common carp. The golden fish forages on the
same sandy flats and along the edge of the current like carp. And like
carp, their diet includes aquatic insect larvae and mollusks.

Redhorse suckers have a tough, leathery mouth with flexible lips,

Above and right: Native redhorse suckers, sleek and fast, can be tricked with nymph patterns. Inset: Tom Powell with a smallmouth buffalo from the Colorado River.

perfectly positioned for hoovering prey off the bottom of the stream. Unlike carp, redhorse do not have a fleshy barbel moustache and are more streamlined. If carp are built for comfort, redhorse are built for speed. They will sometimes chase down a nymph or even a streamer, but the best bet is to drop a nymph (I've had good results using olive or black damsel nymphs and Pat's Rubber Legs patterns) on the bottom just ahead of a foraging fish.

Gray redhorse are native to streams draining into the Gulf of Mexico, and aside from the Rio Grande watershed in northern Mexico, parts of New Mexico, and far West Texas, their stronghold is the Texas Hill Country. They grow to an average maximum length of a little more than 20 inches.

Take a look at one in profile, and most anglers will immediately think, "Bonefish!" In fact, we sometimes refer to the muscular, torpedo-shaped fish as "river bones," and the strength of their runs when hooked justifies the moniker.

River Carpsucker

The river carpsucker (*Carpiodes carpio*) is a beautiful, golden fish that is visually similar to common carp and buffalo ("carpiodes" means "carp-like"), but—as with other suckers—lacks barbels. The river carpsucker also sports an elongated dorsal fin, noticeably longer than in carp.

The widespread carpsuckers are vacuum and filter feeders, with algae and plankton making up a significantly greater proportion of their diets than is the case with carp. Even so, they are sometimes caught by fly fishers, especially on nymphs fished close to the bottom.

River carpsuckers are denizens of deep pools and slow water. With a maximum length of about 24 inches, they are game fighters.

The golden river carpsucker lacks the fleshy barbel moustache of the common carp.

Chapter 10

Panfish: Sunfish, Brim, and "Perch"

SUNFISH—COLORFUL, PREDOMINANTLY PALM-SIZED SCRAPPERS of the genus *Lepomis*—are by far the most numerous sport fish in Central Texas streams. Often lumped together under the heading "panfish" (for their table qualities) or "bluegill" (for the most widespread and common member of the genus), and also called "bream" or "brim," and—inaccurately—"perch," five native and one introduced species are commonly caught in Central Texas (some others, such as the orangespotted, redspotted, dollar, and bantam sunfishes, are either not common enough or do not grow large enough to merit more than a passing mention). Most species in the genus hybridize readily, which sometimes makes field identification problematic.

Sunnies, like black basses (also in the sunfish family, though not in the genus *Lepomis*), are nest guarders and during the spring and summer breeding seasons are easily spotted by looking for the circular depressions of clean gravel in shallow water.

Most of the sunfishes will take a variety of flies, including dries (watching longear sunfish rise to a

Above: Palm-sized panfish, like this green sunfish caught by Merrill Robinson, aren't just for kids. They are plentiful and terrific fun on ultralight fly rods.

> "Without the youthful joys of fishing for bluegill, sunfish, warmouth, rock bass, white and black crappie, and yellow perch, this boater fears he might well have sunk into juvenile delinquency—or, worse, golf."
>
> TED LEESON, "CELEBRATING THE ALL-AMERICAN PANFISH," *BoatUS*

caddis hatch on Brushy Creek is a sublime experience), terrestrials (a bank beetle or foam spider or ant is a favorite offering), nymphs, poppers, and even small streamers. Basically, if a sunny can get it in its mouth, it will eat it.

Bluegill (*Lepomis macrochirus*) are native to the U.S. east of the Rocky Mountains and have been widely introduced elsewhere for both sport and food. Bluegills are one of the heavyweights of the sunfish family, reaching a maximum size of 15 inches.

Bluegills are rather plain (look for the "railroad track" vertical barring) until the breeding season, when males color up.

Bluegills have a relatively small and round opercle flap ("ear") that lacks the white or red margin found in some other species, and their pectoral fins are rather longer and more pointed than in other sunfish. The gill covers and head often are washed in blue (thus the name). Bluegills have five to nine dark vertical bars and a distinct dark spot at the base of the second (soft) dorsal fin. Fish in breeding colors can be astonishingly bright, sporting pink or even purple hues.

Redear sunfish (*Lepomis microlophus*) are the "tanks" of the sunfish family. The current state record is a 2.99-pound, 14-inch specimen from Lady Bird

There's nothing subtle about a redear sunfish, and they grow large enough to bend a 5-weight.

Lake in Austin. The opercle flap is small compared to other sunfishes and, as the common name suggests, edged in red. Otherwise the fish are the drabbest members of the family.

Commonly known as "shellcrackers" for their dietary preferences—mollusks and clams are favored entrées—redears are not often caught on dry or topwater flies, though they will eat nymph and worm patterns.

Green sunfish (*Lepomis cyanellus*) are, with warmouth, more bass-like than other sunnies. They have relatively large mouths, which they put to good use attacking topwater and terrestrial flies and larger streamers. With a spawning season that spans the warm months, they also hybridize readily with most other species of sunfish found in Central Texas.

Green sunfish have larger mouths and longer bodies than most other members of the genus Lepomis, and readily take flies meant for bass.

Green sunfish may be identified by their relatively elongated bodies, overall greenish color, random blue or green spots and lines on the cheeks, indistinct vertical barring on the sides, an opercle flap edged in white, and light-colored edging on the fins. In the breeding season, this latter trait can be quite striking, with dark fins set off by bright white, yellow, or pink edges, similar to brook trout or other chars. Green sunfish put up a tremendous fight on ultralight tackle.

Longear sunfish (*Lepomis megalotis*) are the living jewels of Central Texas streams. What they lack in size, they more than make up for in ferocity and beauty. Longears have an elongated opercle flap, edged in white, but not so long as the opercle flap in redbreast sunfish, which leads to confusion. Allegedly, the type specimen had been the victim of a disfiguring event which left its opercle flaps longer than normal.

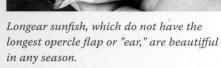

Longear sunfish, which do not have the longest opercle flap or "ear," are beautiful in any season.

Longears are attractive in any season, but during the breeding season males "color up," displaying vivid ruby reds and aquamarine blues that rival the displays of any tropical reef fish.

Redbreast sunfish sport a long, thin opercle flap and a yellow or orange belly that becomes more vivid in males during the summer spawn.

There is a significant variation in color and pattern between populations in different streams.

Because of their preference for clear, flowing water and gravel bottoms, longears are strongly associated with Hill Country streams and are a favorite quarry of Central Texas fly fishers.

Redbreast sunfish (*Lepomis auritus*) are so common in most Texas rivers (in the waters covered in this book, only the Lampasas River does not have a population) that many people believe they are native. In fact, they are a common fish of the American Southeast but were naturally absent from the Gulf slope drainages until the 1960s, when they were introduced.

Most notable for the bright yellow, orange, or red bellies of males during the breeding season, the redbreast or "yellowbelly" sunfish can be distinguished from the longear sunfish by its longer, thinner opercle flap that is not edged in white. Redbreasts are aggressive feeders and will attack flies half their size.

Warmouth (*Lepomis gulosus*) are elongated, olive or brown mottled or barred fish with distinct facial stripes. Sometimes called "stump-knockers" for their preference for heavily vegetated pools and swamps, they are not common in Central Texas streams, but they are sometimes found in deeper pools, especially if there is submerged timber or vegetation.

Warmouth will take crawfish imitations, damsel nymphs, and even topwater flies like the mini Master Splinter Mouse.

Warmouth, sometimes called "goggle-eye" or "stump knocker" can be found in deeper, vegetated or brushy pools. Warmouth have a tooth patch on the tongue.

Chapter 11

Cichlids

THE **RIO GRANDE CICHLID** *(HERICHTHYS CYANOGUTTATUS)*, also known in the aquarium trade as the Texas cichlid, is the only cichlid species native to the United States. Ubiquitous in the clear, spring-fed streams of Central Texas (but absent from the Lampasas River), it is often presumed to be native to this part of the state; however, its native distribution is limited to the Rio Grande, Pecos, and (perhaps) Nueces River drainages as well as parts of northeastern Mexico.

In 1928, for reasons that have been lost to history, the U.S. Fish and Wildlife Service captured some "Rios" near Mission, Texas, and brought them to its National Fish Hatchery in San Marcos where they were propagated until 1941. The fish were distributed into area rivers as early as 1929, where springs provide thermal refugia during the cold months. Today they can be found as far east as Houston and, perhaps, New Orleans, though the New Orleans-area fish may turn out to be the closely related pearlscale or green Texas cichlid (*H. carpintis*).

From about November through March, it's tough to find a Rio on most Central Texas streams. The San Marcos River, which presumably has the longest-established non-native population and also benefits

The Rio Grande cichlid is the only cichlid species native to North America. It has been established in spring-fed Central Texas rivers since 1929.

from a huge volume of spring water in its upper reaches, seems to be the exception. But on Brushy Creek, Onion Creek, and the San Gabriel, Pedernales, and Colorado rivers, good luck finding one during the winter. I've always pictured them huddled around a campfire-like spring in a deep pool, sipping hot toddies and trading lies about their summer adventures.

> "Sometimes you're taking them onetwothreefourfive and justlikethat you want to cry out to the rest of them: Hey clear out, can't you see what's happening?"
>
> ARNOLD GINGRICH,
> *The Well-Tempered Angler*

Rios are strikingly colored fish, usually a dark gray, sometimes tan or olive, with a liberal sprinkling of cream or blue spots. Breeding males develop large nuchal humps on their heads and may appear, from above, to be bicolored, with their heads and the front parts of their bodies nearly white and the after halves dark gray or black.

As striking as their coloration is, Rios' behavior is even more interesting. During the long (March–August) breeding season, pairs form monogamous bonds and clean a circular nest by pecking gravel and debris and depositing it outside the nest (sunfish, by contrast, create their nests by fanning a circular area with their fins). Both the males and females are "brood guarders," meaning that after their (on average two thousand) eggs have hatched, they aggressively protect their young, which remain for a time in the vicinity of the nest and the parents.

They are curious fish, darting out to carefully inspect any new thing in their field of vision. They are known to stalk their prey (insect larvae, small fish, drifting terrestrial insects, even small frogs and snakes) and are most often antagonized into a strike.

Small crawfish imitations like Bailes' Hatchling Craw and nymphs, including the appropriately named Bennett's Rio Getter, work well, and sometimes Rios can be enticed to take a dry fly. A Rio sight fished on a 2- or 3-weight rod is an experience to remember.

Blue tilapia (*Oreochromis aureus*) is the other cichlid species commonly found in Central Texas and is likely an aquaculture hybrid crossed

Like most species of fish, Rios exhibit significant variability.

with Nile tilapia (*O. niloticus*) or other species. Still spreading throughout the area through accidental (and in some cases probably intentional) releases, they are considered invasive.

Similar to the Rio Grande cichlid in body shape (both have long, trailing dorsal and anal fins), the blue tilapia is native to western Africa and is not closely related to the native Texas fish (while Rios are brood guarders, tilapia are "mouth brooders"). A rather drab, slate blue or gray fish with faint barring on the sides, blue tilapia males put on some color for the breeding season, when the heads of large fish turn a metallic blue and their fins may be edged in red or pink.

The bad news about tilapia is that the fish are swimming in our rivers. The good news is that the wild fish are terrific table fare, and you can keep every single one you catch guilt free. More good news for anglers: They are giants among panfish, growing to a maximum length of about 21 inches, and a lot of fun on a fly rod. Try a chironomid pattern in size 12 or smaller.

Invasive blue tilapia continue to expand their Central Texas range. Rob Halford didn't mind the fight from this surprise catch—the first recorded from Salado Creek.

Chapter 12

Other Fishes

WHILE BLACK BASSES, TROUT (SEE THE **GUADALUPE RIVER** chapter), carp, sunfish, and cichlids are the most common fly rod targets in Central Texas, several other native and introduced species provide good sport and are common enough to bear mentioning.

Crappie are the third most popular game fish in Texas, after bass and catfish. White crappie (*Pomoxis annularis*) are more common in Central Texas than are the similar and closely related black crappie (*Pomoxis nigromaculatus*). Both species of sunfish are more often found in reservoirs, but white crappie in particular will become established in deep pools and impoundments of rivers in Central Texas.

Crappie can grow quite large for members of the sunfish family, with some specimens of both species topping 4 pounds. Small streamers, like Clouser minnows, and a sinking or sink-tip line can be effective when fishing for crappie around docks and points in area lakes. In Texas,

> "The fish and I were both stunned and disbelieving to find ourselves connected by a line."
>
> WILLIAM HUMPHREY, "GREAT POINT," *The Armchair Angler*

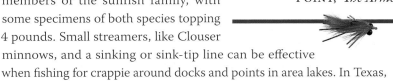

Crappie are common in area reservoirs and can sometimes be found in streams as well. This white crappie (note the spots arranged in vertical bars) was caught on Brushy Creek.

there is a daily bag limit of twenty-five fish, with a minimum length of 10 inches.

Bass

Temperate or "true" basses include white bass (*Morone chrysops*), discussed in the **San Gabriel River** chapter, striped bass (*Morone saxatilis*), and hybrid striped bass, sometimes called palmetto bass, sunshine bass, or "wipers." A fourth species, yellow bass (*Morone mississippiensis*) is a small, slow-growing fish not found in Central Texas.

Note the single, unbroken line that proclaims this fish is a white bass.

Striped bass are native to the Atlantic seaboard and the Gulf of Mexico as far west as Louisiana. Stripers spend most of their lives in saltwater, ascending coastal rivers as much as one hundred miles to spawn.

Stripers do just fine in freshwater and have been introduced into a number of Texas reservoirs, notably Canyon Lake, Lake Travis, Lake Buchanan, Lake Whitney, and Lake Texoma. The latter location is the only reservoir with a free-flowing tributary long enough for striped bass to naturally reproduce most years.

In addition to being fine table fare, striped bass grow to prodigious sizes and are revered as sport fish. Fish stocked in reservoirs often escape or are swept into the river below an impoundment (as has happened on the Guadalupe River) or, during the spring spawning season, travel upstream in streams that empty into lakes. The current rod-and-reel state record, a 48-inch, 53-pound monster, came from the Brazos River, and my friend John Erskine captured the current state fly fishing record

John Erskine with his Texas fly fishing record striper on the Guadalupe River.

A word about identifying whites, stripers, and wipers (hybrids): It's helpful to remember the "rule of two." Striped bass have two spines on their gill covers, two elongated tooth patches, and two or more distinct, unbroken lines that extend to the tail. White bass have one spine and one tooth patch. Hybrid striped bass may have either but usually have two tooth patches. The horizontal lines on a white bass are faint, and only one extends unbroken to the tail. Wipers fall somewhere in between, but they usually have broken lines that nonetheless extend all the way to the tail.

No trout snobs here. If it swims, eats, and pulls, we'll probably chase it.

(43 inches, 36.5 pounds) on the Guadalupe River on a big black-and-yellow streamer.

For stripers on the Guadalupe River, any big streamer, but especially one that looks a lot like a rainbow trout, will do the trick. The daily bag and size limit for striped bass and hybrid striped bass is five fish in any combination, with a minimum length of 18 inches. On Lake Texoma, anglers may keep ten fish, but only two may be over 20 inches.

Hybrid striped bass do not naturally reproduce, but they are regularly stocked in reservoirs throughout Texas, where they can reach weights of 20 pounds and lengths of more than 30 inches.

Catfish

Catfish are, overall, the second-most sought-after freshwater fish in Texas, just not by fly anglers. I've heard trout snobs scoff that muddy or degraded waters are "catfish water," but the clear streams of Central Texas are home to several species that provide good sport and, if you are of a mind, a guilt-free meal.

Channel catfish (*Ictalurus punctatus*) are the most commonly encountered catfish species in the streams of Central Texas, and though they prefer to feed from dusk until about midnight, they can often be seen in the company of foraging carp or freshwater drum. As the common name indicates, channel cats are river fish; in fact, caddis fly larvae make up a significant (40–60 percent) portion of their diet. Larger fish will readily take baitfish patterns intended for bass, but I have had the best luck with lightly weighted damsel nymphs.

Channel cats (like the closely related blue catfish) have deeply forked tails and are a uniform olive brown or dusky gray color with fine black spots that sometimes disappear in older fish. The state record channel cat was a 36.5 pound fish taken from the Pedernales River. The daily bag limit is twenty-five (blue and channel catfish in any combination), with a minimum length of 12 inches.

Blue catfish (*Ictalurus furcatus*) can be distinguished from channel cats by the absence of dark spots (except in the Rio Grande population) and a straight-edged anal fin (it is noticeably rounded in channel cats). Blue cats are the largest of the native catfish, with a 121-pound specimen from Lake Texoma currently leading state records. Blue cats are more frequently found in larger river systems and reservoirs and eat a wide variety of prey, including crawfish, insect larvae, fish, and frogs. The Texas fly fishing record is a 35.5-pound fish that fell to a Clouser.

Mature **flathead, or yellow, catfish** (*Pylodictis olivaris*) shelter beneath rocks, logs, banks, or other structures in deeper pools during the day, making them difficult to target. Interestingly, juvenile flatheads are found only in riffles. These fish regularly reach weights of 50 pounds in rivers; they are primarily piscivorous and prefer to hunt after the sun sets. If

Channel catfish provide good sport as well as fine table fare for anglers inclined to harvest a fish or two.

you are going to give it a shot anyway, a sink-tip line and large streamer imitating a sunfish might do the trick. The daily bag limit is five, with a minimum length of 18 inches.

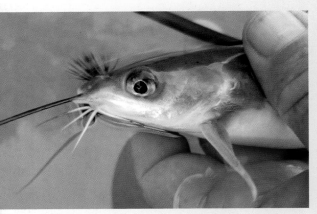

Take care when handling catfish. Catfish, when agitated, will often lock their dorsal and pectoral fins (presumably this makes them more difficult to swallow). The sharp, serrated spines of many species deliver a (usually mild) venom that can result in intense, localized pain and swelling.

Armored and **sailfin catfishes** (*Hypostomus plecostomus, Pterygoplichthys spp.*), commonly called "plecos," "suckermouth catfish," or just "suckers," are native to Central and South America and have established reproducing populations in Central and South Texas, likely as a result of aquarium releases. Similar in shape but widely variable in coloration and pattern, there are at least several genera and species present in our rivers, some of which are hybrids. Plecos are algae grazers and are rare incidental catches for fly fishers; they should be removed from the water, gutted, and—preferably—consumed whenever caught.

Drum

Freshwater drum (*Aplodinotus grunniens*) is a rarely targeted species in Central Texas but is a frequent and welcome incidental catch, particularly on the Lower Colorado and on the Lampasas River, where it often can be found in company with carp. Nearly ubiquitous statewide, gaspergou, or "gou" as they are sometimes called, are the only freshwater representatives of the drum family, which also includes spotted seatrout, redfish, and black drum. The species most closely resembles the latter, minus the stark black vertical bars. Freshwater drum are opportunistic feeders, with adults eating fish, crawfish, mollusks, and larval insects. I've caught them on streamers intended for bass and crawfish imitations meant for carp. They feed at or near the bottom of deeper pools, so a heavy fly or sink-tip line is helpful if you would like to catch one.

Gar

Gars are sometimes called "living fossils" because they have remained relatively unchanged from 100-million-year-old fossil specimens, and they retain primitive traits (like the ability to extract oxygen from both air and water). In Central Texas, the **spotted gar** (*Lepisosteus oculatus*)

Freshwater drum, related to both the familiar black drum and celebrated red drum (redfish) of the Texas Gulf coast, are just as sporty as their flats-dwelling cousins.

is the most commonly encountered species and can provide a thrilling, acrobatic flight on a fly rod.

A quick look at a gar's mouth tells you all you need to know about its dietary preferences: Rows of needle-like teeth are designed to capture fish, which make up about 90 percent of adult gars' diets. The other 10 percent is made up of crawfish and insects. Spotted gar will readily take a streamer, or even a topwater fly, but expect some missed hooksets as their mouths are extremely bony.

Longnose gar (*Lepisosteus osseus*) are found less frequently in Central Texas streams and grow larger (up to 72 inches) than spotted gar, which usually are 3 feet or less in length. Longnose gar can be identified by the namesake snout—noticeably longer and thinner than in any other species—and the lack of rounded dark spots on the head and pelvic fins.

Spotted gar are the most commonly encountered gar in Central Texas and readily take a fly. Setting the hook in a gar's hard, bony mouth is another matter entirely.

Alligator gar (*Atractosteus spatula*), which can exceed 9 feet in length and weigh more than 270 pounds, are found primarily in larger, slower rivers along the Gulf Coast and in East Texas, but they do make their way up both the Brazos and Colorado rivers.

Shortnose gar (*Lepisosteus platostomus*), the fourth gar species found in Texas, is limited to the Red River basin in the northern part of the state.

Oddities and incidentals found in some Central Texas streams include everything from feral goldfish (*Carassius auratus*), which can grow to several pounds, to rare, native mountain mullet (*Agonostomus monticola*). **Gizzard shad** (*Dorosoma cepedianum)* and the similar, but smaller, **threadfin shad** (*Dorosoma petenense*) are found in larger streams and in some smaller creeks (Onion Creek comes to mind), where the former grow to a sporting size of more than 12 inches and will some-times, unaccountably for an herbivorous filter feeder, eat a fly. You can catch **rock bass** (*Ambloplites rupestris*) in the San Marcos River.

These are just a few of the 247 species of freshwater fishes in Texas—not all of which are found in Central Texas and not all of which will take a fly; but you never really know what you might encounter.

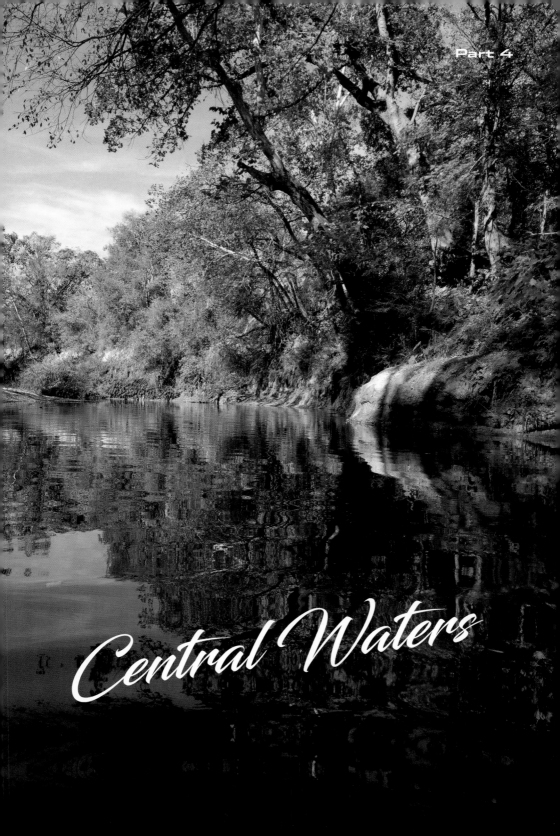

Part 4

Central Waters

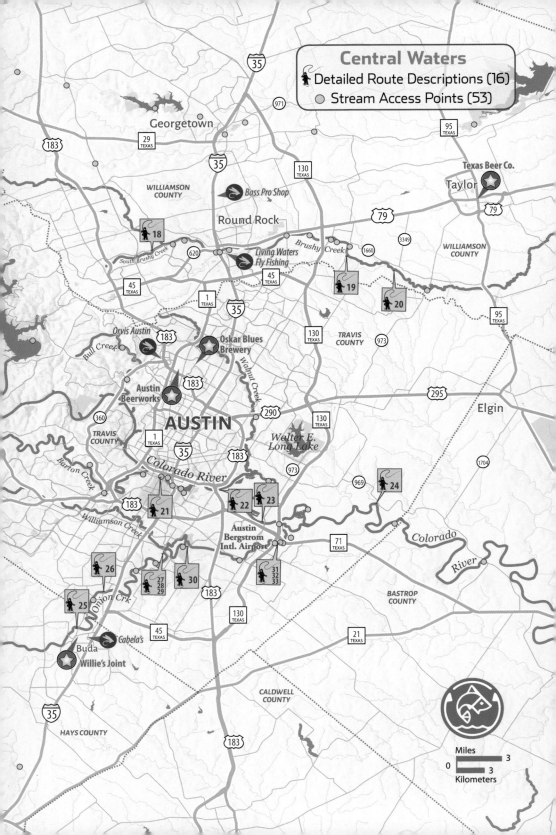

Central Waters

Detailed Route Descriptions (16)

Stream Access Points (53)

Georgetown

WILLIAMSON COUNTY

Bass Pro Shop

Round Rock

Texas Beer Co.

Taylor

WILLIAMSON COUNTY

18

South Brushy Creek

Living Waters Fly Fishing

Brushy Creek

19

20

Orvis Austin

Bull Creek

TRAVIS COUNTY

Oskar Blues Brewery

Walnut Creek

Austin Beerworks

AUSTIN

TRAVIS COUNTY

Barton Creek

Colorado River

Williamson Creek

Walter E. Long Lake

Elgin

21

22 **23**

24

Colorado River

Austin Bergstrom Intl. Airport

BASTROP COUNTY

26

Onion Crk.

27 28 29

30

31 32 33

25

Cabela's

Buda

Willie's Joint

CALDWELL COUNTY

HAYS COUNTY

Miles

0   3

3

Kilometers

Chapter 13

Brushy Creek

Regular insect hatches, genetically pure Guadalupe bass, Rios, ease of access, gorgeous scenery, opportunities to practice tight-quarters casting. Access points: 14.

Brushy is a creek in name only. This fascinating stream rises east of US 183 in western Williamson County and flows 69 miles to its confluence with the San Gabriel River in Milam County, well below Granger Lake. From its headwaters in Leander to Norman's Crossing in Taylor, Brushy Creek falls about 500 feet, in the process flowing off the Edwards Plateau and onto the deep alluvial soils of the Blackland Prairie. Fed by numerous tributaries and springs, it is a lushly vegetated small water with stunning views around nearly every bend.

Let's just get this out of the way up front: Brushy is also fed by discharge from several wastewater treatment plants, which together pump up to 20 million gallons of treated water into the stream every day. Every stream that flows through an urban area has had a brush with wastewater. Don't let it alarm you. Water treatment is managed with recreational contact in mind, and local governments work hard to preserve the riparian

> "[I]n a world where most men seem to spend their lives doing things they hate, my fishing is at once an endless source of delight and an act of small rebellion."
>
> —ROBERT TRAVER (JOHN VOELKER), *Testament of a Fisherman*

corridor and buffer the stormwater runoff. Wastewater returns contribute to baseline flows, too, especially important in summertime. Overall, the water quality in the creek is good, and the little river supports a diverse array of aquatic insects and native fishes.

It's almost impossible to overstate how much this stream is treasured by local anglers. Brushy Creek is home waters for Living Waters Fly Fishing (see the **Appendices**, page 352), and it is a quick and (sometimes) easy local option for Rio Grande cichlids. The bass fishing can be hot here, too. Because the creek is small and isolated from reservoirs and larger rivers, Brushy's native Guadalupe bass have largely escaped the genetic introgression common in some other area streams.

But it's not just the locals who love this river. Anglers have been known to drive three or four hours just to fish Brushy Creek. Maybe it's because this stream is catalog-perfect; it would look right at home in Pennsylvania or in the foothills of the Rockies. Or maybe it's the regular insect hatches—BWOs, caddis flies, and tricos—which reinforce the illusion you are fishing a trout stream. Go ahead and fish it that way. The jewellike, native sunnies and yearling Guadalupe bass rise to the insects, and strikingly patterned, mature bass will be in the pocket water, seams, and deep bends, just where you'd expect to find coldwater trout.

The Spanish explorers who encountered Brushy Creek in 1716 gave it the more lyrical name *Arroyo de las Animas Benditas*, or Creek of the Blessed Souls. Those lucky enough to fish it believe this early appellation to be fitting—until a backcast gets stuck in a sycamore or willow tree. Then the current name makes total sense.

Champion Park and Hairy Man Road, Cedar Park
30.51152, -97.75847
3830 Brushy Creek Rd., Cedar Park, TX 78613
22.2 road miles, 0:28 drive time
Difficulty: Easy

CHAMPION PARK IS A CONVENIENT STAGING AREA, WITH
plenty of parking, restrooms, and potable water, and it's just minutes
from dozens of other access points on Brushy Creek. It's a good place to
begin exploring the upper section of the stream, and the natural pond
created by the creek here holds some good fish.

What You Will Find

If you are eager to wet a line and are approaching from the east, it will take some willpower to make it all the way to Champion Park, which is actually on South Brushy Creek. All along Hairy Man Road, you will be tempted by gravel turnouts along the creek (here's one, at **Great Oaks Drive**: (30.521249, -97.73587) and parking areas across the two-lane blacktop (for instance, dedicated parking for **Brushy Creek Regional Trail**: (30.52547, -97.72351). The parking areas are technically for folks who want to stroll or jog the trail system that follows the creek, but they work perfectly well for anglers, too. The stream along this section is hard-bottomed, shallow, and—in the summer months—sometimes annoyingly clotted with long, ropy strands of algae. Pools and bends hold plenty of fish, though. For a quick and easy guide to the upper sections of Brushy Creek, stop by Living Waters Fly Fishing in Round Rock and pick up their richly illustrated map.

The Hairy Man of Brushy Creek

Aw, c'mon. You saw the street name and really wanted to know, didn't ya? Here's how Hairy Man Road got its name.

A legend dating to the late nineteenth century tells the story of a boy separated from his family when he fell off the wagon, or maybe when floodwaters came between them. The boy grew up alone in the heavily wooded bottomlands along Brushy Creek, or perhaps he was raised by wild animals. However he survived, the boy grew into a frighteningly unkempt fellow who didn't much care for company.

Day-trippers up from Austin would frequently encounter the Hairy Man as he leapt from the underbrush or crouched in the canopy, dropping down to tattoo the tops of their carriages with his feet.

One day the Hairy Man lost his grip and fell in front of a team of horses, which trampled him to death. Folks say his spirit still haunts the winding blacktop that replaced the old dirt path along the stream.

The Brushy Creek Women's Association celebrates the legend with a "Hairy Man Festival" at Cat Hollow Park each fall. The festival naturally features a "hairiest man" competition.

18 The Pond at Champion Park
(Bank and Wade Fishing the Impoundment)

The pedestrian bridge that crosses the lower end of the pond is a good place to start. The easiest access is on the south side, across the bridge. There is room to cast near the southeast corner of the pool, and plenty of brush in the water to hold largemouth bass and sunfish. These fish get harassed pretty regularly and can be finicky. If poppers or other topwater flies aren't working for you, try a damselfly nymph.

The only known wild mint patch in Williamosn County sprawls across a spring on the south bank of the Champion Park impoundment.

Wait a minute … do you smell that? Did a pack of gum explode in your pocket? No, that's a sprawling patch of wild mint you're standing in (probably an escapee, it's the only known wild stand of peppermint in the county). Pretty cool, huh?

The stream spills out of the pond in two channels. The riffle river left, the north bank, sometimes holds carp head-up into the current. Follow either channel downstream, back toward Brushy Creek Road, and you'll find sunfish and Rios in pocket water.

Back on the pond, you can cast from the base of the bridge on either side, but the south bank is the better option. On the upstream side of the bridge, walk back up the hill to the trail and head west a few yards to get around a stand of trees at water's edge, and you'll encounter a beautiful spring braided across a large limestone slope. The mint is lush here. Work your way down and fish immediately below the

The impoundment of South Brushy Creek at Champion Park offers easy access and a variety of water.

Just above the impoundment, the stream narrows and stealth is required to sneak up on the fish.

spring. The bottom looks mucky but is actually pretty solid below a layer of silt. Standing timber upstream river right separates a backwater from the main channel, and both are good for largemouth bass. There are huge carp and smallmouth buffalo in this pool as well.

To get to the head of the pool, your best bet is to cross back over the bridge toward the parking lot and then follow the trail upstream along the creek. A dirt track leads down to the head of the pool. Stealth is key here; approach slowly and quietly, as bass cruise the channel and hang out at the edges of the vegetation. Ease into the water and you can wade back downstream, fishing both banks, or upstream toward the large boulder river right (your left). Above the boulder the channel narrows considerably and the trees on the bank crowd over the water.

The navigability of South Brushy Creek where it crosses private property above this point has yet to be determined conclusively, but the Brushy Creek Regional Trail greenbelt provides near continuous walk-in access along much of the stream, both upstream to US 183A and downstream along Brushy Creek proper through Round Rock.

From downtown, take TX 1 (MoPac/Loop 1) and US 183/183A (tolls on the US 183A section) north to Avery Ranch Boulevard. Turn right and go 1.9 miles to West Parmer Lane. Turn left, drive 0.7 miles to Brushy Creek Road, and turn right. The entrance to Champion Park will be just over a mile down the road on your right.

This low waterfall spans Brushy Creek about a quarter of the way between access points on the Cemetery Wade and marks the beginning of the most productive water.

CR 137, Hutto
30.506854, -97.548799
1213–1031 CR 137, Hutto, TX 78634
28.5 road miles, 0:30 drive time
Difficulty: Moderate

THIS IS A TERRIFIC ONE-WAY WADE UPSTREAM, A BIT MORE than 2 miles between parking spots, with Guadalupe bass, largemouth bass, and carp featuring prominently. The stream's character is varied along this reach, with a hard (and slick) corrugated limestone bed alternating with easy-walking gravel. In many areas there is enough exposed rock along the edge of the water to legally walk with your feet dry.

You will drive past a lot of good water in Round Rock on your way to this access point, including **Chisholm Trail Park** (30.512064, -97.689527) and **Memorial Park** (30.512303, -97.685592), on either side of I-35, and **Veterans Park** (30.514766, -97.675553) just downstream. All afford good access and excellent fishing.

Chisholm Trail Park, one block east of the interstate, is home to the erosional pedestal of Edwards limestone that gives the city of Round Rock its name. The rock was a handy landmark for a ford, so this is also where the cattle trail crossed the creek during the frontier years.

You can also get to the water at the **CR 123 crossing** (30.53093, -97.589405; park on the gravel turnout but don't block the low-water bridge) and at the corner of **Red Bud Lane and CR 123**, 1.25 miles upstream (30.53074, -97.61401; a dirt track parallels the northbound lane; park at your own risk beneath the bridge). It's a 1.6-mile wade between the two access points if you want to go one-way and shuttle.

I don't want to make too much of it, but consider: you could purchase a Rio Getter fly at Living Waters Fly Fishing (103 N. Brown St.), grab some famous Round Rock Donuts (106 W. Liberty Ave.), and catch a Rio Grande cichlid at Memorial Park all within about half a dozen blocks and half an hour, fifteen minutes of which you'll spend in line for your donuts.

What You Will Find

From the unimproved parking area at the CR 137 bridge, it's an easy walk down to the water—just follow the trail. The creek is shallow here, but the bottom is hard, *slick*, and uneven (thus the "Moderate" difficulty rating). Where you can, you will want to walk the gravel bars or dry limestone shoulders.

19 The Cemetery Wade (Wading Upstream to Chris Kelley Boulevard)

Wading upstream from the bridge, the first reach of water is a long, shallow run. Guadalupe bass—our main quarry here—are riffle-loving fish; look for them lying in the corrugations of the channel and also against the slightly deeper, treed north bank (river left, your right).

At about 600 feet you'll encounter a picturesque limestone shelf jutting from the south bank river right (your left). At about 0.3 miles a spring spills into the creek on the same side. Another tenth of a mile upstream you'll see what looks like a tributary entering river right. There's a deep pool here and some timber in the water; it's a fish condominium and worth a pause in your trek upstream.

Just above the pool, at about 0.5 miles, a low waterfall spans the stream. It's pretty, and there is excellent, highly oxygenated pocket water below the drop. Take your time with the broad pool above the falls. A little farther on, you'll encounter another riffle with some interesting backwaters river right, and then a sweeping bend. Here, at the 0.75-mile mark, there is access river left to **Old County Road 137** (30.51807, -97.54644), which runs right past the old Hutto Cemetery. Don't get out yet, though. The best water is ahead of you.

Above: Even though Brushy gets most of its water from tributaries and (gasp!) treated waste water returns, springs contribute throughout its upper reaches, and are always a goood place to look for fish.

Right: Look for this ammonite embedded in the center of the limestone stream bed just upstream from the CR 137 access point.

At 0.8 miles, the center of the channel deepens to about thigh-deep, and you can find fish holding at the edge of the current there. At about a mile above the bridge, in another sweeping bend (this time to the west), the stream deepens along a high dirt bank river right. *Stop*! Or, at least, slow down. The next 200 yards could provide the best fly fishing of the year, so take your time. You will want to wade the shallows and gravel bars on the north bank.

There are big carp in the pool at this bend, and some potential state-record Guadalupe bass. A crawfish-patterned fly, like Matt Bennett's Carp-It Bomb, is a good all-purpose fly for this spot and will fool both big bass and carp.

At about 1.1 river miles you will encounter another riffle, marking the upstream limit of the magic pool. At the 1.3-mile mark, you'll want to slow down again. This pretty pool is waist-deep river left, and deeply

undercut limestone ledges on the
south bank provide terrific cover
for fish.

At approximately 1.75 miles,
you'll wade under the **Riverwalk
pedestrian bridge** (30.52310,
-97.56038). You can climb out here
and take the sidewalk back to the
Hutto Youth Soccer Association
fields, where you have perhaps
left a second vehicle, or continue another half mile through
promising water to **Chris Kelley
Boulevard** (30.52594, -97.56660),
at the 2.2-mile mark, where there
is an easy walk up the bank under
the bridge.

*This mid-winter 15-inch (plus) Gaudalupe bass fell
to a Carp-it Bomb fished slow and deep in a bend
about midway along the Cemetary Wade.*

The best parking at the soccer fields is adjacent to Chris Kelley
Boulevard. To get there, take the dirt road on the north side of Riverwalk
Drive at the east end of the park and loop around between Brushy Creek
and the playing fields.

From downtown, take TX 1 (MoPac/Loop 1) north to TX 45 east
(tolls) to TX 130 north (tolls). In 2 miles, take Exit 426, Gattis School
Road (CR 138), and turn right. Follow CR 138 2 miles to CR 137, and
turn left. Go north on CR 137 for 0.9 miles, pull off, and park on the
other side of the guardrail on the southeast side of the bridge.

Norman's Crossing, Taylor
30.489056, -97.499279
394–428 CR 129, Taylor, TX 76574
31.1 road miles, 0:38 drive time
Difficulty: Easy

NORMAN'S CROSSING IS FAR ENOUGH EAST OF THE I-35
corridor that it gets very little fishing pressure. The creek flows fast and
deep here over a mostly gravel bottom and is shaded in the wet wading
months by a canopy of bottomland hardwoods. Rio Grande cichlids
don't make it this far down the stream, but handsome, genetically pure

Guadalupe bass—a few roughly the size and shape of a football—are plentiful.

What You Will Find

After you've parked, walk back across the bridge and hop the guardrail on the northwest side. A trail at the bottom of the cement bridge apron leads to the gravel bank of the stream. Fishing is good both upstream and downstream, though if you're headed far downstream, a paddlecraft would serve you well. The **FM 973 crossing** (30.469034, -97.463487), about 4 miles downstream in Rice's Crossing, offers good access and great parking beneath a shading oak, but several more-than-head-deep pools with no legal way around make wading difficult unless you're willing to swim. We'll head upstream from the CR 129 bridge instead.

20 **Norman's Crossing** (Wading Upstream from the Bridge)
The pool below the bridge is deep, particularly against the south bank (that's why you had to walk across and approach the river from the north). Sunken brush and logs that have washed down the river collect

The reach above Norman's Crossing alternates between fast runs and broad pools.

against the pillars. If you don't pick up your first Guadalupe bass here, walk upstream about 100 feet on the gravel bank river left (the north bank). A nice eddy forms against the opposite high dirt bank; swing a Brushy Creek streamer or largish olive Woolly Bugger through here for a near certain-take.

The entire shoreline here, up to the first riffle, is productive. There is some nice pocket water and a slough below the riffle river right (your left as you head upstream). Above the riffle, which is at a bend in the stream, a gorgeous pool hints at what lies ahead. The water ranges from thigh- to chest-deep once you step off the gravel bar. You'll want to cover the north side of the pool all the way up to the riffle pretty thoroughly. There are some fine Guadalupe bass beneath the trees here.

Above that riffle, a gravel bar river right parallels a fast, deep run. The pool at the top of the run, about a quarter mile from the bridge, is thigh-deep along the higher north bank; there is some shallow, slack water river right. The next pool is broad but shallow—just ankle- to shin-deep—and you should walk through it.

The pool above is a doozy. Head-deep against the high, dirt bank, it's full of complex eddies. It's worth casting from the lower end of the pool for a while just to see where your fly will go—it's mesmerizing. The pool can be fished equally well from the tail or the head. To get to the head, edge to your left and wade through the muck river right, and then walk along the shoreline (it's the only muck you'll encounter).

The run above the pool looks to be bottomed half in gravel and half in limestone, but it's actually half gravel and half clay. The clay, which is firm and fairly sticky, is an exposure

This standard 8-inch Guadalupe bass came from a shallow pool in stained, but still reasonably clear, water.

Giant extinct oysters, Exogyra ponderosa, litter the stream bed on this reach.

Outside of federal lands, including national parks and parks managed by the U.S. Army Corps of Engineers, it's legal in Texas to pick up fossils on public land; however, cultural artifacts such as projectile points and pottery should always be left where they are discovered.

of the Sprinkle Formation, a rare layer of ancient seabed that did not become limestone. If you look down as you walk upstream, you'll see dozens of fossils of extinct giant oysters (*Exogyra ponderosa*). They're pretty cool, and common in this formation in the few places it crops out in Central Texas.

The next pool upstream gets gradually deeper toward the top—chest-deep against the bank river right. Walk to your right to the exposed gravel bar. The creek makes a gentle S curve here, west and then north again. Continue to walk on the gravel river left to a fantastic pool in the bend at about 0.5 miles. The current runs hard in deep water against the high bank, where eddies, plenty of slack water, and a deposit of silt and leaves conspire to create an insect factory. The little fish love it, and the big fish follow the little fish. Take your time.

The stream shallows as the bend straightens out into a run, but tenacious sycamores cling to the far bank and their exposed roots could pass for mangroves.

The next pool also gets deeper as you head upstream. Keep to the north bank on your right, and at the head of the pool walk up the big gravel mound and around the fallen tree to cross the channel. The deep run here forms an interesting backwater with a jumble of cement

and (usually) some sunken logs. Both are fish havens, and this is a great place to tease some green sunnies.

Around the next bend and at the top of the run, at about 0.75 miles, a vista opens that is beautiful in any season. Springs tumble from the fern- and moss-clad north bank, and elephant ears bunch along the edge of the water. Sycamores, pecans, and oaks form a canopy overhead.

Deeper water lies against the high bank river left, but the entire pool can be productive. The next gentle bend to the west features tons of vegetation and brush river left, up to the log-choked mouth of Cottonwood Creek, which enters from the north about 0.8 miles from the

Blake Smith releases a largemouth bass on the Norman's Crossing section of the creek.

This gorgeous, shady pool features cascading springs and chest-deep water along the north bank and knee-deep gravel and overhanging brush on the south bank.

bridge. This is easy wading, with lots of fish-holding structure in the river all the way up to the next bend to the southwest, at the 1-mile mark.

I can easily take an entire morning or afternoon to fish this first mile, especially if I'm paying attention to the insect hatches or the incredible variety of birds flitting through the trees. It's just a bit more than three more river miles up to the **CR 137 crossing** in Hutto (see page 171). Save it for a long summer day and be sure to bring plenty of water.

From downtown, take I-35 north to Exit 238B and then US 290 east (tolls) toward Houston. Continue on US 290 about 10 miles. Just past the Walmart in Manor, take a left on FM 973. After another 10 miles cross Brushy Creek, take a left on FM 1660 at the small community of Rice's Crossing. At Norman's Crossing, 2.6 miles up the road, take a left on CR

129. The unimproved parking area is adjacent to the bridge guardrail on the southwest side of the crossing.

 Country Cool, Shinyribs

Texas Beer Co. in Taylor is leading the revitalization of the historic downtown area. It's also less than two blocks from Louie Mueller Barbecue, named a James Beard Foundation "American Classic."

⭐ Texas Beer Company

texasbeerco.com

Hours vary, closed Mondays

Many years ago, I briefly worked as a reporter at the *Taylor Daily Press*. I chronicled the first big, painful growth spurt in nearby Hutto, where the city council meetings frequently lasted into the wee hours of the next day and sometimes included threats of bodily injury. I wrote about the usual small-town events and characters, and unwisely took an editorial stand in a local barbecue skirmish. I hadn't been back in a decade when, after a session on Brushy Creek, I met some friends at the Texas Beer Company on the corner of Second and Main.

This was not the Taylor I remembered. A dozen years ago, the blocks of historic, Victorian-era Main Street buildings were locked in a death spiral of moribund, low-rent businesses and boarded-up storefronts. Today these are rapidly being converted into vibrant, modern enterprises.

The Texas Beer Company brewery and taproom, opened in 2016, has been a catalyst for the city's revitalization. Housed in the graceful, fully renovated McCrory Timmerman building—three older buildings joined under one roof in 1911—the brewery sits on a corner that has been the site of a mercantile store, a department store, and a diner. Today, loft apartments occupy the top floor and a gallery, barbershop, coffee bar, farm-to-market deli, winery tasting room, and the taproom fill out the street level. An awning covers the sidewalk all the way around (you can take your beer outside, just stay under the awning). The beer is excellent—I'm partial to the Blacklands Porter—the staff and patrons are Texas-friendly, and there is live music on weekends, when you may also find barbecue from one of the award-winning local joints (for the record, they're *all* good). There is a limited bar menu during the week.

A fairly typical largemouth bass from the Hairy Man Road reach of the stream.

The Outlaw Sam Bass

The outlaw Sam Bass met his end in Round Rock. Originally from Indiana, Bass drifted from job to job along the post–Civil War frontier, eventually settling in Denton, north of Dallas. After driving a herd of cattle to market and gambling away the owners' profits in frontier saloons, he turned to banditry.

As a member of the "Black Hills Gang," he scored big with a Nebraska train robbery that netted $60,000—worth more than $1.4 million in 2018.

Bass returned to Denton and soon enough to robbing stagecoaches and trains. Eventually, with the Texas Rangers hot on his trail, he made his way down to Round Rock, where he planned to rob the Williamson County Bank. On July 19, 1878, Bass and his accomplices rode into town to scout the area. They entered Koppel's (Kopperal's) General Store, newly opened on the corner of Main and Mays, with the intention of buying some tobacco.

Williamson County Deputy Sheriff A. W. Grimes noticed that Bass, whom he did not recognize, was carrying two pistols—one more than the law allowed—and approached him to confiscate the illegal weapon. The gang shot Grimes dead before the deputy could draw his own gun.

The shootout moved into the street, and Texas Ranger Sergeant Richard Ware, getting a shave a few buildings down, ran out with his face still lathered and fired at the outlaws, striking Bass. The wounded bandit was found in a pasture the next day and taken into custody; he died of his wounds in Round Rock on his birthday, July 21. He was 27 years old. His last words, according to some sources, were "The world is a bubble, trouble wherever you go."

Bass is buried in Round Rock Cemetery under a rather grand marker inscribed, cryptically, *A brave man reposes in death here. Why was he not true?* The Koppel building still stands, just two-and-a-half blocks east of Living Waters Fly Fishing.

Chapter 14

Colorado River

*Central location, multiple access points, all of the fish,
and a paddler's paradise. Access points: 24.*

THE COLORADO RIVER IS THE LONGEST RIVER WHOLLY WITHIN
the state of Texas. The river rises at the edge of the Llano Estacado near
Lamesa, Texas; receives its first major inflows from the Concho River;
and flows about 600 miles in a southeastward direction to the Gulf of
Mexico at Matagorda Bay.

The first Europeans to take note of the
river were Juan Domínguez de Mendoza
and Nicolás López, who called it the *San
Clemente* in 1684. In 1687, French explorer
René-Robert Cavelier, Sieur de La Salle,
named it *La Sablonnière* ("Sand Pit").

> "Fishing is a matter of timing in a
> changeable universe."
>
> JOHN GIERACH, "WHERE TO FISH,"
> *Standing in a River Waving a Stick*

The name *Colorado*, Spanish for "red" or
"reddish" was probably first applied to what today we know as the
Brazos River (short for "*Brazos de Dios*," or arms of God), and sometime
during the period of Spanish exploration the names were mistakenly

interchanged. The waters of the Colorado, at least in its long run through
the Texas Hill Country to down below Austin, have always run relatively
clear.

The Colorado is a big river and in most reaches not suitable for walk/
wade trips. For that reason, we will look at it a bit differently than smaller
streams in the area; I will provide a general overview of the opportunities
and access points and suggest some paddling itineraries. Do-it-yourself
trips are quite practical, especially if you have two vehicles or a shuttle,
but the most efficient way to shorten the learning curve, on the Lower
Colorado in particular, is to book a guided trip with any one of several
guides who run shallow-draft jet boats on the reaches east of Austin.

The Highland Lakes

As early as 1854, residents of the watershed were already thinking about
damming the river. Adam Rankin Johnson, the founder of the town of
Marble Falls, marked the location of a proposed dam that year. Buchanan
Dam and Inks Dam, downstream, would finally be completed by the
newly established Lower Colorado River Authority (LCRA) in 1938,
creating the first two of what would become six "highland lakes" along
the river. The six lakes—Buchanan (known for its striped bass fishing),
Inks, LBJ, Marble Falls, Travis, and Austin—manage floods; store water
for residential, commercial, and agricultural use; and generate hydroelec-
tric power. They also provide outstanding recreational opportunities for
Central Texans.

The LCRA maintains a number of public parks and boat ramps on the
reservoirs (visit lcra.org for information), and the Texas Parks & Wildlife
Department (TPWD) operates **Colorado Bend State Park** (2236 Park
Hill Dr., Bend, TX 76824) and **Inks Lake State Park** (3630 Park Road
4 W, Burnet, TX 78611) on the river, both slightly outside the scope of
this book. Both of the state parks offer good bank fishing opportunities
and paddling access. Colorado Bend State Park additionally offers outstanding wade fishing and is a popular destination for fly fishers during
the early spring white bass run.

Lake Travis, just to the west of Austin, is an outstanding Guadalupe
bass and largemouth bass fishery, but you will need a boat of some sort
to access most of it. It's also a popular party lake, with numerous booze
cruise operators and dockside bars and restaurants. Many years it leads
the state in boating accidents and fatalities. **Hippie Hollow Park** (7000
Comanche Trail, Austin, TX 78732), a Travis County property, is the only

clothing-optional public park in the state. Texans have been known to drive hundreds of miles to be shocked and scandalized by the goings-on here.

Lady Bird Lake

Lady Bird Lake
30.26181, -97.74877
650 W. Riverside Dr., Austin, TX 78704
800 feet
Difficulty: Easy

LADY BIRD LAKE, UNLIKE THE HIGHLAND LAKES JUST UPSTREAM, is a "pass through" or constant-level reservoir covering 468 acres in the nearly six river miles between the Tom Miller Dam, which impounds Lake Austin, and Longhorn Dam, east of I-35. For nearly half a century (Longhorn Dam was completed in 1960), the impoundment was known as Town Lake. In July 2007, the Austin City Council voted to rename the reservoir in honor of the former first lady of the United States, who had championed the beautification of this reach of the Colorado River.

Lady Bird Lake offers outstanding recreational fishing opportunities. The impoundment is world-renowned as a Euro-style carp fishing destination (no surprise, really, since the first carp to swim in Texas did so in the waters of Barton Springs) and in recent years has produced some excellent largemouth bass, which can be sight-fished from the bank. Rio Grande cichlids and various species of sunfish, which grow quite large here, round out the most commonly sought fishes. A fish consumption ban, due to high levels of chlordane, was imposed in 1990 and lifted in 1999.

Throughout Lady Bird Lake, anglers should target shoreline structure, including cypress knees, laydowns, and jumbled boulders. The maximum depth of the impoundment is just 18 feet.

What You Will Find

The City of Austin prohibits the use of most gas-powered motors on the lake, and swimming and wading is likewise outlawed nearly everywhere here (Barton Creek is an exception), though you are welcome to paddle the lake, and there are numerous stand-up paddleboard (SUP), kayak, and canoe rental businesses on the water. Nearly the entire impoundment is surrounded by parks, trails, and green space, and there

Right: There is no fishing in the spring-fed Barton Springs Pool, but the half mile below the dam offers some fine opportunities, especially during the cooler months.

are numerous access points from which to launch a kayak or a canoe, and bank fishing opportunities are nearly endless.

Red Bud Isle Park (30.291732, -97.787492) is the westernmost access point on the impoundment. This 17.5-acre park just below Tom Miller Dam is most popular as an off-leash dog park, but offers good access to bank anglers and paddlers who wish to fish the upper end of Lady Bird Lake. The easiest places to launch a kayak or canoe are either side of the parking lot just below Red Bud Trail. I've had better luck fishing the narrow channel on the west side of the island. Be aware that releases from Tom Miller Dam can occur at any time.

Zilker Park (30.264236, -97.768109) is Austin's favorite common area, home to the ACL Music Festival, Blues on the Green and summertime Shakespeare productions, a botanical garden and nature center, playing fields, and the four Barton Springs, which fill historic Barton Springs Pool with an average of 34 million gallons of 72-degree water each day.

Barton Creek itself flows for just 0.5 miles below the dammed springs before it meets Lady Bird Lake, but its clear (and in the winter, warm) waters offer excellent fishing for Guadalupe and largemouth bass, Rio Grande cichlids, and sunfish. There also is a thriving population of tilapia here, particularly during the cooler months; please catch a bunch and take them home and eat them.

Best bets for fishing this short reach of Barton Creek are early mornings on weekdays and wintertime. It can get crowded with paddlers and dogs otherwise. It's easier to paddle up to the dam from Lady Bird Lake than to launch a boat here (though you can rent from Zilker Park Boat Rentals—see **Appendices**—right on the water). If you do bring your own kayak to launch here, a two-wheel dolly is helpful. Note that wading is allowed in Barton Creek, just below Barton Springs Pool.

There are no directions provided from downtown Austin, because this lake is in downtown.

21 Town Lake Metropolitan Park

The public parking area at South 1st Street and West Riverside Drive (30.26181, -97.74877) is near the zero point for our mileage calculations and provides access to the half mile of shoreline at **Auditorium Shores**. Roll your kayak about 500 feet to the water, or fish from the bank

along the Ann and Roy Butler Hike and Bike Trail that circles the lower two-thirds of Lady Bird Lake.

Just downstream, on the north bank of the lake, paddlers can access the water from **Congress Ave. Kayaks** (30.26060, -97.74178), an easy paddle back up to the Congress Avenue bridge to watch the daily emergence of the world's largest urban bat colony—1.5 million Mexican free-tailed bats. Spring through fall, the bats begin flying out just before sunset and will eat between 10,000 and 20,000 pounds of insects before returning to roost in the morning. For more information about Austin's bats, including current emergence times, visit Bat Conservation International (batcon.org).

Worth mentioning: the **YETI Flagship** store is located just a block south of the river at 220 S. Congress Avenue, and the **Patagonia Austin** store is about a half-mile north at 316 Congress Avenue.

East Avenue at I-35 (30.25199, -97.73664) is another close-to-the-water access point on the north bank of the river and a good place to launch a kayak or canoe. **Festival Beach** (30.248630, -97.727783) offers parking and a boat ramp.

Back on the south bank, anglers can access some terrific bank fishing along the hike and bike trail east of I-35, at **Lakeshore at Lady Bird Lake Metro Park**, and at **Longhorn Shores at Town Lake Metro Park**. Park on **Tinnin Ford Road** (30.244095, -97.724670) or **Lady Bird Lane** (30.243672, -97.722457). This area includes some of the Austin Carp Anglers club's favorite "swims" (carp fishing areas) and offers sight casting opportunities for bass, sunfish, and Rios from the bank. Just watch your backcast and don't hook a jogger or her dog.

Montopolis Bridge, Austin
30.24702, -97.69033
6213–6501 Levander Loop, Austin, TX 78721
5.4 road miles, 0:13 drive time
Difficulty: Easy

THE PORTION OF THE RIVER KNOWN AS THE LOWER COLORADO, or "LoCo," officially begins at **Longhorn Dam** (30.24967, -97.71352), or more usually here, at the Montopolis Bridge. The commonly used name is a bit off, as our access point is actually below the concrete spans of the US 183 bridge, not the historic steel truss. The latter bridge, opened in

Lady Bird Lake is best accessed by kayak, canoe, or SUP.

1935, carried more than 29,000 vehicles per day but was decommissioned in 2018 and converted to bicycle and pedestrian use.

It is 61 glorious river miles from Longhorn Dam to the take-out at **Lost Pines Nature Trail Park** (30.07365, -97.30961) south of Bastrop. The river here is flat and meandering, and it's possible to plan canoe and kayak trips that last anywhere from a couple hours to a full day to multiple days, including island campouts. There are several outfitters on the river (see the **Appendices**) who are happy to rent boats, shuttle paddlers, and provide advice on the best itineraries.

We'll look at just a couple of reaches of the river in the heart of the world's best Guadalupe bass fishery, long and short paddles perfect for the do-it-yourself angler.

What You Will Find

Depending on the current state of construction on one or more of the bridges, concrete barriers may block some portion of the dirt track and parking area beneath the bridges. Find the track down and park on the hard-packed dirt beneath the bridges.

The author with a decent, if not quite trophy, Guadalupe bass.

 Trophy Float (Paddling Downstream to FM 973)

The paddle from the Montopolis Bridge to FM 973 makes for a good full-day trip (figure making a little more than 1 mile per hour while selectively fishing hotspots). You'll encounter some scattered limestone and jumbled boulders as well as brushy banks and backwaters, all of which you should slow down to fish. You'll also find bass shallow early and late during the summer months, and long casts will get your fly in front of the fish before you spook them. This is a good reach for carp and big freshwater drum, too.

About 1.5 miles below US 183, the main channel of the river

bears left, and a narrow channel hugs the bank river right. This would be a good spot to beach the boat and wade a bit. Boggy Creek enters in a cascade of sand river left at 2.3 miles below US 183; take some time fishing the backwater below the mouth of Boggy. A mile farther downstream, Walnut Creek (see the **Colorado River Tributaries sidebar** in this chapter) enters, also from the north. Walnut Creek is floatable, and wadeable, well upstream from its confluence with the Colorado and also is worth some time. The usually clear creek's sediment load creates a bit of a fan delta in the Colorado, with sandbars and small islands that are wadeable just downstream of the confluence.

At 4.3 miles below US 183, you'll see the **Texas River School campground** (30.25675, -97.63392—see the **Appendices** for more information) river left. For a small fee, the nonprofit Texas River School offers day use and overnight camping on the one-acre property, as well as canoe and kayak shuttles. Advance reservations are required. For a shorter trip, you can put-in or take-out here.

As you round the bend below Texas River School, a red sign on the bank river left warns of the upcoming low-head Decker Dam at 4.8 miles below US 183. The official portage around the dam is river right. You may want to enter the coordinates (30.25501, -97.62636) of the dam into your favorite navigation app so you aren't surprised, especially at higher flows.

The small impoundment created by the dam is where the water for Lake Walter E. Long (Decker Lake) comes from, since Decker Creek has virtually dried up. The water from that popular bass and carp fishing reservoir re-enters the Colorado via Gilleland Creek, upstream from Little Webberville Park. This is also where the 3.71-pound, 17.25-inch current state and world record Guadalupe bass was caught, on a crawfish pattern fly.

At 5.3 miles below the put-in, another island, river right, and a broad riffle, river left, offer wade fishing opportunities. When you see the highlines—the high-tension power lines—crossing the river at 7.8 miles below US 183, you've got just a hair under two miles to go before you reach the take-out at FM 973. If you've been fishing hard, or otherwise lollygagging, you'll want to paddle like you hear banjos to get there before dark.

From downtown, take East Cesar Chavez Street 3.2 miles to Levander Loop, which curves beneath the Airport Boulevard and US 183 (Ed Bluestein Boulevard) bridges.

FM 973, Austin
30.20850, -97.63853
2818 S. FM 973, Austin, TX 78725
11.7 road miles, 0:19 drive time
Difficulty: Easy

THE FM 973 CROSSING IS A POPULAR KAYAK AND CANOE launch and gets plenty of day use by families who simply want to spend some time on the water. Here you will find plentiful parking and easy access to the water between the bridge pilings. While it is possible to wade in thigh- to waist-deep water here, particularly downstream, this access point is most suitable as a put-in for a float down to **Austin's Colony** or **Little Webberville**, or as a take-out for a trip from the **Montopolis Bridge** (US 183) crossing or **Texas River School**. A paddle upstream or downstream from here is an excellent introduction to the diverse and productive fishery that is the LoCo.

Note that the City of Austin prohibitions against wading and swimming in the river extend only to **Longhorn Dam***.*

What You Will Find
The packed dirt track that parallels the bridge opens up beneath it with ample, unimproved (but hard-packed) parking. You can back right to the edge of the bank to drop your boat. As with many public road crossings, this one is used as an illegal dump on occasion; consider taking some trash out with you when you leave.

23 **Prairie Paddle** (Paddling Downstream to Little Webberville Park)
As a rule, it's always okay to paddle downstream if you have a shuttle, but you should begin your trip by paddling upstream if you plan to take out at the same place you put in. Why? Well, in general, because you might just be dog-tired at the end of six or seven (or more) hours of paddling and fishing under the Texas sun and, if the 1960s taught us anything, it's that it is easier to go with the flow. On the Colorado River below Lady Bird Lake, there's another reason: periodic releases from Longhorn Dam can increase flows by a factor of 20 (say, from 150 cubic feet per second to 2,900 cfs) and raise river levels as much as 4 feet (see the **Inland Tides** sidebar on page 199).

The next access point below **FM 973** is the **TX 130 crossing** (30.20917, -97.62244), a little more than 0.9 miles downstream. There

is ample parking below the divided bridge here, but a large riprap apron makes it a tough place to launch or retrieve a kayak or canoe. At lower flows, though, this can be an outstanding option for wade fishing, particularly the half mile along river right, downstream of the bridge.

A group of volunteers take a river cleanup break. Big rivers need love, too, and the Colorado gets an annual hug from the LoCo Trash Bash, an effort led by All Water Guides and Texas River School.

At 3.5 miles below FM 973, a channel river right leads to an unsequestered, abandoned gravel pit. Gravel pits like these—and there are several on this reach of the Lower Colorado—contribute mightily to turbidity in the stream during high flows, and at least one local nonprofit is working on a solution to fill or dam them when owners cannot or will not comply with the law requiring them to do so.

It is 3.7 miles (an easy half-day paddle) down to **Austin's Colony HOA Park** (30.22543, -97.59165). The homeowners' association is long defunct, and you'll have to jump the curb at the gap in the barriers to follow a well-used, rutted track down to the riverbank. There, in addition to evidence of illegal dumping, you will find signs that clearly anticipate public use of the bank. You can also wade the river at this location—the quarter mile upstream along the north bank (river left, your right) is undeveloped city and county property. Just be mindful of possible releases from Longhorn Dam.

Steve Elliott caught this river monster, a longnose gar, while fishing with All Water Guides.

At about 4.3 miles below FM 973, the river splits around a rather large island. The channel river right is the main channel, while the very shallow channel river left is popular with waterfowlers during the fall and winter duck seasons.

About 4.9 miles below the put-in, the outfall from the **South Austin Regional Wastewater Treatment plant** (30.2081, -97.59507) enters river right. Despite being a bit gross on the face of it, the current (and probably bug life in the nutrient-rich water) is a magnet for white bass and other species. Fish small streamers along the current seams and in the structure along the bank on either side of the outfall.

Onion Creek (see the **Onion Creek** chapter for more on this major tributary) enters river right at 5.4 miles below FM 973. If, like me, you are a bit of a contrarian, you may even want to paddle up Onion Creek to **Texas Highway 71**, just below **Barkley Meadows Park**, a distance of 4.5 miles.

Between the mouth of Onion Creek and your take-out at **Little Webberville Park,** you will encounter at least four large islands; for the first three, the main channel is river right at the time of publication. In the fourth instance, the very large island (some call it "Tire Island," others "Goat Island") at 8.1 miles below FM 973, it is decidedly river left. Tire Island, in particular, is a popular camping spot. In all cases, the smaller channels may provide some good wade fishing opportunities if you have time to stop paddling.

Just below Tire Island, Gilleland Creek enters river left, and—when it's flowing—can contribute quite a bit of silt to the river. Below Gilleland Creek, several gravel pits just off the river on the north bank are opened by periodic floods, screwing up water quality for weeks or months before the owners close them off again (as required by law), and the cycle repeats.

From downtown, take I-35 south to Exit 230 for TX 71 west. Follow TX 71 to FM 973 on your left, just past Austin-Bergstrom International Airport. Cross the bridge over the river at 0.3 miles, cross the south-bound lanes and take an immediate left on the dirt track that parallels the structure.

Little Webberville Park, Webberville

30.22966, -97.51812

100 Water St., Webberville, TX 78621

parks.traviscountytx.gov

23.2 road miles, 0:29 drive time

Difficulty: Easy

TRAVIS COUNTY'S LITTLE WEBBERVILLE PARK IS SIX ACRES OF riverfront, a couple of portable toilets, and—the important part—a paved boat ramp. It's also located smack in the middle of a reach of river that produces trophy-sized Guadalupe bass. There are legit "river monsters" here, too: longnose gar more than 4 feet in length, freshwater drum that outweigh toddlers, and smallmouth buffalo bigger than basset hounds.

What You Will Find

Access at Little Webberville Park, free and open sunrise until civil twilight, is straightforward. Drop your canoe or kayak at the boat ramp, park in the lot, and shove off. The boat ramp was renovated in the spring of 2019.

Colorado River Tributaries

In addition to the **Pedernales River** and **Onion Creek**, each covered in their own chapters, numerous smaller tributaries flow into the Colorado River in the Austin area. Some of these are not considered navigable in fact or by statute (see the **Texas River Law** chapter). Others are, or flow through or adjacent to public lands.

Barton Creek rises near the Hays County town of Dripping Springs and flows 40 miles through rugged limestone hills to its confluence with the Colorado at **Lady Bird Lake**. The creek is intermittent during periods of low rainfall, but somehow the remaining pools manage to hold fish—you may just have to hike a ways to get to them. The Barton Creek Greenbelt Trail follows the creek from just above Barton Springs into the hills of west Austin, and can be accessed at numerous trailheads. One popular option is the trailhead at **South MoPac Expressway** (30.24408, -97.80987). Another— and this will get you closer to some deeper pools, though it's a half-mile hike down to the creek—is **Trail's End Access** on Camp Craft Road (30.27512, -97.82522).

Bull Creek is a steep, 12-mile-long stream that joins the Colorado River at Lake Austin. Much of the lower section, where the stream crosses Capital of Texas Highway three times, is quite shallow, but it is surrounded by parks and greenbelts, and there is plentiful access. **Bull Creek Park**, just off the highway at 30.37088, -97.78528, is one example. Upstream, **St. Edward's Park** (30.40663, -97.79035) offers more than half a mile of bank and wade fishing access. A low-head dam here creates a deep pool with plenty of structure and healthy bass and sunfish populations.

Walnut Creek rises in northwest Austin and flows through business districts and neighborhoods 20 miles to its confluence with the Lower Colorado River. This little gem is an

The Colorado's minor tributaries offer some outstanding bank and wade fishing from greenbelts and public parks like St. Edward's Park, pictured here, on Bull Creek.

easy wade and is terrific for native sunfish as well as some surprisingly large bass for such small water. Bonus: Walnut Creek is a fine place to look for both Cretaceous and Pleistocene fossils—everything from giant *Exogyra ponderosa* oysters to bison teeth. You can sample this creek right off the westbound lanes of US 290 at **Big Walnut Creek Nature Preserve** (30.32851, -97.64740). The easiest wade is upstream.

24 Big Water Float (Paddling Downstream to Webberville Park)

The reach from Little Webberville Park to Webberville Park proper, 5.1 miles downstream, is big (if not particularly deep) water. If you fall out of your boat, you'll be able to stand up in many places, but that's no excuse not to wear a PFD. This is mostly flatwater, but it can be deceptively fast, especially if a slug of water is moving downstream from Longhorn Dam.

You may want to start fishing just downstream and across the river from the boat ramp, where a rocky shoal provides good cover for bass. A little more than 1.3 miles below Little Webberville, Cook's Island stretches for half a mile around a bend. The island itself is cut by a

Professional fly fishing guide Lenée Dedeaux shows off a big-shouldered freshwater drum from the LoCo.

channel and is a terrific campsite with ample wade fishing opportunities around its periphery.

At 2.9 miles below Little Webberville, look for a slough (an abandoned channel) river left, just upstream from a small island. The slack water here is worth some casts. Below this, the river shallows somewhat, particularly along the north bank.

The boat ramp at ("**Big**") **Webberville Park** (30.209488, -97.498906) which underwent renovation in 2019, will be river left just past the highlines. A fun, short paddle from Webberville Park is to the large island that splits the river about a quarter mile below the boat ramp. The channel river right is small water, and the channel river left gets very fishy where Coleman Branch enters from the north bank.

The next takeout is 14.3 river miles below Webberville Park is at **FM 969 near Utley** (30.16779, -97.40324). There are a number of islands suitable for camping in this reach.

 From downtown, take I-35 south to Exit 230 for TX 71 west. Follow TX 71 to TX 130 (tolls) and go north to Exit 444 for FM 969 (Webberville Road) east. Follow FM 969 for 5.7 miles to Water Street. A right on Water Street will bring you to the park, on your right. Anglers driving from south or north of Austin may want to take TX 130 the entire way to FM 969.

 Downtown, Vallejo

⭐ A Bite and a Beer for Every Palate

There are more bars, restaurants, breweries, and food trucks in Austin than you could visit in a year (or five) of fishing trips. Two local breweries that produce great beer, have friendly taprooms with both indoor and patio seating, and support the Central Texas fly fishing community are **Austin Beerworks** (3001 Industrial Terrace, **austinbeerworks.com** for more information) and **Oskar Blues Brewery** (10420 Metric Blvd., **oskarblues.com** for more information). It's convenient that they are a mere 2 miles from each other in north-central Austin, near the intersection of TX 1 (MoPac/Loop 1) and US 183. Both breweries employ avid fly fishers, support local river conservation efforts, and welcome damp anglers. Austin Beerworks has its own, full-time food truck. Check the Oskar Blues calendar for monthly "Tie One On" fly tying nights with Matt Bennett.

Inland Tides on the LoCo

You're wading a sandbar below the TX 130 crossing, and you notice that the water level is moving up past your waist, and pretty fast. Or maybe you've beached your kayak on an island and wandered off to fish downstream. You look up to see your boat floating by.

It's a safe bet that both of these things have happened in the past few years. Indeed, Austin-Travis County EMS has rescued several people on the Lower Colorado River in recent years, including a man who became stranded on an island near the Montopolis Bridge in November 2018: He was airlifted to safety by helicopter.

Sudden rises are expected after big rain events or when flood pools on the Highland Lakes are full. But on the LoCo, water levels fluctuate by as much as 5 feet *nearly every single day*. Flows can jump by a factor of 20, from, say, 140 cfs to 2,800 cfs, turning a placid river into a fast-moving juggernaut.

Local fishing guides refer to it as an inland tidal cycle, and note that the best fishing is at slack low water. Unlike lunar tides, the LoCo's fluctuations are entirely man-made, as a result of releases from Tom Miller Dam on Lake Austin, which in turn trigger obligatory releases from the City of Austin's Longhorn Dam. Tom Miller Dam is controlled by the LCRA, which treats its power generation and contractual release schedule as proprietary market information and refuses to let the public know when releases are coming.

The water doesn't come all at once in a great, roaring wall; rather, think of a big "bubble" of water moving down the streambed. From normal "low tide" conditions to a peak "high tide" is typically a matter of seven or eight hours, with a sharp increase over the three to four hours before the peak. As

A kayak or canoe is the best DIY option for the LoCo. A guided raft or jet boat trip will shorten the learning curve.

the slug of water moves downstream, levels and flows gradually fall back to normal. That is, unless there is a "double bump" on a particular day, in which case a small dip may be followed by a second peak.

With no public schedule or warning system in place, the best way to anticipate a high tide on the LoCo is to check LCRA's Hydromet system (hydromet.lcra.org), which displays real-time and historical stream flow and river stage gauges. Barring weather events, LCRA often conforms to seasonal "patterns" of releases; taking a look at the previous several days or weeks can give you an idea of when to expect the next release. LCRA Site 4558, Colorado River at Austin, and LCRA Site 5423, Colorado River near Webberville, are the most useful gauges. Peak flows at the two sites, more than 27 river miles apart, are separated by about ten hours.

Savvy river users also keep a wary eye on 24-hour rainfall totals and creek inflow on the Lower Colorado, as a heavy rain in North Austin can send huge volumes of water down Walnut Creek, for instance, while leaving the Highland Lakes and upstream Colorado untouched.

A 4-foot increase in the river stage at the upstream gauge trans-lates into a little more than a 1-foot increase by the time the water reaches Webberville, and flow rates will have dropped by half. That's good news if you are camping on one of the islands down that way. Regardless, if you are paddling or fishing the LoCo, check Hydromet regularly and plan accordingly. If not for your safety, then for the fishing.

Chapter 15

Onion Creek

Cypress trees and rugged limestone formations, Rios, extensive public access. Access points: 15

ONION CREEK, JUST SOUTH OF DOWNTOWN, MAKES IT EASY TO get away—on a lunch break, on the way home from work, or for an easy Saturday morning. I think of it as one of the two bookends of urban fishing in Austin. It was the first local stream I spent significant time on, nearly two decades ago, and even though some reaches look a lot different today, it's still a terrific place to fish. Bonus: The lower reaches are surrounded by thousands of acres of city, county, and state lands—more public property now than when I was first introduced to the stream.

Like the northern bookend, Brushy Creek, Onion Creek really is a small river, with numerous tributary streams. The creek rises at springs about 12 miles southeast of Johnson City, in Blanco County, and flows 79 miles, past Driftwood and through Buda in Hays County,

> "The best time to go fishing is when you can get away."
>
> ROBERT TRAVER, *Trout Madness*

to join the Colorado River in Del Valle, just east of Austin-Bergstrom International Airport.

Onion Creek, in many respects, is a perfect warmwater fly fishing stream. It's small enough to easily cover water and find fish; it's accessible in many places; and the water quality and scenery can be spectacular when the river is flowing well. At low flows, some reaches can become a bit … well, gross. Below the natural barrier of McKinney Falls, in the final meanders above the Colorado, you'll find Guadalupe bass and carp. Above the falls and all along the creek, you'll find all of the other usual suspects, including trophy Rios.

Onion flows through spectacular limestone formations and is lined with stately cypress trees much of the way to its confluence with the Colorado River. Its 211-square-mile watershed is large enough to contribute to significant flooding after heavy rains, and the cypress gallery—three ranks deep in some places—has taken a hit on some stretches.So have a number of homes built in the second half of the twentieth century. The fish remain.

Garison Road, Buda
30.09429, -97.83894
901 Garison Rd., Buda, TX 78610
15.6 road miles, 0:20 drive time
Difficulty: Easy

Guadalupe bass don't make it up to the reach below Garison Road, but largemouth bass, like this one fooled by Merrill Robinson, are plentiful.

THE GARISON ROAD (HAYS COUNTY Road 236) crossing of Onion Creek is a fine place to begin your exploration of this beautiful little river. There is adequate, if rough, parking for several vehicles, and access to the streambed from the low-water bridge is straightforward.

What You Will Find

Parking is along the road on the northeast side of the crossing. Gear anglers, bowfishers, and neighborhood kids frequent the area around the bridge. There often is a distressing amount of garbage here, including, at times, construction waste. Be a good neighbor and pick up as much as you can safely carry out.

The sliver of property immediately adjacent to Garison Road is privately owned, but just upstream an eighty-nine-acre, city-owned tract is slated for development as Garison Park no later than 2021 and, reportedly, will include a kayak launch. You can certainly launch a kayak or canoe into the upstream impoundment from the bridge, but the best fishing and prettiest water is downstream. Two sets of cement stairs buttress the downstream side of the bridge, and a trail in the right-of-way on the southeast side of the bridge also offers an easy path to the water.

25 The Bucketmouth Wade (Wading Downstream from the Bridge)

Below the pool immediately beneath the bridge, a series of four small pools that are waist-deep in some areas stretches down the streambed beneath majestic cypress trees. The mostly cobble bottom is easily waded, but go slow in the warm months when the rocks may be slick with algae or silt.

During periods of low flows, these pools may be disconnected on the surface. Several may be fed by springs; I've never seen the larger two dry up, even in drought years.

There is a well-worn trail along the creek river right, but it is on

The last long pool before the weir is relatively deep, productive, and beautiful.

private property; it's best to stick to the streambed. The City of Buda's fifty-one-acre Historic Stagecoach Park overlooks this section of stream but does not include creek frontage.

The stream here is crossed by survey lines, indicating that adjacent property owners do in fact own the bed; however, several opinions by the General Land Office, including one in 2018 for this specific location, have held that Onion Creek is navigable; some say to at least Ranch Road 12 south of Wimberley, some 30 miles upstream. That makes this a "Small Bill" stream, one in which the state retained the public's right to use the waters and bed for lawful purposes.

The fourth pool below the bridge is home to a large cypress tree river right, and the washout around its roots is usually good for a green sunfish or two. Below this pool, there is a short riffle at just under 1,000 feet from the bridge, and then a large, broad section of the river opens up.

At the head of this large pool, spring water drips from maidenhair ferns river right, and overhanging trees and jumbled limestone boulders along the bank river left provide terrific cover for largemouth bass. The first 20 or 30 yards are the deepest, but you should be able to get through without overtopping your chest waders at normal water levels. The remainder of the pool, which stretches more than one-third of a mile, is knee- to waist-deep in most places.

A small creek enters river right at about 400 yards below the head of the pool. The shallow limestone shelf below the creek often holds large bass, and the area is a favorite nesting site during spawning season.

This entire pool is terrific for largemouth bass; probe the clear water next to stands of native coontail moss, and brush piles and boulders along the bank river left. The tail of the pool narrows, with a marshy area river left and scattered boulders in the center and river right. Trophy bluegill and redear sunfish live here, and I've seen catchable-sized shad too. During periods of low flow, this pool can become matted with algae in places. Fish use it as cover, but it makes getting to them difficult.

The creek narrows considerably below this pool, and you'll have to wend your way between cypress and sycamore trees in the cobbled bed. If you brought a canoe or kayak, this is where you'll be dragging a bit.

The next pool starts as a treacherous wedge between cypress trees and a golden limestone cliff river right. Watch your footing here, as the bottom is heavily creviced. Late season spawning longears favor this pool, and they are among the most striking I have seen anywhere, with ruby red backs.

As you continue up the middle through the deepest part of this pool, in waist- to chest-deep water, bang the banks with a deer hair bug or a large streamer. A large boulder river right, more than head high, shelters big bass.

Where this pool narrows, at a little more than half a mile below the bridge, you'll be greeted with the sight of a mushroom-shaped island of limestone in the middle of the channel. Fish the periphery, especially the undercut side facing river left, before clambering up the upstream side river

Local wildlife educator and herpetoligist Brent Ormand tussles with a bass on the Garison Road reach.

right. This is a terrific vantage point for spotting fish or watching paired Rios acting goofy below you during the warm months.

As you face downstream, a shallow, tree-shaded backwater over your right shoulder is good for bass and is easily fished from the rock, as is the deep cut bank with numerous root balls and timber snags river left.

The views of the 0.3-mile-long pool from the top of the rock are stunning. River right, a scalloped and sculpted cliff shelters shallow water (find Rios here), and gravel bars and limestone ledges in knee- to chest-deep water meander down to the weir that marks the end of the pool.

The pool is—just barely—wadeable to the dam. A good strategy is to hug the bank river right past the scalloped overhang and then angle downstream to near the bank river left. In years between high water events, the bottom at the tail of the pool, just before the dam, can get a bit mucky. A spring enters river right, just upstream from the dam, and is a terrific spot for a variety of sunfish as well as Rios.

You can turn around here, at just over 1.0 miles from Garison Road, or portage the dam river left and play with the Rios and sunfish in the narrow, grass-sheltered channel river right. Several larger pools at the end of this long run hold decent-sized bass.

The next access point below Garison Road is nearly 3.4 miles downstream from the weir, at **Twin Creeks Road** (30.12665, -97.82162). Parking on Twin Creeks Road is iffy, with lots of signs posted around the bridges. Use your best judgment.

From downtown, take I-35 south 10.3 miles to Exit 221, and then turn right on Main Street/Old Loop 4 and continue 3.4 miles to Garison Road, just across the railroad tracks. On Garison Road, you'll pass the Hays County Public Works Department on the left and then arrive at a concrete dam and low-water bridge. Parking is on your left, before the dam, between the blacktop and the purple-blazed fence posts.

Old San Antonio Road, Manchaca
30.13274, -97.81070
11904 Old San Antonio Rd., Manchaca, TX 78652
11.0 road miles, 0:15 drive time
Difficulty: Easy

THIS SECTION OF ONION CREEK IS GORGEOUS AND WELL WORTH a visit, and access is likely to get even better. The City of Austin reportedly will replace the low, one-lane bridge with an elevated, two-lane structure. The good news is that, currently, the plan is to leave the old bridge as a pedestrian and bicycle crossing.

The wedge of land immediately adjacent to the road is county-owned and hides an extraordinary spring; just on the other side is the fifty-five-acre City of Austin Old San Antonio District Park. This park is undeveloped, and the locked gate just up the road still bears the previous ranch owner's "no trespassing" sign. The north bank of the creek downstream of the bridge (and all the way to I-35) also is city-owned property, labeled on maps as the Old San Antonio Greenbelt.

What You Will Find

Parking here is on the rutted shoulder on the southwest side of the bridge. Please note that the bridge is one-way traffic only; the convention is for the vehicle closest to proceed while oncoming vehicles wait in their lane.

The easiest access also is on the southwest corner, a gently sloping cement apron to the creek bed. Just before you step into the water, be sure to take a look ahead and to the left. There, you will see two parallel lines in the limestone, angling downstream. These are ruts gouged by iron-hooped wagon wheels. This crossing has seen a lot of history.

The King's Highway

The Old San Antonio Road, OSR, or *El Camino Real*, was perhaps the earliest of a network of trails that connected Spain's Mexican colonies with its eastern frontier on the present-day Texas-Louisiana border.

The route that crosses Onion Creek was documented by Domingo Terán de los Ríos, the governor of Spanish Texas from 1690 to 1692. Terán wrote that, on July 22, 1691, his party followed a narrow trail through the woods to *Arroyo Garrapatas* ("Tick Stream," an unflattering early name for Onion Creek), where he encountered bison, ticks, and chiggers. One can almost hear the itchy exasperation in his words.

This route, then called the *Camino Real de los Tejas*, would gradually be supplanted by other trails to the south and east.

The nearby Manchaca Springs (we say "Man-shack," though even "Manchaca" is an anglicized corruption of the name of Texas Revolutionary War hero Capt. Jose Antonio Menchaca), just west of Onion Creek between the Garison Road and Twin Creeks Road crossings, became a popular stagecoach stop on the route between Austin and San Antonio (an eighteen-hour journey in the mid-1800s).

In his 1857 volume, *A Journey through Texas*, journalist and landscape architect Frederick Law Olmstead (of Central Park fame) recounted, wonderingly, a stop at Manchaca Springs. The route continued to be used by stagecoaches through at least 1877, when Scott's Stage Line advertised a stop at the springs.

The wagon ruts in the streambed just upstream of the OSR crossing almost certainly date from the second half of the nineteenth century.

Today, modern highways, including a portion of I-35 just south of Buda, continue to use the ancient route.

26 The Camino Real Wade (Wading Upstream from OSR)

The stream close to the bridge is shallow, ankle- to knee-deep during normal water levels, and heavily crevassed. Watch your step. The best wading is down the center or river left (your right, the north bank). There is a well-worn trail across and above the limestone ledges and boulders on the north bank, but this is private property and should be avoided.

Gradually ease to your left as you head upstream; there are numerous deeper seams, submerged ledges, and stands of coontail moss that provide good cover for fish, but the deepest parts of this long pool will be river left. A reminder: The entire south bank here, to your left, is city property. If you must get out of the river, this is the side to do it on.

Tree falls on this side provide additional cover for large bass, and the graveled bottom of the head of the pool, about 300 yards above the bridge, is home to some dinner plate-sized Rios. A long riffle above the head of the pool marks the place where city ownership crosses the

Cory Sorel takes advantage of a warm, November afternoon just upstream from the Old San Antonio Road crossing.

In addition to bass and the full complement of sunfish, trophy-size Rios lurk in Onion Creek's pools.

streambed and encompasses both banks. The seam and backwater along the fast chute emptying the run above is usually good for a smallish bass.

Two beautiful, longish pools, knee- to waist-deep, stretch around the bend above the riffle. In the first one, look for fish along the brushy south bank and in the pocket in the north bank at the head of the pool. In the second, you will find deeper water, and some rocks, along the south bank, river right. There is a significant washout around the old cypress tree that stands sentinel at the head of the pool, and the deeper (waist-deep in places) water around the tree, along with the current falling off the shallow run above, combine to create a spot with a high probability of actively feeding fish.

The shallow run above the second pool begins about 0.4 miles above the bridge and stretches the length of two football fields. The Old San Antonio District Park boundary crosses the stream at 30.13064, -97.81822, and from this point upstream you will be surrounded by private property.

At the top of the run, which is ankle- to shin-deep walk-through water, the channel narrows and winds a bit with deeper pools and then opens up into the first of two deep pools with some terrific river bass at 0.6 miles above the bridge. Wade these pools river right. Bear Creek enters river left at a bit more than 0.8 miles above the bridge, and the **Twin Creeks Road** bridge looms at just over 0.9 river miles.

The next easy access point downstream is at **Brandt Road** (30.15876,

-97.77584), beneath the East Slaughter Lane overpass. The north bank, between Brandt Road and the creek, from Slaughter east to Bluff Springs Road, is part of the Onion Creek Greenbelt and is public property.

Getting There

From downtown, take I-35 south 7.4 miles to Exit 225, go right on FM 1626 and then take a left on Old San Antonio Road at the first intersection. Continue 0.9 miles to the parking on the southbound shoulder, just across the one-lane bridge.

Onion Creek Greenbelt Park, Austin
30.17179, -97.74355
7004 Onion Creek Dr., Austin, TX 78744
austintexas.gov/onioncreekpark
8.3 road miles, 0:17 drive time
Difficulty: Easy

THE ONION CREEK GREENBELT PARK (THE PARKING AREA ALSO shows up on maps as "Dog Park Blue") is a ninety-nine-acre portion of the Onion Creek Greenbelt redeveloped in 2018 by the U.S. Army Corps of Engineers (USACE) and the City of Austin. An off-leash dog park, it offers covered picnic areas, parking, and restrooms on the north bank of a sweeping bend of Onion Creek. This leafy, former neighborhood retains street signs and ribbon curbs; it's a bit surreal, as only the houses are gone.

An adjacent two-hundred-acre greenbelt follows the north bank of the creek to its confluence with Boggy Creek, 2.25 miles upstream, and the 391-acre Onion Creek Metropolitan Park, which remains mostly undeveloped and is favored by equestrians, stretches along the south side of the creek upstream to Gelle Lane, creating a contiguous green space twice the size of Austin's sprawling and popular Zilker Park.

Downstream, Onion Creek flows through the Austin Soccer Complex and the Roy Kizer Golf Course, two more city properties, before entering McKinney Falls State Park. Below McKinney Falls Parkway, 5.6 miles from the upper end of Onion Creek Metropolitan Park, a patchwork of city, county, and private lands border the creek all the way to the Colorado River.

What You Will Find

There is ample, paved parking here and well-maintained restrooms at the east end of the lot. If the parking spaces are full, you can park along the curb. Entry to the park is free, 24 hours a day. You are likely to face a joyous ramble of dogs sniffing, running, fetching, and just generally having a terrific time in the off-leash area between the parking lot and the creek, and you will probably be greeted by more than one happy canine on your walk to the water or the trailhead.

You will see the creek from the end of the parking area and can enter the water there (or, really, anywhere above the East William Cannon Drive bridge) or head upstream on the level, hard-packed dirt trail (look for the gate on your right as you walk toward the water) if you decide to walk the trail.

There is so much good access here, it is simple enough to plan a full-day's adventure, covering the more than 2.0 miles of creek bordered by the greenbelt and Onion Creek Metropolitan Park, to bail out anywhere along the way, or to plan a shorter wade of a quarter mile or so. You also could launch a kayak at the dog park and paddle upstream to **Brandt Road** or even **Old San Antonio Road**, or downstream to **McKinney Falls State Park** with only minimal dragging at normal flows.

27 Dog Park Blue (Wading or Paddling to the First Trail Crossing)
The entry to the creek here is straightforward. You'll want to head upstream, away from swimming dogs, in knee- to waist-deep water, angling toward the far bank. The bottom here is mostly limestone with some meandering gravel bars. The north bank, river left (your right), is the where you'll find the deeper channel along most of this reach and is undercut with widely spaced snags and brush piles that provide excellent cover for largemouth bass.

The bank river right is a high bluff, in some places a chalky cliff, with a limestone shelf jutting into the stream at or below the level of the water. In fact, the reclaimed homesites along Dixie Drive provide a good vantage point to scout for fish or make some interesting photographs of anglers in the creek below. A trail leads down to a stark white limestone "beach" at 30.16901, -97.74339.

During the spring and summer, look for sunfish and Rio nests on the gravel bars closer to the south bank here.

At just short of 0.4 miles from the dog park, a deep eddy river right is a good place to look for fish waiting for the current to bring

A rough trail leads from the bluff on Dixie Drive down to a bleached limestone shelf just upstream from Dog Park Blue.

them something to eat. Try drifting a damsel nymph through the
backwater.

Just upstream of the backwater
river right, a small creek enters the
stream. Continuing upstream, you
will see riffles and shallow runs
alternating with deep, slow pools. At
just over 0.6 miles, you will want to
head back across toward the north
bank, which here is the shallow side
of the stream.

*Once you get away from the canines, look for Rios
nesting on the gravel bars during the warm months.*

A spur of the **Onion Creek
Greenbelt Trail** (used by both hikers and equestrians) crosses the stream
at a broad riffle at 30.16481, -97.75131, 0.7 miles above the dog park. If
you prefer to hike to this point and start your fishing here, it is an easy
0.6-mile walk on a level, hard-packed dirt trail to the turn-off, and then
about 300 feet down to the creek.

 ## 28 The Prettiest Quarter Mile
(Wading or Paddling to the Second Trail Crossing)

The reach between the first trail crossing to the **second crossing**
(30.16691, -97.75493) is perhaps the prettiest quarter mile on lower
Onion Creek. The sound of traffic has faded to a whisper, and the only
signs of humanity are the flood debris caught in the branches of overhanging trees. Shallow rock ledges and jumbled boulders river right and
an undercut bank river left provide good cover for bass and sunfish.

A pair of red-tailed hawks lives along this section of stream, and you
are likely to see them soaring above the river, or at least hear their distinctive *kee-eee-ar* call, the one Hollywood sound engineers often dub over
images of soaring bald eagles, which don't sound like that at all.

The pool immediately below the broad riffle where the trail ends is
glorious, with a long tongue of current banging into a brushy bank in
chest-deep water. My friend Alana Lyons caught her personal best largemouth (to date) on a mouse pattern here.

The trail along the north bank ends here, or more accurately crosses
the creek and continues as an equestrian route, 0.9 miles from the trailhead at the dog park. A shortcut to the hike, or the wade up the creek, is
to park at the end of **South Pleasant Valley Road** (30.16974, -97.75395),

Alana Lyons with a healthy largemouth on the prettiest quarter mile of Onion Creek.

in view of Perez Elementary School, and follow either branch of a loop trail about 0.3 miles to the water.

 Wild Onion
(Wading or Paddling Upstream from the Second Trail Crossing)

Onion Creek above the second trail crossing feels remote, and with a broader channel here, it is a bit shallower in most places. The easiest wading in the first long pool is river left, where a limestone ledge provides solid footing. A deep channel follows the middle of the stream, and the brushy, undercut south bank is outstanding bass habitat.

Near the head of the pool, an old car is wedged among the trees about halfway up the cliff. It may have been rolled down from the top years ago or, more likely, was swept downstream in one of the floods that have plagued this watershed.

When the creek is flowing well, water quality is excellent, and the upstream sections feel much more remote than they really are.

A little more than 300 yards above the riffle that marks the second trail crossing, another short riffle leads to a smaller pool with limestone ledges along both banks and a deep, graveled channel down the center. I have seen "gangs" of half a dozen 2-pound bass cruising here. The creek is narrower and faster here, and you should look for fish at the edges of the current. At about 0.3 miles above the second trail crossing, seeps and springs drip from a profusion of maidenhair ferns on the high north bank.

Just ahead, the streambed, which you have been following generally northwest since the first trail crossing, begins a sweeping meander to the west and then the south, and large gravel banks

Cory Sorel sends a cast toward a slowly cruising bass above the second trail crossing at Onion Creek Greenbelt Park.

emerge along the north bank. Look for eddies and backwaters on both sides of the creek; that's where you'll find most of the fish.

At just over 0.5 miles from the second trail crossing, you will find a waist-deep pool where the north bank, on your right, is heavily overgrown with vegetation. This is a perfect spot to try out that mouse or hopper pattern.

At 0.6 miles above the second trail crossing, and 1.7 miles above the dog park, Boggy Creek enters river left. A washout at the confluence is neck-deep but can be easily bypassed by edging to your left; you can also fish the deep cut along the west side of Boggy Creek by following the north bank of Onion Creek into the much smaller tributary. There are a few good, small pools within 50 yards of the larger creek.

If you continue upstream on Onion Creek from here, you will soon be headed almost due south in a broader, shallower streambed until you reach the boundary of Onion Creek Metro Park river right at 30.16417, -97.76363, about 2.0 miles from the dog park.

From downtown, take I-35 south to Exit 228, and then cross over I-35 on East William Cannon Drive and continue east for 1.4 miles to South Pleasant Valley Drive. Take a right on South Pleasant Valley Drive and, at the bottom of the hill, a left on Onion Creek Drive. Follow Onion Creek Drive to the parking area (though you can park along the curb anywhere here).

McKinney Falls State Park, Austin
30.180834, -97.721986
5808 McKinney Falls Pkwy., Austin, TX 78744
tpwd.texas.gov/state-parks/mckinney-falls
9.7 road miles, 0:17 drive time
Difficulty: Easy to Moderate

THE 709-ACRE MCKINNEY FALLS STATE PARK IS A POPULAR urban park and will reach capacity on most weekends when the weather is decent. Visitors with campsite reservations will be allowed entry even if the park is at capacity. The daily entry fee (gates are open 8 a.m.–10 p.m.) is $6 per adult. Children age 12 and under are free. Campsites with potable water and electricity start at $20 per night. As is true for all **state** parks in Texas, no fishing license is required if fishing within the park boundaries.

With approximately 1.75 miles of Onion Creek frontage between the upstream boundary of the park (30.17479, -97.73182) and the high bridge at McKinney Falls Parkway downstream, there is ample fishing opportunity.

There also is a lot of history here. The ruins of the namesake settler's homestead and mill, dating from the 1850s, still stand. Above the lower falls, the Camino Real de los Tejas (see The King's Highway, page 207), the Spanish colonial trail, crosses the creek. Elsewhere in the park, visitors can see a 6,000-year-old rock shelter used by ancient residents of the area or visit "Old Baldy," a cypress tree more than 100 feet tall and between 500 and 600 years old. This same tree likely sheltered early eighteenth century expeditions that camped here on their way to missions and forts on the frontier of French Louisiana.

What You Will Find

The park headquarters and office are open during normal business hours. You can check in, pay your fee, and pick up free maps here (as well as, for a price, natural history guides). From the headquarters, you can follow the main road to a big loop that offers parking and access to the Onion Creek Trail, which parallels the creek, and to the Upper Falls.

The erosion-resistant limestones of the Upper and Lower Falls of Onion Creek are remnants of beach deposits that accumulated over ash from nearby Pilot Knob, an extinct volcano that last erupted an estimated seventy-nine million years ago. The creek can easily be forded above either of the falls, which are popular summertime swimming holes.

If you'd like to see both, the distance between the two is only about three-tenths of a mile and can be walked above the creek on the north bank or on the Rock Shelter Interpretive Trail.

The stream along Onion Creek Trail, above the Upper Falls, is relatively broad and slow, and there are multiple access points (a good one, just above the **Upper Falls,** is (30.18472, -97.72582). This is where you would launch or retrieve a kayak for an upstream adventure.

Alternatively, you can take the first right and follow the road to the parking area for the Lower Falls to fish between the falls and downstream to the bridge. The latter is the reach I will focus on here.

30 Below the Falls (Wading Downstream from the Lower Falls)

The Lower Falls form a natural barrier to fish, including Guadalupe bass and carp, moving up from the Colorado River. Williamson Creek enters from river left just above the falls and is worth a side trip. The state park boundary follows the east and north side of this tributary stream more than 0.9 miles to a point near 30.19051, -97.72700. A municipal golf course, which borders much of Onion Creek in the park, continues along the south bank of Williamson Creek upstream of the park boundary.

Williamson Creek can be good for sunfish and small bass, and also for fossils. The lower reach, especially, is worth a visit.

The Lower Falls at the state park form a natural barrier to Guadalupe bass and carp, which are not found upstream.

Fall comes late to Central Texas, and the majestic cypress trees along Onion Creek may still be showing color in November.

Back on Onion Creek proper, anglers can drop down to the water from the Homestead Trail on the north bank, or—a better option—skirt the pool below the falls along a broad gravel bar that follows a bend in the river for about 300 yards.

I prefer to get in the water just below the Lower Falls pool; the creek is relatively narrow and fast here, and it is quite pretty with a high canopy shading the water. There is some terrific pocket water among jumbled boulders and cypress trees river left. You should be able to stay in knee- to thigh-deep water at normal flows, particularly if you bear to the right.

Just after the creek enters a long, straight run below the bend, you'll see a single large boulder ahead river left; there's a good washout there around the base, and you should be able to find Rios and possibly bass in its shadow.

At about 1,000 feet below the pool, you'll encounter a rock garden river left, with another large rock in the middle of the creek. Opposite and just ahead, river right, you will see a nicely shaded, deeper pool river right. Wade up the middle in waist- to chest-deep water to cast to both sides for bass, or skirt the rocks river left and look for carp in the silty, vegetated shallows beyond the jumble of rocks.

Just below this spot, the creek jogs west and then east through a narrow chute. Large limestone boulders and a magnificent cypress tree invite you to stop for lunch or watch mayflies rise from the pool below the riffle. The water here can flow fast and deep, especially if there has been any rain in recent weeks, but the margins of the pool—particularly the "seams" along the fast current—can produce some very nice Guadalupe bass.

Here you will need to wade the edge of the pool river left, or walk along the gravel bank bordering the first half of the pool. Oddly, only the upper half of this pool is in the state park, so stay in the streambed if you continue to the McKinney Falls Parkway bridge.

Below the bridge, the City of Austin owns the north bank to about 30.18174, -97.14520, 460 yards downstream. The next good access point downstream is Travis County's **Richard Moya Park** (30.16991, -97.66507) offers good shots at carp and would be a reasonable put-in for a 3.8-mile paddle down to **Barkley Meadows Park,** but expect some portages around snags.

From downtown, take I-35 south to Exit 231 for TX 71 (East Ben White Boulevard) east, toward the airport. Take the Judson Road exit, go right on Judson Road, and then go left on Burleson Road at the next intersection. Follow Burleson Road 2.0 miles to McKinney Falls Parkway, and go right on McKinney Falls Parkway. The park entrance will be ahead on the right.

Barkley Meadows Park, Del Valle

30.18653, -97.62625

4529 TX 130, Del Valle, TX 78617

parks.traviscountytx.gov/parks/
barkley-meadows

14.2 road miles, 0:20 drive time

Difficulty: Easy to Moderate

THE 256-ACRE BARKLEY MEADOWS PARK OPENED IN SEPTEMBER 2014. It is one of the newest units of the Travis County Parks system and a key link in a planned 21-mile Onion Creek Regional Trail system that will connect the patchwork of county, city, and state lands along the lower reaches of the creek and is slated to include kayak and canoe launches.

Entry to the park is free, and the gate is open every day from 8 a.m. until civil twilight. Amenities include paved parking, picnic tables, portable restrooms, a playscape, and miles of cement trails. There are improved kayak launches both on the creek and at the large, catch-and-release-only Berdoll Pond in the park.

At this point along Onion Creek's course, close to its confluence with the Colorado River, the stream has fallen off the Edwards Plateau entirely and cuts through the rich, deep topsoils of the Blackland Prairie. Despite this, the water remains relatively clear, and there is good wading on a gravel bottom. The variety of fish species here, below the natural barrier of the falls at McKinney Falls State Park, is as broad as you will find in one place anywhere in Central Texas: Guadalupe bass and largemouth bass, Rio Grande cichlids, gar, redhorse suckers, carp, and all of the sunfish.

What You Will Find

There is plenty of paved parking here (grab a spot under the towering pecan trees for shade), a playground, well-maintained portable restrooms, and picnic tables. A network of cement sidewalks leads to good creek access and to the kayak launch (30.18524, -97.62573) on Berdoll Pond.

The five-acre pond has good structure—including standing timber in the southern end—but so far as I have been able to determine, not a whole lot of fish. Your time here will be better spent on the creek.

There are three good access points on the creek here. We will work our way up from the most downstream point.

 Highway 71 Wade (Wading Upstream from TX 71)

The most downstream access point in the park is beneath the **TX 71** bridge (30.18857, -97.61829). Parking is available from the eastbound lane. To get there from the Barkley Meadows parking area, follow the cement sidewalk 0.6 miles (across the historic, one-lane, stone Highway 71 bridge) to the creek.

Onion Creek here is still a classic drop and pool stream, and the pools can be deep—waist- to chest-deep. The best wading is river right.

Of the Guadalupe bass habitat below McKinney Falls, this section of the creek—close to the native species' stronghold in the Colorado River—is

Every once in a while, you're reminded you are fishing an urban creek.

perhaps the best. Drift damsel nymphs along the edge of the current at the heads of the pools here.

This also is a good place to find gray redhorse suckers. During the spring spawning season, the golden fish will gather below shallow riffles and then move through them repeatedly in mixed schools of four to eight fish. Many species seem to be prepared to forego food while concentrating on reproduction; not so the redhorse. They will happily snack and make babies at the same time. I caught three in a row here one spring morning before walking on.

32 Spur Trail Wade (Wading Upstream from the Spur Trail)

About 1,000 feet above the TX 71 crossing, you will find a broad gravel bar on the south bank, your left as you wade upstream. You can access this spot, the terminus of the **Spur Trail** (30.18932, -97.62120) directly from the main trail; it is an easy half-mile walk from the parking area. The pool opposite and upstream from the gravel bar is deep with some interesting backwaters and fallen timber below the north bank.

Cross below the end of the high dirt bluff river right (your left) and keep to the shallower water and gravel bars along the north bank here. About 500 feet

In the spring, look for redhorse suckers stacked up below gravel bars on the reach of Onion Creek above TX 71.

above the beach at the end of the spur trail, you will encounter a long, very productive pool. Gar and Rios are plentiful here, and lunker largemouth lurk in the snags and beneath the banks on both sides of the stream.

Deep pools alternate with narrow runs above the spur trail. There's plenty of shade.

Inset: Fierce redbreast sunfish are a ball on a TFO Finesse 1-weight.

This pool gets deep and is best waded in the warmer months when you are not worried about filling your waders. Take your time getting through this pool—both to find the shallowest route and to adequately cover the water; it is a lot of water for a creek.

About a quarter mile above the spur trail access, the pool ends in a beautiful, shaded riffle braided through gravel bars. Often a green heron has this riffle staked out, and it is a great spot to take a break and watch the birds.

The next pool, also long but not quite as deep, continues to offer opportunities to cast to Guadalupe and largemouth bass along both banks, but particularly the south bank on your left, where there are cypress knees and other structure. You'll wade under the northbound lanes of TX 130 at the bottom of a riffle, a little more than 0.4 miles from the TX 71 access.

33 Toll Road Paddle (Paddling or Wading Upstream from TX 130)

Access to the creek between the northbound and southbound lanes of **TX 130** (30.18845, -97.62710) was designed with kayaks in mind but is perfectly suitable for the wading angler.

For a long time, this was a quick, 30-minute fishing break on my bimonthly drive home from work on the coast. For almost as long, I caught the same *hangry* 12-inch Guadalupe bass from beneath the over-hanging grass at the edge of the fast current river left. That fish was a sucker for a chartreuse mini master splinter mouse.

Then, one time, the fish didn't appear. Thinking maybe she had finally wised up, I switched flies. Nothing. I shrugged it off and continued on my way. Two weeks later, I stopped again, this time working both upstream and downstream and cycling through most of the flies in my box.

Later that week, while visiting the Hendrickson Lab at the University of Texas to talk fish with the experts there, the subject turned to the Guadalupe bass on Onion Creek and the predilection of

Mike Barker plays a Guadalupe bass in a pool above the TX 130 toll road.

Upstream from Barkley Meadows Park, the banks get a bit jungly—in a good way.

many fish to stay in the same general area. I mentioned my pet fish and the specific location, and suddenly Adam Cohen, manager of the ichthyology collection, blushed and stammered, "Uh, well …."

"You collected that fish, didn't you?" I asked.

"Yeah, I think we did," he said, laughing, and then described a recent electro-shocking trip. "Nice Guad."

At least that bass served science. It could have been worse. On a South Texas creek, over a period of many months a particular lunker largemouth was a frequent dance partner for both me and my buddy Jess. Then, one day, Jess couldn't raise the fish he'd named "Mr. Perdido." On the hike out, he found its filleted carcass lying on the bank. It was of legal size and apparently someone made good use of the fish, but still …

All of that to say this: The deeper channel river left, across from the kayak launch, is good Guadalupe bass habitat. Drift a fly along the edge

Lower Onion Creek is a true grab bag of Central Texas fish species—from largemouth bass like this one to Rios to carp.

of the current through there before you get in the water.

Also: Bass are homebodies with short memories for punches to the face. If you release one in good condition, chances are you'll have an opportunity to catch it again.

The pool immediately above the southbound lanes of TX 130 is complicated, with a broad, silty bar river left, a deep cut bank river right, and tons of structure. You may be able to wade it, but I'd save that wade for summer. You also could follow the trail along the north bank, but it's on private property (the south bank is county land, but is brushy and high), so that's not a great idea.

My solution, after wading about halfway across this pool twice, was to launch a canoe and paddle upstream. Just above this first pool, the creek is imminently wadeable, and even if you are paddling, you will want to beach your boat on convenient gravel bars and walk much of it.

At about 300 yards above the bridge, and depending on what the latest flood has left behind, you may have to portage river left around a giant snag caught in the bend where the creek curves back to the south and then west.

At 0.4 miles, you will encounter a deep, almost circular pool below a giant cypress tree. Mike Barker and I sight-casted several fat Guads from this pool; they were chasing baitfish in the shallows and were happy to eat Brushy Creek streamers.

There is possible access from county land along the south bank of the creek here. Check it out and report back, will ya?

Currently, the last public access point on Onion Creek is at the sprawling, rugged, and secluded **Southeast Metropolitan Park** (30.19440, -97.60990). Hike the primitive trail for the solitude and the views of Austin's skyline through a notch in the hills, or take the caliche maintenance road a little more than half a mile to creek access at 30.19901, -97.60889. The two large ponds along the trail here are scenic and worth a look as well.

Travis County is in the process of designing a boat ramp and trailhead for a spot off of Dr. Scott Drive, at the confluence of Onion Creek and the Colorado River.

 From downtown and points north, take I-35 south to Exit 230, TX 71 East toward the airport. Just past Austin-Bergstrom International Airport, take a right on Farm Road 973. Continue across Onion Creek to Pearce Lane, and turn left, crossing under TX 130. Go left again on the frontage road. The entrance to the park will be on your right.

 Swept Away, Jon Dee Graham

⭐ Willie's Joint

williesjoint.com
Opens 11:30 daily. Closes 1 a.m. weekdays, 2 a.m. Fri. and Sat. Kitchen open all day Wed.– Sun., dinner only Mon. and Tues.

Willie's Joint (see what they did there?) is a dive bar, honky-tonk, beer garden, family restaurant (until 9 p.m., anyhow)—take your pick. The house cocktail list, inked on a wall, is a *who's who* of Texas and Red Dirt music; try a Cory Morrow, a Turnpike Troubadour, or a Stoney LaRue. Come by for the legendary steak night, the first Thursday of the month. Or swing by for Chicken Sh*t Bingo on Saturday or Sunday. Try the Stevie Ray Vaughn tacos (pulled pork with pineapple coleslaw) any day. This is a blue-collar establishment, and they are used to folks wandering in grubby from a day at work. If you smell too bad, or you're dripping a puddle on the floor, they may ask you to sit outside. That's probably where you want to be anyway, in the shade of one of the massive oaks.

The Ghost Neighborhoods of Onion Creek

High above the water, on a chalk bluff overlooking the south bank of Onion Creek, the ghosts of Dixie Drive bear silent witness: sidewalks that end in grass, empty patios offering expansive views of aquamarine water, the vestiges of flower gardens. There were houses here once.

Just downstream, on the other side of the river, ribbon curbing and street signs lead to lots shaded by towering pecan trees. Bright white patches in the curbs mark where driveways once led to garages. There were houses here, too. More than two hundred of them.

The neighborhoods of lower Onion Creek were developed in the 1970s, before the extent of the flood plain was understood, before the flood of 1998, before the flood of 2001, before the Halloween Flood of 2013. In that event, Onion Creek rose 11 feet in 15 minutes and crested at a record 41 feet. At least four people died, more than five hundred homes were damaged or destroyed, and insurers paid out more than $30 million in losses.

The Halloween Flood kicked mitigation efforts into high gear. Together with homes that had already been removed from the path of floodwaters before 2013, a cooperative effort between the City of Austin, U.S. Army Corps of Engineers, and the Federal Emergency Management Agency (FEMA) has paid $190 million for buyouts of more than 930 homes (and counting) in the Onion Creek watershed. Travis and Hays Counties have funded additional buyouts on a smaller scale.

Federal guidelines require that the land is returned to green space in perpetuity. Along lower Onion Creek, that resulted in the creation of parks and greenbelts that, with existing parklands, protect more than six miles of riparian habitat and provide outstanding public access.

Notwithstanding the tragic circumstances from which the mitigation efforts arose, the result is a rare restoration of riparian habitat and public access in a region where developers regard waterfront property as a prized amenity.

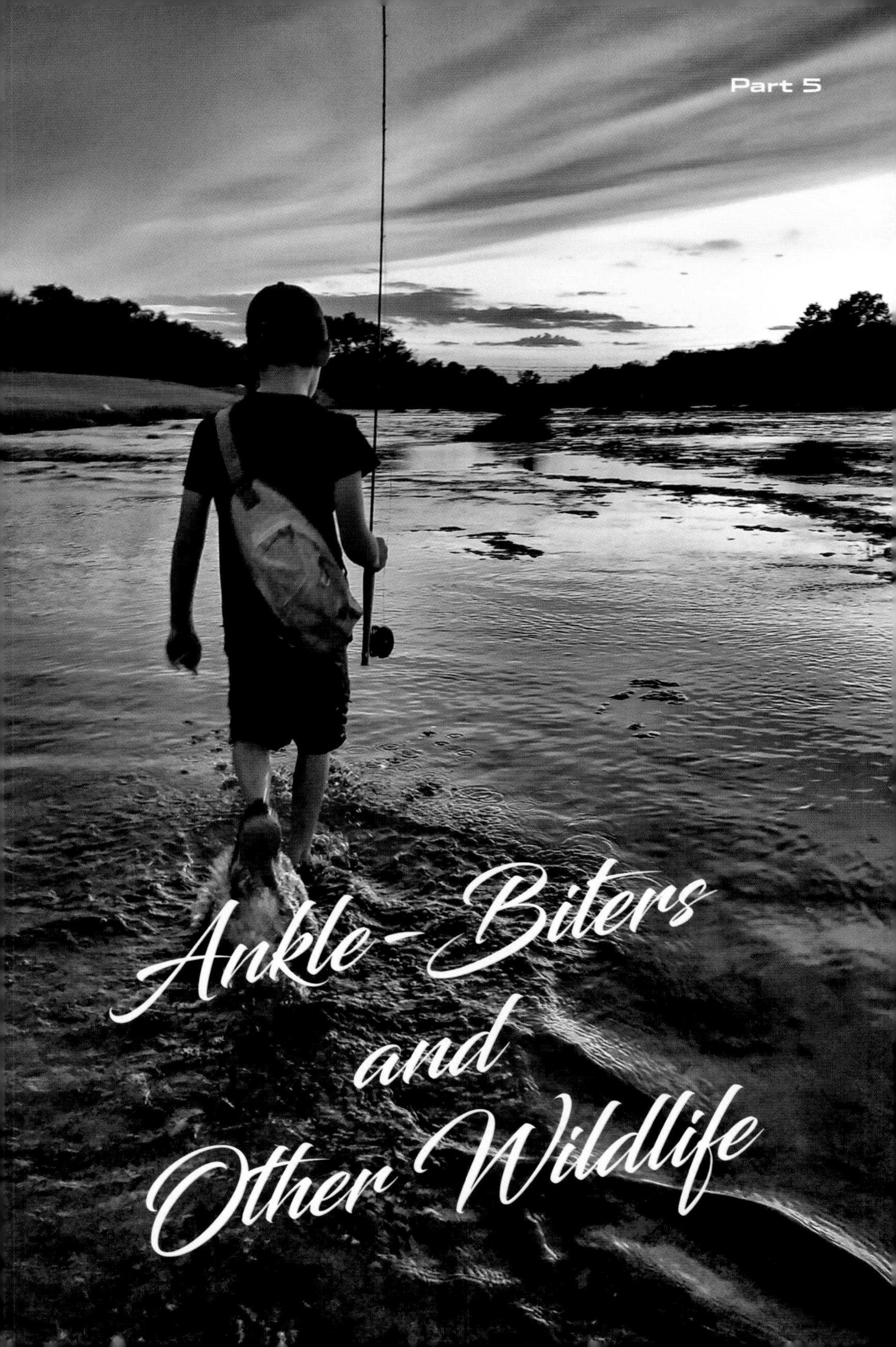

Part 5

Ankle-Biters and Other Wildlife

Deighan Cherry, at 9, has been fly fishing nearly half her life thanks to thoughtful, low-pressure tutelage from her dad.

Chapter 16

Take a Kid Fly Fishing

MY 9-YEAR-OLD, CONOR, WILL ROLL CAST TO THE SAME SPOT for fifteen minutes, trying to get the fly just a little farther out there. Then he's off to turn over logs to look for snakes and lizards. My 7-year-old, Aidan, is good for half a dozen short casts before he sets the rod down to throw a rock or chase after his brother. I have to remind both of them that we "fish first, swim later."

My 21-year-old, Patrick, takes a 3-weight down to the creek near his college just to cast. He says it makes for a relaxing study break. When we fish together, he usually stops before I do. "I've caught enough," he says, and then wanders off to examine animal tracks in the mud or sift through a gravel bank for fossils or artifacts. I remember when he did those last two things as a young boy, and also threw rocks, chased frogs, and splashed in water I hoped to fish.

There is something special about a fishing trip with Dad—or with Mom, Grandma, or Grandpa ... any adult, really. What I remember from my own childhood is this: the getting ready—finding old clothes, clothes almost ready for the rag bag, at Mom's insistence. Gathering up tackle boxes and fishing poles. My dad waiting for the coffee to perk and me watching the proverbial pot, waiting for it to boil for my hot chocolate.

On the way to our spot, we'd stop at the all-night bait stand and ponder the choices: finger mullet? Pinfish? Shrimp! Live or dead? If I'd been good and let Papa have a little quiet time on the drive, there might be a candy bar for me at the counter. Then the anticipation of that first cast, the tug of a fish, the angler's discourse ... time slowed to ten words per minute. My hardworking, often-absent father there, right there, with me. Fishing.

> "I mean, you can't force kids out there because they'll rebel against it. That's why it's so important for parents to find their own enthusiasm and discover nature with their child. My parents took us fishing. And I'll tell you there's nothing that stimulates the senses like hearing your mother swear quite a while after she's lost a fish. I mean, it's an exciting experience."
>
> RICHARD LOUV, "SAVING KIDS FROM NATURE DEFICIT DISORDER," *Morning Edition*, NPR

Whether its cane poles and night crawlers dug from the garden and a stroll to the local creek with Grandma, or crankbaits and hula poppers from the deck of a boat on a bassy lake, most angling origin stories are at least thematically similar. My own boys will remember fly rods as being part of their stories, though there is some spinning gear in there too. I hope they'll remember that it was a lot of fun, that the learning wasn't too painful, and that I was present. Entire books have been written about how to make that happen. Here are a few of the things I think are important:

Taking Your Kid Fishing Isn't Really About Catching Fish

Young children have short attention spans. If my younger boys actually fish twenty minutes out of an hour, that's a lot. And that's not going to be twenty minutes straight, but a couple of casts here, a couple there, all between climbing trees, skipping stones, and swimming. If your kids do that, too—that's okay. Don't get frustrated. The important thing is that the kids are having fun and they will want to do this again.

But Try to Catch a Fish Right Away

It's not really about catching fish, but sometimes it is, and an early and easy payoff is the best way to reinforce that. Thankfully, in my neck of the woods, we have plenty of dumb, willing sunfish that will happily smack a foam spider; they are easy to find, easy to fool, and provide a visually

For my boys, at least, some measure of independence ("I want to do it myself!") has been important in maintaining their interest.

exciting take and a thrilling fight on a 2- or 3-weight rod. Plus, they are pretty in hand. Heck, I like to catch them myself.

By getting that first fish out of the way, you have provided a win right at the top of the program. Fishing mission accomplished! Now there's plenty of time to have fun. You've also reinforced the idea that catching fish on a fly rod is an attainable goal.

Gear Matters

I've found that "snack break" is an important component of a fishing trip with the kids.

Imagine being 47 inches tall and 50 pounds, as my 7-year-old is, and trying to effectively wield a 9-foot, 5-weight rod. That's a tall order.

There's not a whole lot of quality gear out there sized for the littlest fisherfolk. TFO's Bug Launcher, in 7-foot, 4/5-weight or 8-foot, 5/6-weight probably comes closest. At less than $100, it's not too spendy, and the grips have been shaped for smaller hands.

Rajeff Sports offers the bright and cheerful ECHO Gecko, a 7-foot, 9-inch, 4-weight rod with an extended lower grip for two-handed casting. It retails for around $100 and also is a decent choice. Redington's entry for the youth market is a medium action 8-foot, 5-weight, the Minnow, for around $90.

Both the Bug Launcher and the Gecko are fast or "medium-fast" carbon rods. For durability, the ability to feel the rod load, and pure fun on smaller fish, I much prefer to put a light fiberglass rod in my kids' hands. Alas, no one makes a glass rod just for kids.

Fortunately, big-box retailer Cabela's makes some fine, inexpensive fiberglass rods—the CGR (Classic Glass Rod) series. The 6-foot, 3-inch, 2-weight and 5-foot, 9-inch, 3-weight are what I settled on for my younger boys. The full-flexing, slow action provides plenty of feedback during a cast, protects tippet, and makes a 6-inch sunfish feel like a monster.

Paired with Cabela's click-and-pawl reels I got on sale for $10 and spooled with colorful Maxcatch weight-forward floating lines (they both do well with a WF3F line), I was able to outfit each of the younger boys with his own rod and reel for less than $100 (I picked up the rods, normally about $70, during one of the frequent sales). If a kid breaks a rod, I can take it into Cabela's and swap it out; even if I couldn't, at that price, they haven't also broken my heart.

By the way, if you opt for the CGR for your child, buy an extra for yourself. These little rods are huge fun on a creek.

Working on Casting

My experience has been that the easiest cast for a young child to master is a roll cast. With a slow, full-flexing rod a new caster can easily achieve twenty-foot casts, and that's plenty on most small waters.

My 9-year-old is about ready to move on to overhead casts, and I may just send him to an FFI-certified casting instructor friend for the next step. It's not that I couldn't teach him, but Chris could teach him better and faster. A lesson might just save both Conor and me some time and frustration. I've found it also helps, sometimes, to have an authority other than Mom or Dad do the teaching.

Girls Can Fish, Too

It should go without saying, right? And maybe these days it does. But if more men had taken their daughters, as well as their sons, fishing a generation ago, Orvis might not be pushing their "50/50 on the Water" program today.

Jud Cherry put a 9-foot, 5-weight fly rod in his daughter Deighan's hands when she was 4. Now an accomplished angler at the grand old age of 8, "Li'l D" (follow her adventures on Instagram @march-browneyedun) has been featured in *Dun* magazine and, to my knowledge, released at least two potential world-record fish in 2019.

Plentiful and willing sunfish make "catching" an easy part of any outing with children.

Cherry, a life-long fly angler, says his daughter is a natural but that he also stacked the deck a little at the beginning: Every fishing outing included a stop for ice cream or hot chocolate, there were a lot of pink flies and pink accessories in the mix, and he encouraged her to invite—and teach—her friends.

"I'm sure that teaching or encouraging girls to fly fish is different than boys," Cherry told me. "It's not my goal to make her a perfect fly fishing woman. If I allow her to love it, I will not be able to stop her from learning. If she continues with it through her adult life she will always see it as a gift from me and not something I forced her to do."

Let it Be Their Thing

Fly fishing is your thing, right? Maybe it's *everything* to you, outside of your family. Naturally you want to share your passion with your children, to make memories they will cherish as geriatric trouters on some quiet

"Fish first, swim later" is one of our family rules, but we try to leave plenty of time for play and exploring.

spring creek a lifetime from now.

Montana fly fishing guide and shop owner Hilary Hutcheson echoed Cherry recently in an episode of JT Van Zandt's "Drifting" podcast.

"It's their experience and their fish, and the mistake I think I've made is just *wanting it so bad* for them," said Hutcheson, talking about taking her girls fishing. "And then I'm, like, 'Wait a minute, this is for them. It's not about me.' I really want them to enjoy this and catch a fish, but I have to want it for them."

Sometimes my kids want to go catch fish. Most of the time they just want to go to the river. Or maybe they just want their dad's undivided attention for a few hours. I'm okay with all of that. It gives me a chance to talk to them—about where water comes from and where it goes; about the wildlife we see; and, yes, about fish and catching them.

In the quiet and chaos of a fishing trip with my boys, I've learned the most extraordinary things about them and about myself. It may be the next best thing to actually fishing.

 In a Wink, Jamie Lin Wilson

There's really no way to know if a kid will stick with fly fishing, or return to it later in life, but there's little doubt that the time on the water is well spent.

Chapter 17

River Critters

ONE GOOD REASON TO GRAB A FLY ROD AND HEAD FOR A Central Texas stream is the opportunity to enjoy an incredible diversity of wildlife. Rivers and creeks provide excellent—and sometimes the only remaining—habitat for all sorts of creatures and serve as natural corridors between larger, undeveloped tracts of land. I often think of my fly fishing journeys as nature hikes with a stick in my hand, a not entirely unique approach to fly fishing, I imagine.

Mammals on the Land and in the Water

The largest predator remaining in this part of Texas is the **mountain lion** (*puma concolor*), also known as the cougar, panther, or puma. Among cat species, mountain lions are larger than all but lions, tigers, and jaguars, even though cougars are not considered to be one of the "big cats" due to their inability to roar. Males can reach lengths of more than 8 feet from nose to the tip of the tail, and weigh more than 150 pounds.

Mountain lions have the largest north-south range of any land animal in the world, with populations found from the Yukon Territory in Canada through the southern Andes in South America. In Texas, the cat was believed extirpated from the eastern half of the state by the middle of the twentieth century, but it seems to be making a comeback.

Cougars have always been present in the Texas Hill Country, and every few years a sighting in suburban Austin sends local news anchors into a frenzy. Friends have seen them along the banks of both the San Marcos River and the Colorado River while fishing. Males have immense home ranges of eighty to two hundred square miles, with females usually making their homes in half that space.

Cougars are ambush predators, typically leaping onto the backs of large prey like white-tailed deer and wild hogs and killing with a suffocating bite to the neck. There have been just four attacks on humans in Texas since 1980, all in the remote western areas of the state.

Mountain lions are secretive animals and prefer to avoid humans whenever possible. If you are fortunate enough to see one, enjoy the opportunity (and log your observation on iNaturalist!).

If a cougar appears interested in you or approaches, make yourself appear as large as possible by waving your arms or holding your shirt or jacket out. Throw rocks and sticks if they are handy. Speak loudly and firmly, and do not break eye contact with the cat. Whatever you do, don't turn your back on it or run. In the unlikely event you are attacked, fight back. Adults, and even children, have successfully fought off mountain lions.

> "Catching fish is low on my agenda when I go fishing. I'm much more interested in savouring the day and exploring the wildlife of the river."
>
> FENNEL HUDSON, *A Meaningful Life, Fennel's Journal No. 1*

The only other wildcat you may see in Central Texas is the fairly common **bobcat** (*Lynx rufus*), which is about twice the size of a domestic cat and poses no danger to humans.

Canids you may encounter include the **coyote** (*Canis latrans*) and the **gray fox** (*Urocyon cinereoargenteu*). I have seen both while fishing in Central Texas, and hear coyotes "singing" most nights from my home in Georgetown. Neither are a danger to humans, and both can be great fun to watch if you see them before they see you and disappear into the trees.

White-tailed deer are plentiful in the region, and you are just as likely (maybe more likely) to see one browsing someone's begonias while you drive through a suburban neighborhood as you are to encounter one along a river. Likewise, **eastern cottontail rabbits** (*Sylvilagus floridanus*) and **black-tailed jackrabbits** (*Lepus californicus*) are common sights, especially at dawn and dusk.

Other common mammals include **nine-banded armadillos** (*Dasypus novemcinctus*), **raccoons** (*Procyon lotor*), **opossums** (*Didelphis virginiana*), any one of four species of skunks (**striped skunks**, *Mephitis mephitis*, are most common along Central Texas streams), **eastern fox squirrels** (*Sciurus niger*), and the striking black- and gray-colored **rock squirrels** (*Spermophilus variegatus*). With the exception of the squirrels, these animals are largely nocturnal, and you are most likely to see them at dawn and dusk. I've been fortunate to see two **porcupines** (*Erethizon dorsatum*) on fishing trips, one of which was hanging out in a tree over the water.

The mostly nocturnal nine-banded armadillo can most often be seen very early or very late in the day. Armadillos have poor eyeseight, and one can often approach quite near a wild animal.

Less common mammals you may encounter include the expanding population of **river otters** (*Lutra canadensis*). I have seen just one, on the mainstem San Gabriel, but they are reported from a growing number of area streams. **North American beavers** (*Castor canadensis*), most active at night, are often detected by the evidence they leave behind. Brushy Creek is home to a healthy population and is the only place I've actually seen the animals (both times right before dark).

You are likely to find fresh beaver "chews" before you see a beaver, but that should be your cue to start looking for large burrows into a high dirt bank, right at or just below the water-

The presence of North American beavers is most often betrayed by their handiwork, like this felled tree on the Lampasas River, and a half-stripped limb, or "beaver chew."

line. Unlike beavers in the Eastern states or the Mountain West, Central Texas beavers rarely build lodges or dams.

I have yet to see my first **ringtail** (*Bassariscus astutus*), or ringtail cat, in the wild, but the little nocturnal predator in the raccoon family is certainly present throughout the region. I know some cliff-bounded reaches of river that must harbor them.

Creeping, Crawling, and Hopping Reptiles and Amphibians

Venomous snakes are very rare on Central Texas streams, but this cottonmouth, on Salado Creek, could definitely ruin your day if you were to inadvertently step on him.

Diamondback watersnakes grow to imposing lengths and they may swim toward a disturbance in the water, but are harmless to humans.

More than thirty species of snakes occur in Central Texas, including the **Texas coral snake** (*Micrurus tener*), the **copperhead** (*Agkistrodon contortrix*), the **cottonmouth** (*Agkistrodon piscivorus*), and at least three species of rattlesnake, of which the **Western diamondback rattlesnake** (*Crotalus atrox*) is by far the most common. All of these venomous reptiles will bite defensively; in the unlikely event you encounter one, allow it to flee.

Of the other two dozen or so nonvenomous species of snakes, you will certainly encounter water snakes, particularly **diamondback water snakes** (*Nerodia rhombifer*) and **plain-bellied water snakes** (*Nerodia erythrogaster*) (formerly known as the "blotched" water snake). These harmless animals are sometimes curious and will swim toward a disturbance on the water just to see if it's something they want to eat. Finding that it is not a fish, frog, or crawfish, they will go on their way.

Garter snakes and ribbon snakes, particularly the endemic **redstripe ribbon snake** (*Thamnophis proximus rubrilineatus*), also are common in and around area streams. **Eastern rat snakes** (*Pantherophis obsoletus*) can grow to lengths of more than 6 feet. Not particularly associated with water, you are most likely to notice one if you see (or hear) a mixed flock of songbirds and jays raucously "mobbing" something as-yet unseen in a tree or on the ground. Birds really, really dislike the arboreal rat snakes.

Common lizards, often observed basking (or skittering away if you get too close) on limestone cobbles in a streambed, include the **Texas spotted whiptail** (*Cnemidophorus gularis gularis*) (look for the tail twitching back and forth, like a cat on the hunt), the **Texas earless lizard** (*Cophosaurus texanus texanus*), and—more often along trails leading to the water—the **six-lined racerunner** (*Cnemidophorus sexlineatus sexlinineatus*).

Common turtles you will see basking on a log or rock, or swimming in a stream, are the **red-eared slider** (*Trachemys scripta elegans*) (the vivid red marking behind the eye gives it away), the **Texas map turtle** (*Graptemys versa*) (look for the yellow racing stripes on the head and the serrated posterior carapace with dark spots), the **Texas river cooter** (*Pseudoemys texana*), and—most often seen in the water—the **spiny softshell** (*Apalone spinifera*). The long-tailed, heavily keeled **common snapping turtle** (*Chelydra serpentine*) is often mistakenly called the "alligator snapping turtle," a different species not commonly found in this part of the state. Snapping turtles are not baskers; instead they hang out on muddy river bottoms waiting for a meal (usually a fish) to come along.

While many Edwards Plateau springs harbor endemic (and threatened or endangered) species of salamanders, you are not likely to notice them unless you turn over rocks in the water and look closely.

The tiny (0.6 inch) **Blanchard's cricket frog** (*Acris crepitans blanchardi*), on the other hand, is prolific and ubiquitous and will scatter and dive into the water with every step you take along

The redstripe ribbon snake, a subspecies of the western ribbon snake, is endemic to the Edward's Plateau.

Speedy and wary earless lizards are commonly seen in streambeds during the warm months.

Red-eared sliders are the most frequently kept pet turtles in the world and are native to Central Texas. The keeled carapace, obvious in this juvenile from Brushy Creek, becomes more flattened in older turtles, which can live to thirty years in the wild.

Texas river cooters are one of the most common basking turtles found in area rivers.

The common musk turtle, or stinkpot, seen here next to a racoon track, grows to a total length of about 5.5 inches.

a stream's bank most months of the year. Note how closely the overall color of the cricket frogs matches the prevailing substrate and contemplate a size 8 or 10 Dahlberg diver. You will hear cricket frogs as well; their calls sound like pebbles clicking together.

Other commonly seen frogs include the **Rio Grande leopard frog** (*Rana berlandieri*), which supplants the southern leopard frog found in the eastern third of the state, and the **American bullfrog** (*Rana catesbeiana*), which you are likely to hear before you see.

The tiny, half-inch-long Blanchard's Cricket Frog is ubiquitous along Central Texas streams in all but the coldest months.

Below: The Rio Grande leopard frog is another common resident of Central Texas rivers and creeks.

Birds in the Trees and on the Water

Texas boasts an incredible diversity of birds—more than 650 species at last count—and getting out on a river or creek is a great way to see and hear some of them. In the central part of the state, the Edwards Plateau is home to two endangered songbirds, the **golden-cheeked warbler** (*Setophaga chrysoparia*) and the **black-capped vireo** (*Vireo atricapilla*). Both are small birds and not especially numerous, but many of the waters described in this book flow through their remaining habitat.

Birds of prey are perhaps the most conspicuous winged critters

Right: Zone-tailed hawks are something of a Texas specialty, but also may be found in New Mexico and Arizona.

Below: Red-tailed hawk.

Bald eagles, like this one on the Guadalupe River, are making a comeback in Central Texas and are most often seen fall through spring.

Bald eagles, including this one on the San Marcos River, nest on several Central Texas streams.

you will encounter. **Bald eagles** (*Haliaeetus leucocephalus*) are making a welcome comeback in the area and, as fish-eaters, are usually found around larger rivers or lakes fall through spring; I have seen nesting pairs on the San Marcos, Guadalupe, and Colorado rivers, but there are undoubtedly others. **Ospreys** (*Pandion haliaetus*) also make their living on the water and can be found year-round on most larger streams, though they are more common in the winter when migratory birds join the few that hang out through the summer.

Common hawks include the **red-tailed hawk** (*Buteo jamaicensis*), **red-shouldered hawk** (*Buteo lineatus*), and the **Cooper's hawk** (*Accipiter cooperii*); the last of these is falcon-like, with a long, narrow tail and preference for dining on smaller birds.

Of the true falcons, you almost certainly will see the diminutive but fierce **American kestrel** (*Falco sparverius*), and if you are lucky, you may glimpse a **peregrine falcon** (*Falco peregrinus*). An interesting member of the falcon family that has in recent years expanded its range into Central Texas from points south is the **crested caracara** (*Caracara cheriway*), a striking white-and-black bird that I think of as the Cajun of raptors: It will eat just about anything that moves and some things that don't. Caracaras hunt on the wing or on foot and are not above eating roadkill. Caracaras, alone among the falcons, have a "naked" face, usually yellowish-orange.

Caracaras dominate **black vultures** (*Coragyps atratus*) when dining on the remains of a medium or large animal. **Turkey vultures** (*Cathartes aura*), which probably arrived at the carcass first (they have a better sense of smell than the other carrion eaters), are relegated to the children's table

Great blue herons are common along Austin-area waterways.

by both and must wait their turn. Turkey vultures roost communally, often near water, and a large colony can quickly foul a short stretch of river. Turkey vultures can be distinguished from black vultures by their naked, red heads and wobbly soaring.

Wild turkeys—the native subspecies in Central Texas is the **Rio Grande turkey** (*Meleagris gallopavo intermedia*)—never stray too far from water and can be seen (and heard) on the banks of many area streams.

Naturally, a number of wading birds frequent our rivers and creeks. Among them, the **great blue heron** (*Ardea herodias*)—a bird I always think of as the "grumpy old man" due to its color and voice—is the largest and always recalls to me my Gulf Coast childhood.

Green herons (*Butorides virescens*) are common and fascinating birds, one of a handful of species known to use tools to obtain food (they haven't graduated to fishing poles yet, but they will sometimes drop twigs—or even insects—into the water to get their prey to rise). Green herons are loath to give up prime fishing spots and will frequently allow a quiet angler to approach closely, and then fly upstream a few hundred feet until again disturbed.

Other common wading birds include two white herons: the magnificent **great egret** (*Ardea alba*) and the smaller, yellow-footed **snowy egret** (*Egretta thula*). An interesting tidbit about snowy egrets: for inland birds, crawfish make up about 40 percent of their diet, and the snowy egret's nesting season in Central and East Texas corresponds to the greatest availability of crawfish there. An angler sighting one or more snowy egrets may want to consider digging out a crawfish pattern.

A few more birds bear mentioning. A Central Texas stream is one of the few places where you will have a reasonable chance of encountering all three kingfishers native to North America. The **belted kingfisher** (*Ceryle alcyon*) is the common, mid-size chatterbox of the continent and is ubiquitous.

The tiny, jewel-like **green kingfisher** (*Chloroceryle Americana*) likes smaller, moving water and can be glimpsed perched above a riffle or zooming by cussing at your intrusion. Finally, the heavyweight of New World kingfishers,

A great egret above its nest on Brushy Creek.

the **ringed kingfisher** (*Megaceryle torquata*), can be found on some streams in the warmer months.

Green kingfishers are the smallest of three native kingfishers you may encounter on the river.

Vermillion flycatcher.

The latter two kingfishers are tropical birds (I first saw the giant ringed kingfisher in Panama) that reach the northern edge of their range in Central Texas. Unusual in the bird world, ringed kingfishers in particular display something called reverse sexual dimorphism; that is, the females are more colorful than the males (think of cardinals or peacocks for an example of typical sexual dimorphism). Kingfishers nest in vertical dirt banks along streams, and you will see their burrows on some of our waters. Listen for their rattling calls, not entirely unlike the scolding of a fox squirrel and, some say, akin to pebbles being shaken in a tin can.

Of course there are many, many more bird species that are common in the area. *The Sibley Guide to Birds*, which covers both Eastern and Western species (ranges overlap in Central Texas) and offers multiple illustrations of each species, including immature individuals and birds in flight, is hands-down my favorite guidebook and is well worth throwing into your pack when you head out to stomp a creek.

 Gotta Know, by JJ Grey & Mofro

Texas River Flora and Fauna

Sometimes beauty can be found in small things, like this lichen-and-moss-covered rock in the middle of the stream.

Looking for a little luck while wading? All water clovers have four leaves.

Above: Coontail Moss.

Below: Delicate Mexican primrose-willow can be found near flowing water.

Above: Humped bladderwort, a carnivorous plant that captures aquatic insects, can be found in shallow backwaters of many area streams.

Left: Taro, commonly known as "elephant ears," is non-native but flourishes along some stream segments.

Below: American water willow.

Above: Leavenworth's eryngo is prickly and very, very purple.

Above right: American beautyberry is an important food source for birds and other wildlife.

Right: Cardinal flowers, like this specimen along Salado Creek, are primarily pollinated by hummingbirds.

Members of the order Odonata, dragonflies, like the roseate skimmer (left) and damselflies, like the blue-ringed dancer (right), are a major food source for Central Texas fish, both in their aquatic, nymph stages and as adults. Dragonflies rest with their wings splayed-out, while the more slender damselflies rest with their wings folded. There are dozens of species in a rainbow of colors.

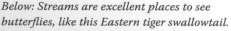

Below: Streams are excellent places to see butterflies, like this Eastern tiger swallowtail.

Above: Spinybacked orbweavers look a bit like crabs, and can be found in an array of colors throughout the area.

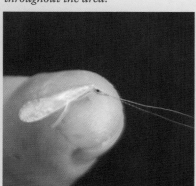

Above: A caddis fly, possibly a "white miller," on Brushy Creek.

Right: The red swamp crawfish is the largest and perhaps most common of dozens of Texas species.

Clockwise from top left: Plain-bellied water snake; redstripe ribbon snake; porcupine in a tree; white-tailed bucks fighting during the rutting season.

Part 6

Southern Waters

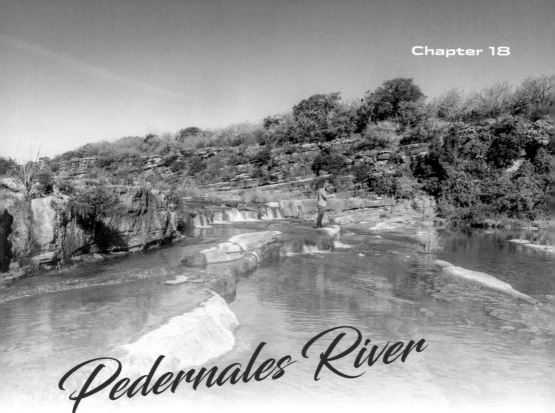

Chapter 18

Pedernales River

Extensive public park frontage, common carp, Guadalupe bass, solitude, and plentiful wildlife. Access points: 3.

THE PEDERNALES RIVER IS A 106-MILE TRIBUTARY OF THE Colorado River that rises in springs just west of Harper, Texas. Its confluence with the larger stream is hidden deep below the waters of Lake Travis, completed in 1942.

Like many other Central Texas streams, this one received its name from eighteenth-century Spanish explorers. Pedernales is Spanish for "flints;" chert nodules are common in the riverbed and were an important source of raw materials for tools and weapons for indigenous peoples.

The river, commonly pronounced "Purr-din-alice" because that's how native son President Lyndon B. Johnson and other locals said it, can be a difficult stream to fish but is well worth the effort: each of my many visits has been rewarded with some new insight, not to mention solitude, wildlife, and an all-star cast of Central Texas fish species.

At low to normal flows (and normal looks low by the standards of many streams, as the river runs beneath the limestone in some places),

Chert or "flint" stone seen on Pedernales river.

it's a terrific river to fish with a friend or two. Numerous pools connected only below the surface (if at all) on some sections can be fished from nearly any direction. On better-watered reaches, public lands allow anglers to "leapfrog" one another in search of fish.

And there are plenty of fish. There is also lots of other wildlife. At each of the locations described below, I've seen at least one of the following: porcupine, armadillo, coyote, gray fox, spiny softshell turtle, Rio Grande turkey, osprey, ringed kingfisher, and screech owl. Interpretive displays in the state and county parks helpfully point out native plant species and geological features. At Milton Reimers Ranch Park, look for the small, black Texas persimmon fruits ripening in late summer.

RM 1320 Near Hye
30.27176, -98.54561
1412–1850 RM 1320, Johnson City, TX
78636
57 road miles, 1:02 drive time
Difficulty: Moderate

THE RANCH ROAD 1320 CROSSING IS THE WESTERNMOST crossing that provides both easy, legal access and quality water. During some flows and seasons, sections of the river at crossings upstream from this one can be choked with heavy algae mats, most likely a result of fertilizer runoff from the burgeoning vineyards in the Stonewall and Fredericksburg areas. Moreover, low-head dams at the Lyndon B. Johnson National Historical Park near Stonewall and elsewhere upstream from the RM 1320 crossing create impoundments that are not easily wadeable.

Of course, wine is an objectively good thing, but so are clear, healthy streams, and I'm hopeful that as viniculture matures in Texas, so will practices for managing fertilizer and pesticide application and runoff. For now, the water above and below the RM 1320 crossing is in good shape, and even when flows are low or nonexistent, pools stay clear and cool.

The river here can be fished both upstream and downstream. We'll look at the longer, upstream route first.

What You Will Find

There may or may not be water in the river at the bridge. If there is not, rest assured that there are some terrific pools a short distance both upstream and down.

I have run into a couple of other anglers here, though we have never arrived at the same time. There may be a *#flybraryproject* in the vicinity. Take a look around, and if you need a fly, take a fly. If you have a fly, leave a fly. **Here's another thought:** *Leave a note taped to the inside of your road-facing window indicating whether you've gone upstream or down. That way no one is spending time fishing in your footsteps. Or, alternatively, they can come say howdy.*

34 Carptopia (Wading Upstream from the Bridge)

The upstream section of river at the RM 1320 crossing can be stellar. You'll have approximately 1.8 miles of walking and wading in that direction before you encounter any serious obstacles, and you'll likely have many shots at common carp, big largemouth bass, feisty Rio Grande cichlids, and Guadalupe bass. Depending on flows, it will be a combination of rock hopping and knee- to waist-deep wades, or clambers and strolls across corrugated limestone and gravel to sample numerous deeper pools.

The first of the pools stretching across the river is a mere 100 yards above the bridge. It is relatively shallow and unproductive (but check the shaded water beneath the trees river right). The pool just beyond is better, and it holds a variety of fish. A small school of carp makes its home beneath a towering stand of invasive carrizo cane (*Arundo donax*) on your right, though you can find them feeding in any part of the pool, and clumps of pondweed provide shelter for bass. The center of the pool is nearly waist-deep; when moving on, walk through the shin-deep water on your right.

Many of the pools in this river are oriented across the riverbed rather than in the direction of flow as in other streams. Hard deposits of limestone that have resisted erosion point generally toward the Llano Uplift to the north and west (the massive granite dome of Enchanted Rock is a prominent feature 23 miles northwest as the shrike flies). The meanders of the river cause the limestone ridges to run across the streambed in some places, diagonally in others, and up and down in still others. Behind some of these dikes, pieces of granite, swirled in floodwaters, have abraded the softer limestones and created pools as deep as 8 to 10 feet. From the air, the riverbed looks like a long, wrinkled sheet thrown carelessly on the landscape.

The first large pool on this reach is the next one, about 400 yards above the bridge. Common carp are the stars here, though you may also encounter a relatively rare native, the river carpsucker.

Look for the carp in the shallows river right (your left) feeding along the submerged ridges that run diagonally upstream across the river. It's possible to wade straight up the middle here, in deeper water, but go slowly as there is a lot of up and down over the corrugations and they can be slick with fine sediment when the water has been low for a while.

You can also wade against the bank river right, or pick one of the exposed, or nearly exposed, limestone dikes and follow it diagonally from the south bank to the middle of the pool before hopping into deeper water.

Exit the pool near the south bank, ignore the large landlocked

Right: Fly fishers new to targeting wild river carp are rarely successful on the first outing. Cory Sorel worked for this fish.

Below: John Henry Boatright slips into ninja fishing mode as he prepares to cast to a feeding carp.

Big largemouth bass also inhabit this stretch of water.

pool directly ahead of you (it may well have fish, but I've never seen any), and rock hop around the smaller pools here for shots at Rios and sunfish.

From this point, a high ridge of dark, heavily oxidized limestone will carry you about 800 feet due west with the main channel of the river on your right. The ridge provides an excellent vantage point for sight casting the braided channel below you and ends at a long, narrow pool that is home to some solid Guadalupe bass and Rio Grande cichlids. The bass may be lurking beneath an undercut ledge here or at the head of the pool beneath a large tree.

About three-quarters of a mile above the bridge, you will reach a broad pool that spans the streambed even during low flows. None of it should be over chest-deep at normal levels, but the knee- to waist-deep side is river right (your left) below the heavily vegetated south bank. This also is where the carp are, reliably, so go slowly and keep an eye out for shadows, tails, and bubble trails.

At the head of the pool, at a bit more than 0.8 miles, cross over on dry limestone or in shallow water to the north bank to cast beneath the trees downstream. This is prime bass habitat, but it has also turned up all sorts of welcome surprises.

At the 1-mile mark, a small pool along the north bank is worth some casts, and the deeper pool just above it has yielded 5-pound bass, giant channel cats, and carp. Walking here is easy on gravel bars along the south bank. A flood-ravaged fence extends into the riverbed—just step over it.

From here, you will be walking noticeably uphill in the streambed, and pocket pools, mostly river right, provide phenomenal, easy fishing. The pools stay relatively clear and cool, even in dry periods, and each is home to a carp or two, a few big largemouths, and channel catfish.

> "So while it's true that there are many things I am unsure of, there are several things I do know for sure: some anglers fish for numbers regardless of their age, some fish for camaraderie with fishing buddies, and some fish just to get outside. But we all fish to learn, to feel like we've figured a part of nature out, to be proud of ourselves when we succeed in our pursuit."
>
> April Vokey, "Seeking Solitude," *Fly Fusion*

At 1.25 miles above the bridge, you will reach perhaps the prettiest of these pools—we call it the "red rock pool"—where a jumble of granite boulders spills down the riverbank. It is easily fished from either the upstream or downstream side.

The next quarter mile will be mostly dry during normal flows. At nearly 1.5 miles above the bridge, the river again looks like a river, with a long, narrow pool stretched along the south bank. It is best waded along the edge of the north bank (this is actually an island, created by a second, narrow channel of the river—if you can find where it enters the main channel, in the vicinity of 30.26727, -98.56747, it makes for a good alternate route to the top of this section) or along the limestone ridge that runs down the middle. The water is deep here, and the rocks can be slick, so take care.

Near the top of this nearly 1,000-foot-long pool, a backwater river left is terrific bass habitat and worth a stop. At the very top of the pool, it will be a steep clamber over a small waterfall up to the next section of river: a final, deep pool with some stunning geology.

Straight ahead you'll find deep, aqua water that can be fished from the periphery nearly all the way around; the exception is a section of the north bank, where a sheer, limestone cliff rises 50 feet or more above the river. As you face upstream here, another deep pool is hidden by the trees over your right shoulder.

There is an abrupt rock wall about 7 or 8 feet high at the head of this pool, at 1.8 miles above the bridge. It creates a beautiful cascade when water is flowing over it. Iron Rock Creek enters from river left above this falls.

35 Deike Ranch Reach (Wading Downstream from the Bridge)

The downstream reach at RM 1320 offers a bit less variety in both topography and fish species but contains beautiful, large pools that are easily waded. The surrounding land is owned by an amiable old-timer, Levi Deike, whose family once fielded a remarkable all-brothers baseball team and included the longest-serving postmaster in U.S. history; Mr. Deike's namesake mailed Lyndon Johnson's first letter from nearby Hye.

The first, and smallest, of these pools is a mere 40 yards downstream, but it is hidden from the bridge by heavy vegetation. Walk down the center of the streambed or on the limestone ledges river left. A channel braided through the rock, mostly river right, connects this pool with others downstream. The next narrow pool (560 feet below the bridge) is deep and has several submerged ledges that provide cover for fish.

I "dabbed" a carp here one hot summer morning, after tracking bubbles and the occasional swirl of a tail. With only my leader dangling from my rod tip directly above, it did not work out well for me. The carp must

The downstream reach, which runs through the Deike Ranch, is more easily negotiated at low flows.

*John Erskine stalks a carp
below Ranch Road 1320.*

have been pleased, once it ejected the barbless hook from its lip.

There will be shallow water across the river in some places here, even during low or normal flows; river left is easier walking, but the opportunities to wade downstream river right should be obvious.

There are plenty of willing Rios in this reach of the river.

At about 0.3 miles, a broad pool stretches downstream. At first, it may seem intimidating, but the wading is easy here over a mostly firm sand-and-gravel bottom with a few limestone ridges to step across. A large, square limestone block about 40 feet out into the pool river left makes for a fine casting platform and puts the shaded shallows beneath the pecan trees on the north bank in reach. Cast to the edges of the block before wading out to it.

Another tenth of a mile will bring you to some exposed limestone center-left; it separates a shallow pool river left and a deeper pool river right.

Rocky Creek enters from the south bank at 0.7 miles. There's a nice plunge pool in the streambed here, as well as a good pool just upstream in the creek (don't travel beyond that first pool in the tributary, though, as the navigability of this creek is disputed). Beyond the narrow pools river right just downstream of the confluence of Rocky Creek and the river, it's about a 0.4 mile walk to the next good water. Rocky Creek is a great place to call it a day and turn around to return to the bridge.

From downtown, take TX 1 (MoPac/Loop 1) south to US 290 west. At the Y intersection in Oak Hill (where US 290 and TX 71 split), stay left on US 290 toward Dripping Springs. Continue through Dripping Springs to the junction with US 281, turn right, and continue on US 290 through the town of Johnson City. From the Hill Country Science Mill in town (a huge, colorful silo on your left as you head west), it is 8.6 miles to Ranch Road 1320 on your right. Take RM 1320 north 1.8 miles to the low-water bridge and park off the road on the southeast side under a large, shading oak tree, or on the left if need be.

From Leander, Georgetown, and points north, take TX 29 west to Liberty Hill, turn left onto Ranch Road 1869, and go west until it dead-ends into Ranch Road 1174. Go south (left) at the T and enjoy the spectacular vistas as the road winds through Balcones Canyonlands National Wildlife Refuge. RM 1174 dead-ends at Farm Road 1431 (you can also take FM 1431 from Cedar Park, but you'd miss that incredible drive through the wildlife refuge). Go right to Marble Falls, and then south on US 281 to Johnson City and follow the directions above. This route will take about 80 minutes from Leander.

Pedernales Fall State Park, Johnson City
30.308043, -98.257662
2585 Park Rd. 6026, Johnson City, TX 78636
tpwd.texas.gov/state-parks/pedernales-falls
41.0 road miles, 1:00 drive time
Difficulty: Easy to Moderate

PEDERNALES FALLS STATE PARK, THE FORMER CIRCLE BAR Ranch, was acquired by the Texas Parks & Wildlife Department (TPWD) in 1970 and opened to visitors the next year. The 5,212-acre park includes more than six miles of frontage on the Pedernales River. Along more than four miles of the river, park property spans the stream and visitors can legally use either bank. On the upper 1.7 miles of river, only the south bank is within park boundaries.

The terrain here is rugged in places, but trails to and from the water are well maintained, and the park offers anglers some amenities not found at public road crossings: parking lots, restroom facilities and potable water, marked trails, camping, and legal bank access. As in all Texas state parks, anglers need not purchase a fishing license to fish within the park boundaries (that goes for both resident and nonresident anglers); however, visitors 13 and older must pay the park entrance fee ($6 per person per day).

What You Will Find
The park headquarters, where you must check in, has a store with natural history guidebooks, maps, swag, vending machines, ice, and more. Park staff are friendly and helpful and can give you the lowdown on current conditions.

If you arrive before the headquarters opens at 8 a.m. daily, pay the $6 per person fee at the honor station. You'll get a note on your windshield sometime during the day reminding you to come by the office, just in case you were planning to camp and need to get an assigned campsite; if you aren't camping, there's no need to stop by the headquarters. Campsites fill up fast for summer weekends and holidays, so make reservations online at least three weeks in advance if you are planning an overnighter.

With more than six miles of river, there is a lot of good fishing in the park. My favorite reaches are at either end; in the middle you're more likely to have a group of tubers float through or have to navigate a family splashing in a riffle. The park's road system, parking, and trailheads are all on the plateau; you'll have to follow well-maintained trails down into the canyon to get to the river. Remember to leave a little gas in the tank for the climb out at the end of your day.

To reach the uppermost stretch of river in the park, the enchanting reach above the falls, take the road from park headquarters until it dead-ends at the Pedernales Falls Trailhead.

To reach the downstream section, take the second right from the park headquarters, park in a designated space between campsites 33 and 34, and take Trammell Crossing Trail down to the river.

36 Above the Falls (Rock-hopping above the Falls)

From the trailhead parking lot, it's a short, easy walk downhill to the interpretive area above the massive Falls Formation, where the river plunges 330 feet in about three-quarters of a mile. Take the upland trail to your left as you face the river or head straight down to the sandy beach below.

The river bed above the falls is a labyrinth of stone and water.

The streambed above the falls is a series of slides and plunge pools, twisting channels carved in gray limestone, and potholes as deep as 10 feet. You might follow a likely looking and convenient line of boulders only to find you have dead-ended at another aqua pool. It's a bit of a labyrinth, but in a fun way.

A series of unfortunate events shortly after the park opened led the state to adopt a "feet dry" rule for this section of the river (as well as a short reach just below the falls). No swimming, no wading, no paddling, no tubing. Visitors can, however, rock hop across the streambed and fish the numerous pools so

Large pools above the falls are always worth a look, but so are the small potholes that may hold water year round.

It's easy enough during low-to-normal flows to pick your way between the pools without running afoul of park rules and getting your feet wet.

long as they stay out of the water and off the far bank, which is outside the boundary of the park.

Some of these pools, like the pair along the north bank beginning about 1,000 feet above the base of the falls, offer anglers the opportunity to sight cast to fish 10 or 20 feet below them. It's pretty cool to have a bird's-eye view of a catfish rising to a slow-sinking damselfly nymph pattern, or to watch a Guadalupe bass pace a mouse, waiting to pounce.

Think about how you'll actually land that fish before you do that, though, if you want your fly back. In some places you'll be able to pick your way down to the water's edge. In others, not so much.

Other pools, like the L-shaped lagoon centered on a stumpy cypress tree at 0.3 miles above the falls, can be fished like any other pool on any other

river. There are some gorgeous Guadalupe bass and Rio Grande cichlids here, as well as sunfish.

A little more than one-tenth of a mile above the cypress, a narrow pool spans the river and may require you to take to the sandy trail above the bank river right (your left) to remain within the rules. Once you have skirted this pool, you can continue on in the riverbed to a largish pool along the south bank at 0.7 miles. There are several more pools that slash diagonally across the river just upstream from here. Look for carp in all three, and on the ledges in the deep pool below the north bank right at the park boundary (30.33683, -98.2629), which is a little more than 0.8 miles from the base of the falls.

You can continue upstream, now in a southwesterly direction, past the park boundary so long as you remain in the riverbed. The prohibition against wading no longer applies at this point, though the logic may remain.

At the 1.2-mile mark, a long and deep pool provides one last, good shot at carp from the ridges of limestone that reach their fingers into the water. Depending on water levels, you would likely have to swim to legally continue upstream from the bottom of this pool.

37 Trammell Crossing Reach
(Wading Downstream from Trammell Crossing)

From the designated parking area between campsites 33 and 34 at the trailhead, follow Trammell Crossing Trail a little more than 0.3 miles down to the river. It's a pleasant, mostly shaded stroll … on the way down. But you've got some round-trip trudgery through sand (it's pink sand, so that's interesting, anyhow) ahead of you, and you may not be feeling very sprightly on the way back up.

It's about 2.25 miles from Trammell Crossing to the downstream park boundary, and the river here looks a lot more like a typical river than it does upstream from the falls, with long runs and clear pools, many shaded by stately cypress trees.

When you reach the river, head across to the far bank in ankle- to

If you are planning a long wade downstream from Trammell Crossing, be sure to leave some gas in the tank for the hike out of the valley.

knee-deep water. Both banks are within the state park here, but this entire reach is best walked along the north bank (river left). This north bank is fairly level but it alternates between deep sand and inconveniently sized cobbles, and you may find walking easier in the water in some sections.

I usually take the bank past the first pool (though the deeper hole where Twin Falls Creek enters river right is worth a few casts), which is a popular family play area. The second pool, beginning about 1,000 feet below the crossing, can be productive up the middle, casting to the treed bank river right.

At the tail of this pool, continue on the bank river left. Cypress trees provide intermittent shade during the warm months, and the slight elevation of the bank will allow you to scout for fish as you walk. You've left the worst of the sand behind you for the moment.

At about 0.8 miles you will see a head-high boulder sitting all by itself river left. The washout at the base of the boulder shelters breeding pairs of Rios during the summer and is worth some time. The pool that opens up beyond the boulder is home to common carp, monster grass carp, freshwater drum, catfish, and largemouth and Guadalupe bass. If you continue along the north bank, a sand-and-rock ridge covered in springy grass will carry you to a vantage point a good 10 feet above the last quarter of the pool.

This spot affords you a rare opportunity to look down on the fish and cast to targets below and away. This is especially advantageous when fishing for carp, which with their large lateral lines are extraordinarily sensitive to the approach of anglers at the water's level. From the high point of the ridge, just before a tree blocks your further progress, a rock ledge below and downstream will often hold feeding fish, as will the shallow water below the bank. Larger fish cruise in and out of a

The reach between Trammell Crossing and the park's eastern border boasts clear water and plenty of shade.

Guadalupe bass on the Pedernales (there are no spotted or smallmouth bass here) are atypically pale, with golden rather than dark dots on their bellies.

laydown against the north bank, just around the corner (but within reach if you cast carefully). If you do get an eat, there are several places where you can take a steep, short slide to knee- to thigh-deep water.

To continue downstream, find your way around the small grove of trees and back down to the streambed. You'll be dealing with some sand again, but with any luck it will be damp and not quite as deep as on the bank upstream.

At the 1-mile mark, a series of small pools and a backwater river right offer opportunities for bass and small carp, which often feed head-up in the riffle here. The river continues in a narrow channel along the south bank. Walk the next half mile mostly in the shade of the cypress trees.

This is one of the spots where my friend John Henry likes to find a convenient cypress knee here, make himself comfortable, and wait for a slowly cruising or feeding carp to come to him, casting when it is just past so as not to spook it.

At 1.4 miles, the river spills down a long, graveled riffle into a sandy pool. This is another terrific carp hole, with bass and sunnies lurking along the deeper north bank. Start on the sand river right and ease into the water to wade down the middle.

At 1.5 miles a large riffle creates an island in the channel (there is some excellent Guadalupe bass habitat at the edge of the fast water in that tangle of roots), and a large, carpy backwater river right. From here, continue on beneath the cypress trees, or slog through deep sand behind them. Note that the south bank, river right, is private property here.

The river here gets wider and deeper all the time, and at 1.75 miles you will find a jumble of boulders in the middle of the channel. This makes for a terrific turnaround point as well as a great place for a cooling frolic in the water. Some of the water will be over your head.

If you continue from here, you'll find the river remains wide and relatively deep, flowing just a little east of north for about a quarter mile. Look for carp in the shallows river left and big bass around the occasional jumble of boulders river right. At about 2.0 miles, the river shallows and narrows and cuts a channel back over toward the north bank. About 1,000 feet beyond this cut, you'll reach the park boundary (30.30626, -98.22326).

You can continue on, say to the mouth of Flat Creek, which enters from the south just around the bend, but you'll need to remain in the streambed to avoid trespassing on neighboring ranches.

From downtown, take TX 1 (MoPac/Loop 1) south to US 290 west. At the Y intersection in Oak Hill (where US 290 and TX 71 split), stay left on US 290 toward Dripping Springs. Continue through Dripping Springs 32 miles to Ranch Road 3232 and turn right. Head north 6.4 miles to Ranch Road 2766, and take a right and then an immediate left onto Park Road 6026. The park headquarters (check in and pay the entry fee) is 2.5 miles up the road.

From the north or west side of Austin, or if you need to make a fly shop stop en route to the water, take Bee Caves Road west from TX Loop 360 (Capital of Texas Highway) to TX 71; Sportsman's Finest (see **Appendices**) will be on your right at the junction (12434 Bee Caves Road). Continue west on TX 71. In the small city of Bee Cave, take a left onto Ranch Road 3238 (Hamilton Pool Road) and continue 6.8 miles to the junction with Ranch Road 12 (look for the Texaco station). Go south on RM 12 7.4 miles to US 290 and then west on US 290 from Dripping Springs as described above.

Milton Reimers Ranch Park, Dripping Springs
30.33370, -98.12231
23610 Hamilton Pool Rd., Dripping Springs, TX 78620
parks.traviscountytx.gov/parks/reimers-ranch
29 road miles, 0:40 drive time
Difficulty: Easy to Moderate

MILTON REIMERS RANCH PARK IS THE LARGEST UNIT OF THE ever-expanding Travis County Parks system and is a longtime favorite among rock climbers and mountain bikers from across the state. The 2,427-acre park includes nearly three miles of Pedernales River frontage, with public access and trails along the south (here it is east) bank.

Cory Sorel keeps an eye out for carp as he wades below Trammell Crossing.

The park has for decades been a popular fishing spot during the spring run of white bass (rancher Milton Reimers long allowed anglers entry for a small fee). It also features all the other Pedernales River species, plus some lake-dwelling species like white and black crappie year-round.

When Lake Travis is full (at a pool elevation of 681 feet, a rarity in recent years), the riverbed fronting the park is nearly completely inundated, and is best fished from a kayak or canoe, or from the bank. At lower lake levels, the channel is braided and sometimes disappears altogether beneath the sand between pools, particularly downstream from the "River Beach" below the paved paddlecraft launch. The fish are necessarily concentrated in the deeper pools then, and stalking and sight casting opportunities increase.

Reimers Ranch is a day-use-only park, open from 8 a.m. until dusk, and visitors must pay a $10 per vehicle entry fee on weekdays, $15 per day on weekends and holidays from May through September.

What You Will Find

The road and trail system along the river looks a lot larger on a map than it is in reality. You can easily walk and fish the nearly three miles of river in a day and have a leisurely walk back to your vehicle, wherever you park. The second parking area, called "River Bend" parking on some maps, leads down to the kayak launch and swimming hole; it is the most central. The last parking area, used primarily by rock climbers, offers the most difficult climb down to the river. There are restrooms and potable water at all of the parking areas except at the climbers' trailhead.

38 Reimers Ranch (Upstream and Downstream, Multiple Access Points)

From the second parking area, you can follow the hiking trail down to the river or walk down the paved road to the kayak and canoe launch (it's pick-up and drop-off only at the launch; you still have to park uphill).

From the large pool, the "swimming hole," you'll have 1.6 miles of river downstream (to 30.38028, -98.10194, near the mouth of a creek that enters river right) and a little less than that upstream (to 30.35972, -98.12722) before you leave the park boundaries. The county owns the southern bank of the river all the way to the Hamilton Pool Road crossing, upstream, but portions are still reserved for the Reimers family at this time. What you can do with that stretch of water depends entirely on the lake level.

When the lake is below full but above "really low," the river is walkable between pools or wadeable over a sand-and-gravel bottom. Even at low levels, there will be fish in the intermittent pools, and in the deeper, permanent pools you can find huge river largemouth bass; I've seen catches of 4, 5, and even 7 pounds from this stretch.

When the lake is full or nearly full, you'll want to paddle or float the river. You can get out and wade where you find sand or gravel bars (usually upstream of the swimming hole) and won't run out of floatable water until you are above the park boundary.

You can also fish the river from the banks, typically from boulders jutting into the channel. Two trails parallel the river nearly the entire length of the park's frontage. Lower River Trail gives you the better opportunity to scout for fish and access the water's edge. Upper River Trail is used mostly by rock climbers headed to cliff faces at the top of the canyon.

Upstream from the swimming hole about 0.3 miles, a long, deep pool begins. This pool is not wadeable even during low water levels, except at the head and the tail. You'll have to use Lower River Trail, river right, or hug the sandy north bank. Note that the trail (and currently public park property) ends before the pool does, and if you continue past the old iron fence posts, you will be trespassing on private property.

Cory Sorel slowly strips a fly past an unsuspecting carp in low-water conditions on the Pedernales River.

During the annual white bass spawning run, about the time the redbud trees begin budding out (late February through the end of March most years), you'll need to arrive early, especially on weekends. The rest of the year, especially on weekdays, you may have the river almost to yourself.

 From downtown, take TX 1 (MoPac/Loop 1) south to Southwest Parkway, go west on Southwest Parkway to avoid the Y intersection at Oak Hill, take a right on TX 71 west, and continue through Bee Cave to Ranch Road 3238, Hamilton Pool Road, on the left. It is approximately 11.5 miles to the entrance to the county park on your right. If you cross the Pedernales River, you've gone too far.

 Seven Year Drought, Jamie Lin Wilson

⭐ Pecan Street Brewing

pecanstreetbrewing.com
Open 11 a.m. to 9 p.m. daily

Pecan Street Brewing is located on Johnson City's historic town square, across from the Blanco County Courthouse (free parking). The atmosphere is casual and friendly, but if you're extra grungy from a morning on the river, you can always ask to be seated in the biergarten out back; it's pet friendly, too.

So far as I can tell, and I'm still working my way through the menu, everything here is good: the beer, brewed on site, as well as standbys like the Texas Old Fashioned hamburger and chicken fried steak. The more creative offerings, which rotate, are worth a gamble: the Brisket Tejano served as street tacos is one of the most memorable lunches I've enjoyed while taking a break from exploring a river.

The Drought of Record and the Flood of '52

In 1949, farmers and ranchers in Central Texas were having a hard time. Below-average rainfall and above-average temperatures were stressing herds and crops. By 1951, the entire state was in a severe drought. At the beginning of September 1952, the federal government launched "Operation Haylift," flying bales in from wetter regions of the country, and the city of Llano began buying train cars of water because the Llano River had completely dried up.

From September 1 to September 9, the Pedernales River at Johnson City registered zero stream flow. Then it began to rain. Just a little at first, and then a whole lot: the Hye and Stonewall areas received 26 inches of precipitation in less than 24 hours. On the morning of September 10, the Pedernales began to flow. By noon the river was 3 feet high and running at 137 cubic feet per second (cfs). At 6 p.m., the gauge height was 9.2 feet and the river was rolling at a brisk 3,200 cfs.

The flood continued to gain steam, with flow doubling nearly every hour until, at 10 p.m., the river was a raging monster moving at an astonishing 390,000 cfs and rising to 40.8 feet. The Pedernales peaked at 42.5 feet and 441,000 cfs in the dark, morning hours of September 11. Then, just as quickly as it rose, it fell back to a 7.3-foot flood stage and a discharge of 5,520 cfs by midnight. Floodwaters raised Lake Travis 57 feet, from 30 percent of capacity, its all-time low, to full capacity in less than 24 hours.

As the waters receded, residents surveyed the damage: century-old cypress trees splintered to matchsticks; mature pecan trees swept downstream; entire fields of rich topsoil stripped to clay and gravel; a tractor trailer carrying a nineteen-ton load swept off US 290; and the US 281 bridge in Johnson City destroyed.

The deep, pink, granite-derived sand in Pedernales Falls State Park is a relic of the '52 flood, washed down from the upper reaches of the river.

The devastating flood did not end the drought—it would continue until the spring of '57, and by the time normal rains resumed, nearly a hundred thousand farms and ranches were out of business.

The 1952 flood, while the worst in memory, is far from the only such event on the Pedernales and other area streams. Meteorologists call this region of Central Texas "Flash Flood Alley." A steep gradient and thin, rocky soils limit the ground's ability to quickly absorb rains.

The '52 flood was devastating but spared human lives. Other fast-water events, even minor flash floods on small creeks in the area, have not been as forgiving. Nearly every year vehicles are swept from low-water crossings, and people who think a rushing river looks inviting die as they take a closer look. Don't be one of them. Pay attention to weather forecasts, seek higher ground at the first hint of a rise, and never, ever drive through floodwaters across a road.

Chapter 19

Blanco River

Smallmouth bass, scenic beauty, the shops of Wimberley. Access points: 7

THE BLANCO (WE SAY "BLANK-OH") IS A LITTLE RIVER WITH A big reputation, and not just for its outstanding beauty. You probably saw it featured on national newscasts during and after the devastating Memorial Day flood of 2015. You may have heard about the big river bucketmouths lurking in its deep pools, or the smallies tucked into the rock gardens dotting its clear waters. Or, just possibly, you drove up past Fischer to check it out and at nearly every road crossing got the distinct impression you weren't exactly welcome.

That's the Blanco, an 87-mile-long study in contradictions.

People can't even agree on where the stream starts. Some say in springs on a ranch in Kendall County, others insist the source is a little farther up the valley. The river even disappears about midway between the town of Blanco and the village of Wimberley, rejoining the underlying Trinity Aquifer for some 15 miles before re-emerging in springs in the dry streambed below Pleasant Valley Road and on Cypress Creek, a 14-mile-long tributary of the river. That latter spring, Jacob's Well, is a legendary Hill Country swimming hole, corkscrewing 140 feet down into the aquifer.

Right in the middle of what many people call the "Dry Blanco," the streambed dips down into the aquifer at a fantastic geological formation known as "The Narrows." The pools there reportedly are a glorious swimming hole, but they are jealously guarded by adjacent landowners.

In 2015, a group of landowners found an exceedingly odd vehicle to achieve their goal of limiting access. In fewer than sixty words, H.B. 3618 outlaws camping or building campfires in the bed of the Blanco River. The intent seems as clear as the waters of the river: keep the public out of The Narrows, which requires a 15-mile roundtrip hike on the streambed to access legally.

While the intent is clear, the statute's constitutionality is less so. A 1917 San Antonio appeals court ruling, *Dincans v. Keeran*, recognized that "Hunting, camping, and fishing are reasonable uses of the navigable waters …"

The jealousy with which many riverside landowners guard access is often coupled with a sincere conservation ethic.

The effort to keep folks out of The Narrows is consistent with other actions some landowners

RIPARIAN RESTORATION AREA
this GROW ZONE provides:
• protection for young trees
• erosion control
• cleaner Blanco River
• and many more benefits!

For more info: BlancoTrees.org   TreeFolks

have taken along the stream—posting "No River Access" signs at crossings where, clearly, there is river access, and prevailing upon Hays County commissioners to pass an ordinance prohibiting parking within 500 feet of a bridge, or *anywhere* along the five miles of Chimney Valley Road.

It's not that there are not friendly folks here; there are, both in the small towns of the valley and among waterfront landowners. But the status quo is so firmly entrenched that many prospective anglers—those without private access—have given up on much of the Blanco.

> "To find the best places on the Blanco River, you must spend the better part of a day wading and paddling, or you have to know someone who will grant you access."
>
> WES FERGUSON, *The Blanco River*

The official and unofficial limitations on river access in the area are a bit jarring, though, especially given the Wimberley Valley's (in particular) reliance on vacationers and day trippers to bolster the largely agricultural economy.

Part of the problem arises from the date the first survey of the valley was completed: 1835, two years before the Republic of Texas forbade the drawing of property lines across navigable streams. Landowners here do in fact own the streambed. But thanks to the 1929 Small Bill and ensuing legal opinions, the public still gets to use it, even in areas where it is dry (see the **Texas River Law** chapter)

The flip side of such fierce protectiveness is that the owners of some large tracts, including the ranches surrounding The Narrows, and—notably—the historic Halifax Ranch downstream, have actively worked to protect the river and surrounding habitat through conservation easements.

The Blanco River was first mentioned by a Spanish Franciscan friar, Isidro Félix de Espinosa, in a diary entry for April 16, 1709. He called the river San Rafael Creek. By 1727, a Spanish army officer, Pedro de Rivera y Villalón, noted that some called the stream the *"Arroyo Blanco."* The name gained currency and eventually stuck.

For all the drama and contention along the Blanco, there is access. You could get in the river at the popular road-side access point at the base of the **Wayne Smith Lake dam** (30.10032, -98.44307) on Farm Road 1623 (River Road) upstream from the town of Blanco or launch a kayak or canoe to fish the impoundment at **Blanco State Park** (101 Park Rd. 23, Blanco, TX 78606). Some other spots will require anglers to ignore threatening signs (the "No River Access" ones, not the "No Parking" ones—ignore the latter and you'll likely find a ticket under your windshield wiper).

Here are three that don't.

G.W. Haschke Lane Crossing, Wimberley
29.990545, -98.199831
702 G.W. Haschke Lane, Wimberley, TX 78676
41 road miles, 0:55 drive time
Difficulty: Moderate

ON A MAP, THE FISCHER STORE ROAD (HAYS COUNTY ROAD 181) crossing looks as if it might offer access to the Blanco River; it doesn't. The high bridge here, rebuilt after the 2015 flood, is forbidding. Go just a little farther, though, across the bridge and up the hill, and you'll see G.W. Haschke Lane to your left. Follow this road to the low-water crossing, nine-tenths of a mile downstream from the Fischer Store Road.

The upstream section, between the low-water crossing and Fischer Store Road, is deep and swift and clear and looks bassy as heck along the edges; I haven't fished it out of sight of the bridge, but you definitely should.

The downstream section is a wonderland of jumbled boulders, deep runs, and tumbling riffles. We'll look at a nearly 0.5-mile section here.

What You Will Find
After you have wound through the neighborhood, G.W. Haschke Lane is a long, straight glide path into the Blanco's valley, and you will find parking on the shoulder of the two-lane road on your left, before you get to the post-and-cable barriers that prevent people from driving onto the flood plain. The one-lane, low-water bridge offers easy access. If the water is over the bridge, by the way, wade with extreme caution; that's a lot of current, and it would be easy to be swept off your feet.

39 The Old Man of the River Reach
(Fishing Downstream from the Bridge)

Start in the small pool below the bridge, from the edge of the road. The richly oxygenated water here is home to Guadalupe bass and sunfish and catching one here before you get your feet wet is a quick and easy way to ensure you keep the skunk off.

Enter at either downstream corner of the bridge, but you will want to edge toward the bank river left for the best wading through the upper section of this reach. At about 200 feet below the bridge, a jumble of boulders in the center of the stream offers good cover for Guads and sunnies.

Begin wading back toward the center of the channel to cast to the deeper pockets below the cypress knees and boulders river left, and pick your way across the stream to the (now shallower) bank river right. A little more than 500 feet below the bridge there is some really interesting pocket water river left, approach-able across the rough karst riffle.

The first small plunge pool, hard against the bank river left, is usually good for a couple of Guadalupe bass, and the next, much larger pool, has everything from giant, undercut boulders to—in the very back of the pool—sub-merged timber. In anything above low flows, you will want to walk back across the top of the riffle and negotiate the scenic drop, a small waterfall, really, river right.

At normal flows, you can cross the river in the broad pool below the falls and fish back up into the pocket behind the huge boulder right at the edge of the channel. I have seen some trophy small-mouth bass here, as well as some respectable largemouth bass.

At about 900 feet below the

I've nicknamed this rock feature, just beyond the big bend in the river, the "Old Man of the River."

Hunter Barcroft casts to the base of a cabin-sized boulder near the end of the wadeable section.

bridge you will see a home on the hill river right and "No Trespassing" signs along the river bank. Cross the river here, and hug the bank river left, where there is a broad, limestone shelf. The shelf will be exposed in low flows, and shin- to knee-deep in higher flows. The channel below the shelf is at least chest-deep, and the ledge itself provides cover for all sorts of fish.

From this point downstream you will want to wade river left, though it's easy enough to walk out into the broad, shallow run that begins at about 1,000 feet below the bridge to cast to the slightly deeper channel against the bank river right.

At 0.3 miles below the bridge, you will reach a large gravel bar river left. Several boulders in deeper water are worth probing and you should approach the silty flat ahead, river left, carefully, as you may see carp or red-horse suckers foraging there.

Cory Sorel casts to a bass lurking beneath the remnants of a cypress tree. The 2015 flood took out many century-old trees along the river.

In this same pool, in a sweeping bend of the river, look for bass in the deeper channel in the center and along the native vegetation in shallower water river right. A small creek enters here, river right, as well.

Continuing downstream through a series of fast runs and riffles, the easiest wading will be river left, but the best bass habitat is river right. This is an incredibly scenic reach, with a towering, rugged cliff river right (look for the face of the "Old Man of the River" up there). At 0.4 miles, the fast water bangs into a huge boulder river left, creating a wash-out and eddy that holds fish. Skirt this small pool river left, in soft sand and gravel, to fish the head of the next pool.

Here, you will find a jumble of cab-in-sized boulders river right. The water just beneath these rocks is relatively shallow and home to some good bass. You can reach it easily by wading into waist to chest-deep water in the channel.

The pool that stretches ahead is wide and deep and full of huge boulders; it's too deep to wade at normal flows or higher, so this is probably where you turn around unless you are paddling. If you are in a boat—and that's not a bad idea—the next legal access point is 2.7 miles downstream at the "**Slime Bridge**" on Wayside Drive (29.96750, -98.18949). If you do use the Slime Bridge, note that legal parking is about 900 feet uphill, above the intersection with Bandigoca Road.

From downtown, take TX 1 (MoPac/Loop 1) south to TX 45 (tolls) and go right to Farm Road 1826. Take a left on FM 1826 and continue to Hays County Road 150 to Driftwood. In Driftwood, take a right on Hays County Road 170 (Elder Hill Road) to Ranch Road 12. Go left on RM 12 and then, just north of Wimberley, take a right on Jacob's Well Road (Hays County Road 182) and follow it to its intersection with Ranch Road 2325. You'll go right and stay on RM 2325 for 1.4 miles before taking a left on Fischer Store Road (Hays County Road 181). Follow Fischer Store Road across the river and take the first left on G. W. Haschke Lane. This sounds more convoluted than it is, and it is a scenic drive that shows the Texas Hill Country to good advantage.

7A Ranch (Pioneer Town), Wimberley

29.98636, -98.11048

333 Wayside Dr., Wimberley, TX, 78676

(512) 847-2517

7aranch.com

38.2 road miles, 0:52 drive time

Difficulty: Easy

IF YOU ARE LOOKING FOR BLANCO RIVER ACCESS IN WIMBERLEY, this is it. Founded in 1948 as a seven-acre riverfront family resort, the property today encompasses 142 acres and half a mile of well-groomed riverfront. With nineteen cabins and several larger accommodations, the resort offers an ice cream parlor, game room, and camp store. Rumor has it that the "cantina" in the faux western town (built in 1956) may soon house a functioning bar, as well.

Overnight guests have unrestricted access to the river, but the resort also offers day passes for $10 per person during the summer and $5 per person in the off-season. Day passes are sold on a first-come, first-served basis with a limit of fifty per day, and visitors can come and go between 10 a.m. and 6 p.m.

The river here is eminently wadeable below the low water crossing at Hays County Road 1492; the upstream section is best paddled. Visitors must park in the lot near the office, up the hill, but may unload and load paddle craft at the low-water crossing. The resort also offers single and tandem kayaks for rent by the hour and the day.

What You Will Find

All visitors must check-in and pay the day-use fee at the ranch office. You'll want to be there right at 10 a.m. during the summer, as the resort often sells out all fifty passes. You will have to leave your vehicle in the office parking lot, though you can load and unload kayaks or canoes at the low-water crossing (29.98501, -98.10938).

The resort property, on the north bank of the river, stretches 190 yards (about the length of two football fields) below the bridge and about 660 yards above the bridge.

40 7A Ranch Wade (Wading Downstream from the Bridge)

The stream along the north bank downstream of CR 1492 is a rocky, shallow run with a deeper channel river right, below the cypress trees that survived the 2015 flood. A deep pool against that far bank, at about 450 feet below the bridge, is a refuge for bass, even during drought years. As you draw even with Wayside Drive, on your left, be sure you are walking in the streambed—the resort's property ends at the downstream side of the intersection.

At 0.4 miles Wilson Creek enters river left, and you'll want to wade across the river toward the shallower south bank, where you can cast back across the river to scattered boulders along the bank river left. At a little more than 0.5 miles, the limestone shelf along the south bank runs out, and you'll have to ford a waist- to chest-deep pool to reach the next shallow stretch—about 400 yards of heavily seamed walk-through water in a sweeping bend of the river.

The next good pool starts about 0.8 miles below the low-water crossing and can be waded either side, though river left will give you a bit more room to maneuver.

At about 1.1 miles below the bridge, **Cypress Creek** enters river left (29.99146, -98.09487).

41 Pioneer Town Paddle (Paddling Upstream from the Bridge)

The upstream section of the river here is deep—really deep, becoming over-your-head deep a short distance above the bridge. There is good bank access river left for about 200 yards, but you'll be dodging swimmers and rope swings. A better bet is to paddle this reach, and in fact there is no reason not to continue farther upstream, beyond the 7A property line.

You can target cypress knees along the south bank on your way up, and at about one-third of a mile above the bridge, some large boulders along the north bank provide good fish holding structure. The river shallows along the south bank here, as it enters a bend, and at 0.5 miles you'll most likely have to get out and drag your boat for 300-400 feet to the next deep pool.

Right: This pale bass is most likely a Guadalupe bass, though smallmouth bass also are found in the Blanco.

Bottom: Riley Huggins stalks a Guadalupe bass in the clear waters of the Blanco River.

This pool, which stretches a little less than a quarter mile, is more productive for bass than the heavily fished, deep water bordered by the 7A Ranch.

At about 0.75 miles, the river shallows again, into a broad run. At about 0.9 miles above the bridge, sandy islands and vegetation river left (your right as you head upstream) provide good cover for bass and sunfish. This is also a terrific reach of water for carp.

About 1.0 miles above the bridge, the river becomes a drag at low flows, and two-tenths of a mile above that, you'll run out of water altogether in all but high flows.

Getting There

From downtown, take TX 1 (MoPac/Loop 1) south to TX 45 (tolls) to Farm Road 1826. Take a left on FM 1826, which will end at Ranch Road 150; go left (south) 0.5 miles to the tiny burg of Driftwood. At the vintage gas pumps on your right, take a right on Elder Hill Road (Hays County Road 170). This scenic two-lane will take you to Ranch Road 12, where you will go left and continue into Wimberley, where you will take a right on Ranch Road 2325. In 0.3 miles, take a left on Green Acres Drive (Hays CR 279) and continue 1.3 miles to Wayside Drive (CR 179). The 7A Ranch office is about 750 feet down the road on your right.

Old Martindale Road Crossing, San Marcos
29.871882, -97.916842
1220 County Rd. 295, San Marcos, TX 78666
31 road miles, 0:41 drive time
Difficulty: Moderate to Difficult

ON THE WAY TO THE OLD MARTINDALE ROAD CROSSING, THE last legal access point above the confluence of the Blanco River with the San Marcos River, you'll pass easy access at **Hays County's Five Mile Dam Park Complex** (two county parks with more than a quarter mile of Blanco River frontage, 4440 Old Stagecoach Road, Kyle, TX 78640).

By the time you reach the Old Martindale Road crossing, the river has fallen off of the plateau and is carving a deep and broad channel through the beginnings of the coastal plain. The river here is not muddy, but it is often chalky due to the underlying clay formations.

The Blanco here is fishy as heck, and the broad pools off the main river channel offer a rare chance to fish some slower water on a Central

Texas stream. You could wade upstream, too, all the way to the big pool below Texas Highway 80 in lower flows, but we'll look at the downstream reach.

What You Will Find
The upstream corner of the bridge, the northwest corner, is fenced and wildly overgrown. The southwest corner offers better access, but you will have to ease your way down a concrete and stone abutment into the shallow channel. An alternative is to walk across the bridge, hop the guardrail, and walk down on the southeast side.

42 The River's End Reach (Wading or Paddling Downstream)
As always, you should take a moment to check out the water closest to the access point. In this case, the slack between the bridge pilings and any shallow pools that have spread out between the abutments. Old Martindale Road is pretty quiet, and this piece of river doesn't get a whole lot of pressure, so the fish remain largely unperturbed.

In the first 400 feet below the bridge, the river runs swift and deep in a channel along the bank river right. Wade river left (the bottom can be a bit soft here) and swing a streamer or crawfish pattern along the far bank.

A gravel bar and a deep washout around a battered cypress tree river left marks the end of the first run and the beginning of the first big, backwater pool. This pool, and the one just downstream from it, offers relatively shallow, slow water and a jungle of spatterdock "lily pads" that provide excellent cover for largemouth bass.

Wading here is a bit tricky; at lower flows, you can follow the gravel bar into the main channel and wade in waist- to chest-deep water and cast to the pool river left; alternatively, you can skirt the pool along the bank in some pretty sticky silt.

A really interesting feature of this part of the river are the clay "islands" that have resisted erosion and dot the streambed. Often there are graveled channels between the clay mounds, and carp, in particular, will alternate between the protected labyrinth of channels and the flat tops of the clay pedestals as they forage for prey. The clay, by the way, is an exposure of the Sprinkle Formation, the same deposition of volcanic ash we saw on the lower reaches of Brushy Creek. It also is as slick as frog snot, so watch your step.

At about 1,000 feet below the bridge, you'll see a long section of abandoned pipeline lying at an angle to the shore river left. The deeper side of

The lower Blanco River is home to a wide variety of fish, but heavy largemouth bass top the list.

the old pipe, the one that faces the channel, is a prime ambush spot for bass and sunfish. Try a deer hair bug or popper stripped from the shoreline over the pipe.

At the end of the first big pool, you will encounter a shallow run and a long gravel bar river left. The bar is in the streambed, and you can walk it to fish the backwater river left. As the gravel bar subsides into the river, the pool deepens; fish down the middle in waist-deep water or cross to the graveled shoreline river right at 0.3 miles below the bridge.

The river remains deep and broad here, with a shallow gravel bottom river right and a deeper "cut bank" river left. That cut bank is home to some nice bass—fish it slowly and thoroughly.

At a little more than 0.4 miles, the river races down a long, shallow riffle that ends in a fine, deep pool half a mile below the bridge. If you want to fish that pool, cross at the riffle and walk the gravel bars river left. You'll run out of gravel at about 0.6 miles, at a deep pool that is not easily wadeable at normal flows. The river here, generally, is putting on its big boy pants as it meanders past abandoned gravel mines and prepares to meet the San Marcos River, 2.1 miles below the bridge. The very last section is better paddled than waded.

From downtown, take I-35 south to Exit 204B and stay on the frontage road past Riverside Drive and the San Marcos Discovery Center on your right, and then take the right that loops back under the interstate. Now on the northbound frontage road, take the first right, River Road, and follow it 1 mile to County Road 295, Avoca Ranch Road. Go right on Avoca Ranch Road 0.2 miles, and then take a left to follow CR 295, now Old Martindale Road, and park on the shoulder on your left, at the first big bend. The bridge is just down the hill.

 105, Guy Forsyth

Devil's Backbone Tavern

devilsbackbonetavern.com

11:30–midnight every day, except Saturdays when the bar is open until 1 a.m.

We pretty much have to drop in on the historic Devil's Backbone Tavern, don't we? After all, I first heard about it in a Tom Snider song, *The Ballad of the Devil's Backbone Tavern.* Opened in 1937 adjacent to a farrier (for the mail horses) and, later, convenience store and gas station, this is a basic neighborhood bar in a neighborhood of sprawling ranches and weekend road-trippers. Some patrons are so loyal their ashes rest below the old, wooden floor. The Devil's Backbone Tavern doesn't take credit cards, but it does have an ATM. You can get food in the four major food groups: potato chips, peanuts, beef jerky, and beer. You'll find Shiner Bock listed under the "exotics" on the beer menu. Ol' Virgie is no longer behind the bar, but the staff is still friendly (maybe even friendlier these days). There is a fireplace and a terrific jukebox, and the recently renovated dancehall hosts some first-class live Texas music on weekends.

 Real Ale Brewing Company

realalebrewing.com

Real Ale, founded in 1996 in the basement of a Blanco antiques store, today is distributed statewide (but **only** in Texas) and boasts a bright, friendly taproom that offers both indoor and outdoor seating on a sprawling property at the edge of town. The brewery also is home to a distillery, Real Spirits, and sells bottles and cocktails made from single barrel and blended whiskeys as well as Texas Hill Country Gin, which includes bottlebrush as one of its ingredients. The spirits are distilled from Real Ale beers and are crafted wholly in Texas. The head distiller, Davin Topel, is a part-time fishing guide and the man behind **whiskeyriverchronicle.com**.

Real Ale has long been a generous supporter of the local fly fishing community and is an almost mandatory stop when fishing the Blanco or Pedernales River.

Chapter 20

San Marcos River

Huge volume of spring water on the upper reaches keeps this river fishing well year-round; look for Rios in wintertime, massive sunfish, and a melting pot of bass. Access points: 6.

THE SAN MARCOS RIVER WAS FIRST DESCRIBED BY EARLY Spanish explorers in the 1690s, and at various times it went by the name *San Agustin* and *Los Inocentes* (possibly for the friendly Tonkawa Indians early visitors found living there). By 1716, the stream's current name was firmly established.

The river rises in the heart of San Marcos, from the San Marcos Springs. The cluster of three major artesian fissures and more than two hundred smaller springs together pump an average of 200 million gallons of 72-degree water each day to form Spring Lake and headwaters of the river. The Tonkawa, who farmed in the area from as early as 1300 A.D., called the springs *Canocanayesatetlo*, or "warm water." Ongoing archeological investigations suggest that the springs may be the oldest, continuously inhabited location in the present United States, with evidence of Clovis culture inhabitants dating back 12,000 years.

An anchor system is helpful when fishing the San Marcos. Paddlers also can beach their boats on gravel bars and wade fish in some locations.

The San Marcos River is one Central Texas Stream where anglers can catch Rios year round.

Early visitors reported abundant wildlife, including bears, mountain lions, and alligators. Glass-bottom boats were introduced to the springs in 1921, and you can still take a ride in one today by visiting the **Meadows Center for Water and the Environment** (29.89413, -97.92966), a research center at Texas State University that occupies the former Aquarena Springs resort complex.

The San Marcos River flows 75 miles in a southeasterly direction to its confluence with the Guadalupe River 2 miles west of Gonzales.

"My attitude is, if it won't take a fly, use lures. If it won't take lures, use bait. I'm not one of those guys who only fly fishes or only uses dry flies. Those guys are missing out. I'm going to catch the damn fish one way or another."

LEFTY KREH, ISSUE 5 OF *The Mission*

There is ample access to the river in San Marcos proper, where it is a popular recreational stream (think inner tubes and kayaks). You can try **City Park** (29.88603, -97.93512) or **Rio Vista Park** (29.87845, -97.93393), just to name two possibilities.

For anglers, kayaks, canoes, and rafts are the primary means of accessing the river, as much of the stream is not suitable for wading. The Texas Water Safari, "the world's toughest canoe race," begins at the headwaters of the San Marcos River, and competitors have one hundred hours to paddle 260 miles to Seadrift on the Gulf Coast. The race is held the second Saturday of June every year.

Mostly due to that race, the San Marcos is well-mapped, and an enterprising angler with rudimentary internet sleuthing skills can find detailed accounts of pretty much the entire river, including the location of the numerous snags and strainers, portages, and access points.

To give you a taste, we'll look at one potential wade and a paddle.

FM 1979, Martindale
29.83240, -97.84235
203 FM 1979, Martindale, TX 78655
36.2 road miles, 0:43 drive time
Difficulty: Moderate

MOST PEOPLE WHO KNOW THE SAN MARCOS THINK OF THE tubing and kayaking opportunities near Texas State University, in the town of San Marcos. Or maybe, like me, they were lucky enough to make their Open Water certification dives in Spring Lake. Most fly fishers dream of downstream reaches, centered on the Martindale area. The Farm Road 1979 bridge offers a rare opportunity to wade the river.

What You Will Find

Walk down to the water along the guardrail on the north side of the road. As with the entire mineral-rich San Marcos, water here is not murky, exactly, but neither is it gin clear like the headwaters springs or some of the more northerly streams in these pages; rather, when it is healthy and flowing well, it will be a deep, emerald green

43 **The Martindale Dam Wade** (Fishing Upstream from the Bridge)
You'll begin this wade in thigh- to waist-deep water river left (your right—the bank from which you entered). The bottom is mostly tightly packed gravel, but you will encounter areas of silt deposition in some places.

At a little more than 400 feet above the bridge, you'll come to the first bend in the river. The gravel bars here are rearranged with every flood. There are boulders in the water river right, just across from the bend, and they provide excellent ambush points for bass. In this reach of the San Marcos, you may encounter largemouth bass, smallmouth bass, Guadalupe bass, or spotted bass; more than likely, any fish you catch will be a largemouth or some mix of the latter three species (see the **Know Your Central Texas Bass** chapter).

Around the bend, and for the next 500 feet or so, the stream is shallower and rocky, more good habitat for the riverine basses, which you will find in the seams of the current. This is also outstanding Rio and sunfish territory, and the sunnies in this reach of the river attain record sizes.

Continue upstream river left to a silty backwater and laydown on the same side at three-tenths of a mile above the bridge. This is a good place to look for carp or the more prevalent smallmouth buffalo. Just above this backwater, you will find a large gravel bar river left. The river bank here is part of the City of Martindale's **Allen Bates River Park** (29.83717, -97.84265), free and open to the public during daylight hours. This also would be a fine place to start or end a wade on this section of the river.

Above the park, when you run out of gravel river left, cross the river in waist- to chest-deep water to the south (here it is west) bank to continue upstream. Standard practice on the San Marcos River, especially during the warmer months, is to "bang the banks" with poppers or deer hair

Griffin Douthitt shows off a beautiful San Marcos River smallmouth he captured while fishing with All Water Guides.

Sycamore and cypress trees put on some fall color to delight San Marcos River paddlers.

bugs. It is particularly effective on segments like this one, with steep banks and heavy tree cover.

At about 0.5 miles above the bridge, you'll see a gravel island in the center of the river—look for Rios here in the summer and bass chasing sunfish in the shallows, especially on the downstream side. A Rio Getter or Hatchling Craw will work on the Rios, and a Lunch Money or Brunch Money streamer (see **A Central Texas Fly Box**, page 45). will trick the bass. Above the small island, laydowns and a riffle provide more good habitat. Take your time wading through this section.

The next pool is wide and deep; keep river right (your left) and portage the one-lane, wooden bridge at just under 0.6 miles above the put-in, on the west side. Above the wooden bridge, another large pool is wadeable, in waist- to chest-deep water, river right. This pool ends at the Martindale Dam (portaged river right if paddling downstream). The highly oxygenated water pouring over the dam is terrific for huge sunfish; try drifting a lightly weighted damsel nymph in the current.

The San Marcos is not a particularly large river, but a huge volume of spring water means it iusually runs fast and deep. It is best paddled or floated.

Getting There

From downtown, Take I-35 south to Exit 205 in San Marcos. Go left, under the interstate highway, on Texas Highway 80. Follow TX 80 5.9 miles to FM 1979 where you will go right and continue for 0.9 miles. As you approach the bridge over the San Marcos River, you'll want to park off the road on the north side.

Spencer Canoes & Shady Grove Campground, Martindale

29.83019, -97.84275

9515 FM 1979, Martindale, TX 78655

36.4 road miles, 0:44 drive time

Difficulty: Moderate

SPENCER CANOE'S IS A VENERABLE CENTER OF TEXAS WATER Safari activity only lightly used by recreational paddlers and anglers year-round. Pay the $5 per vehicle fee (plus $5 per paddler) at the office or (more usually) at the honor box. Spencer no longer offers shuttles, but you can arrange your own or go with a buddy and take out at the "house on stilts" (owned by the same folks) at the Staples Dam. The 5.2-mile reach of water down to Staples offers easy paddling and perhaps the best, easily accessible fishing anywhere on the San Marcos River.

What You Will Find

Once you pay, follow the drive down to the usual launch site (29.83180, -97.84190) to drop off your boat. You'll need to return your vehicle to the parking area. There are showers and restrooms available at the put-in as well. The San Marcos River at normal flows (250–350 cfs at the Martindale gauge) is a fast river, but experienced recreational paddlers won't encounter anything technically challenging. Inexperienced paddlers should keep a sharp eye out for snags and strainers, and make sure any gear you are not using is secured to the boat.

44 The Green Mile (Paddling Downstream)

As you head downstream from the launch, your first stop should be spatterdock-choked backwater river left. The native "lily pad" usually is a sign of a softer bottom and is excellent habitat for insects, amphibians, and small fish that bass love. You'll see several of these off to the side of the main channel on this paddle and should take some time with each of them. Don't neglect the south bank, river right—just past the launch you'll find some laydowns under the heavily treed bank, another bass hideout.

Just 500 feet below the put-in, a gravel bar creates a long riffle; river left is the best option here. At a little more than 1,000 feet below the put-in, as you come around the tip of another big gravel bar (this one exposed), you'll see a large cypress tree and eddy river right. Stop to fish this for Rios and big sunfish. From the cypress tree down to the 0.3 mile mark, where another large gravel bar—actually part of an old concrete retaining wall—emerges river right, you'll find boulders and laydowns along the south bank; this is prime habitat for big bass. Bang the banks with deer hair bugs or sliders, or throw big streamers.

At just over 0.5 miles, negotiate a short, steep riffle to more placid water below. The deeper channel is river left along this section. Over the next mile, the river narrows and sweeps through a series of S bends—the water is faster here, and you will see flood debris (mostly from the Blanco River, the major tributary upstream) caught in the bends.

From about 1.3 miles to a little over 2.0 miles, the river slows and flows due south and then south-southwest. There are broad gravel bars on this reach that are suitable for taking a lunch break, or beaching your

Adventurer, musician, and writer Riverhorse Nakadate displays a healthy San Marcos River largemouth bass.

boat to stretch your legs with a bit of wade fishing. From 2.1 miles below Shady Grove to about 2.9 miles, the river again narrows and snakes back toward the east. At 3.2 miles, you'll see the last good lunch-break gravel bar on this reach, on your left.

At about 4.2 miles, Morrison Creek enters on the north bank. This mud-bottomed tributary holds good numbers of bass in the spring and summer. Just beyond Morrison Creek, the river bends sharply to the south again, marking the start of the "Green Mile" above the **Staples Dam** (29.78272, -97.83104). The house on stilts, and your take-out, is river left just below the Farm Road 1977 bridge.

Follow the directions to the FM 1979 Crossing, and continue across the bridge. Spencer's Canoes & Shady Grove Campground will be on your left.

 Down to the River, Darrell Scott

 Railyard Bar & Grill

railyardbarandgrill.getbento.com/
11–11 daily, 11–12 Friday and Saturday

To grab a hot meal or a cold beer after a trip on the San Marcos, head back into town to the Railyard. This casual, family- (and dog-) friendly bar offers a full menu, pool tables, darts, and horseshoes, and live music on weekends. If you're too gross for the indoor area (doubtful), try the picnic tables outside.

Chapter 21

Guadalupe River

Rainbow and brown trout; striped bass; fast, cold water and gorgeous scenery. Access points: 8

THE GUADALUPE RIVER IS THE MOST POPULAR RECREATIONAL stream in Texas, and namesake and home water for the nation's largest Trout Unlimited chapter. Rising in two forks in Kerr County, it flows 250 miles to San Antonio Bay on the middle Texas Gulf Coast. The stream was named for *Nuestra Señora de Guadalupe* by Alonso de Leon in 1689. In the 1840s, the area became the focus of German immigration led by Prince Carl of Solms-Braunfels.

Noted for its rugged beauty, the Guadalupe is really three rivers: the upper Guadalupe, a typical Hill Country stream above Canyon Lake; the lower Guadalupe, the cold, tailwater fishery below Canyon Lake Dam; and the lazy, turbid river that meanders across the coastal plain. The upper portion of the river and its tributary streams offer fine warmwater fishing opportunities but are outside of the scope of this book.

The Canyon Lake tailwater has two distinct seasons: Roughly May through September is "tubing" season on the river, and people come from all over the state to float and drink beer on the reach between the dam and the city of New Braunfels. That city, at about 80,000 souls, is the largest on the stream and receives more than three million visitors annually, mostly in the summer months, and mostly people who come to play in the water. By the end of the summer, visitors will have deposited several tons of beer cans and plastic water bottles in the river.

From November through March, when trout anglers who reside in more northerly latitudes put away their waders and rods, sit down at their vises in front of a crackling fire, and dream of spring "ice-out," the southernmost trout fishery in the nation is in full swing. Skip the middle weeks of March (spring break), and come back for a six-week shoulder session before the tubing starts in earnest the middle of May. During the fall and winter, outfitters and campgrounds, which during the summer months maintained a frenetic pace shuttling families and young adults, enter a state of brumation; everything slows down, and the local businesses turn to providing parking and river access to fly anglers. Tire inner tubes give way to guide rafts in much smaller numbers.

> "Nymphs: they are borderline amusing to read about in Greek mythology, but not for fishing Texans. Matching the hatch is certainly obsessive and cute, yet finding your own style in life is far more interesting."
>
> NATHANIEL RIVERHORSE NAKADATE, "SPRING CREEK MASTER," *The FlyFish Journal*

My relationship with the Guadalupe is complicated. I'm a native fish guy, mostly, and when it comes to salmonids, I prefer to hunt wild trout in the headwaters streams they were made for. Unfortunately, there are no longer any of those in Texas.

I also really enjoy being the only person, or one of just a handful of people, wading a particular stream on a given day. There are opportunities to experience that on the Guadalupe, but it won't be every time you visit, and it surely won't be on a weekend at the height of the winter season. Those weekends, and perhaps some intemperate comments on the water and on social media, have earned the stream a nickname: the "Dramalupe."

In some ways, the Guadalupe is a victim of its own success. It is an incredibly productive trout stream, and people have noticed. Like every North American tailwater east of the Rockies, the Guadalupe is

Bobby Albin, of Rockport, Texas, releases a rainbow trout on the Guadalupe River.

an entirely manmade fishery stocked with non-native fish. In the case of the Guadalupe, stockings are done multiple times each year between November and March with farm-raised rainbow and brown trout. There are "holdover" fish most years, naturalized trout that look and act wilder with every passing month, and the rainbow trout that make it to the fall are as fine as any you'll find anywhere.

What makes the Guadalupe River unique is that, well, it's in South-Central Texas—roughly at the same latitude as Houston and Orlando and well south of San Diego. The Guadalupe has been named one of the hundred best trout streams and fifty best tailwaters in the U.S.

Between the Texas Parks & Wildlife Department (TPWD) and the Guadalupe River Chapter of Trout Unlimited (GRTU), something like 24,000 trout are stocked in the first dozen miles below the dam every winter. That's a fish every yard or so, on average. TPWD stocks more fish in more locations, but Trout Unlimited stocks bigger fish; GRTU-stocked fish average 15 inches in length, and rainbows in excess of 20 inches are not uncommon.

Some of my favorite childhood memories are of elementary school spring break vacations catching rainbow trout (the small ones) on canned corn or cheese at Camp Beans. The campsites are long gone, but that stretch of river is still one of my favorites. Thanks to the hard work of TU members and the state, the Canyon Lake tailwater is an even better place to put a kid on a feisty rainbow these days. For more experienced anglers, it is an excellent stream to learn the ins and outs of indicator nymphing, mending line, and making drag-free drifts—skills that are useful on any tailwater fishery in the country. You can also catch trout here on streamers (that's all some stubborn Texans will throw) and, especially late in the season, dry flies.

Unlike almost every other Texas stream, there is little right-of-way access at road crossings, and even less parking. With the exception of the U.S. Army Corps of Engineers (USACE) park just below the dam, all of the streamside property in the tailwater section is privately owned. Access to the river is through a shifting network of private and leased sites. Mostly due to the large numbers of anglers, tensions can sometimes run high. This is a river where booking a float trip with a guide, for your first visit at least, would be a worthwhile investment.

Salmonids in Texas

Salmonids—trout, char, and salmon—have a somewhat fraught history in Texas. Some biologists believe the historical record supports the notion that there were, as late as the second half of the nineteenth century, several populations of native **Rio Grande cutthroat trout** (*Oncorhynchus clarkii virginalis*) in the mountains of far West Texas. One of those populations, in the Davis Mountains' Limpia Creek, was extirpated.

The other, in the Guadalupe Mountains' McKittrick Creek—if it in fact existed (I like to think that it did)—was supplanted by stockings of **rainbow trout** (*Oncorhynchus mykiss*) that began in 1917 and continued through 1940. Those fish comprise the only truly wild, naturally reproducing population of trout in the state and are protected by National Park Service regulations that prohibit fishing there. Trout Unlimited and several state and federal agencies have expressed interest in restoring the Pecos strain of the Rio Grande cutthroat to McKittrick Creek, a project that at the moment appears to be stalled but—since the species currently inhabits only about 10 percent of its historic range—certainly seems like a worthwhile effort.

The historical record suggests that Rio Grande Cutthroat trout like this once swam in Texas.

Since fish stocking by government agencies first started in Texas in the 1870s, there have been numerous attempts to introduce everything from both Pacific and Atlantic salmon to cutthroat and brook trout. Some of these fish were planted in streams (and, later, reservoirs) that, ultimately, would not support salmonids' requirement for cold (usually less than 74 degrees Fahrenheit) water.

The creation of Canyon Lake in 1964 changed that. Even before the reservoir was constructed, it was understood that the cold water flowing from the base of the dam would have a negative impact on native, warmwater fishes.

The water comes out of the dam at about 54 degrees and stays cool enough to keep trout happy for 36 hours, or 7 to 16 river miles, depending on the time of year and how fast the water is moving.

In 1966, San Antonio's Lone Star Brewing Company sponsored a three-year rainbow trout stocking program in the tailwater. It was wildly popular, and soon the state picked-up the ball and ran with it, stocking reservoirs and tailwaters across the state. Today, TPWD plants more than 330,000 rainbow trout in community fishing lakes and streams every year. With the exception of the Guadalupe River, these are put-and-take fisheries; in most cases the fish wouldn't make it through the summer.

On the Guadalupe River, Trout Unlimited additionally annually stocks 12,000 pounds of rainbow trout and 2,000 pounds of **brown trout** (*Salmo trutta*). Some regularly survive the summer down to the "Ponderosa" area of the river, about seven miles below the dam. Special regulations are in effect to protect this year-round fishery.

Stocked rainbow and brown trout aren't the only attractions on the Lower Guadalupe; here you will also find escapees from the (also stocked) striped bass population in Canyon Lake. The stripers that have made their way into the river gorge on high-fat rainbow trout and grow to impressive sizes. Smallmouth bass, also stocked in Canyon Lake, do well in the cold water, too. Smaller numbers of sunfish and largemouth bass, as well as Guadalupe bass, persist below the dam. Nymph-eating redhorse suckers are regular incidental catches.

It's worth checking with every campground and resort along River Road to see if they will let you park and access the river for a small fee. Some have exclusive agreements with GRTU (see **Lease Access Program,** below), and others may not allow day users. During the

2017–2018 season, TPWD leased four free public access sites; in the 2018–2019 season, there was only one. For the current year's lease sites and stocking schedule, visit tpwd.texas.gov and search for "Guadalupe River trout."

The access points below have for many years welcomed day users for a small fee (usually $10 per person), and Guadalupe Park is free.

Guadalupe Park, Canyon Lake
29.869756, -98.196098
South Access Rd., Canyon Lake, TX 78133
54.5 road miles, 1:03 drive time
Difficulty: Easy to Moderate

THE FREE PARK BELOW CANYON LAKE DAM, NOT TO BE confused with Guadalupe River State Park above the lake, is open sunrise to sunset and is the only truly public land on this part of the river. There are no facilities. The access road leads to two parking areas; one serves the cemented and safety railed spillway observation deck river left (29.87056, -98.19417). (There also is a short stretch of rocky shoreline between the deck and the mouth of a small creek). This short reach just below the spillway is deep, and you'll want a sinking line or split shot to get down to the fish. Across the river, along the south bank, a hiking trail provides access to nearly 1 mile of water. That's the section we'll look at here.

What You Will Find

From the parking area, look for the well-maintained South Trail, known locally simply as the "nature trail," really two parallel hiking trails specifically designed (in part) with anglers in mind. The trail does have steps (railroad ties embedded in the river bank) and several bridges, but overall it's an easy walk in the shade of the riparian forest.

45 South Trail Reach (Bank and Wade Fishing below Canyon Lake Dam) The South Trail follows the course of the river at a bit of a remove, so you'll have to look for spur trails leading down to the water. Wadeable water begins about 350 feet below the spillway, at the first bend in the river. This long, rocky run continues for more than 700 feet.

At about 0.2 miles below the spillway, a stepped limestone ledge river right provides good access to the narrow pool along the north bank.

The South, or "nature," trail below Canyon Dam—shown here during high flows—offers access to a fine reach of fast, cold water.

This is not only a good place to find trout, but in the summer months it can also be productive for all of the bass species in the river. Probably because it's a good place to find trout, by now preferred forage for striped, smallmouth, and largemouth bass. The ledge continues past a riffle at about 0.3 miles, where the river slows and deepens. The South Trail continues for some distance beyond this point, nearly to the end of the USACE property at 29.86695, -98.18113, just before the first really big bend in the river, but access to wadeable water becomes more difficult.

Keep in mind that unlike many warmwater species (Guadalupe bass excepted), trout actively feed in fast water. They prefer to have the current bring food to them and are adept at using seams, crevices, and even small rocks in the riverbed—anything that alters the flow of water—to conserve energy. That said, when biologists survey the river using electro-shocking, they find the most fish in deeper pools.

From downtown, take I-35 south to Exit 195 and go right on Watson Road, which dead ends at Hunter Road (Farm Road 1102). Go left on Hunter Road and continue to Hoffman Road. Go right on Hoffman

Road, and then right on Farm Road 306. If you miss any of these turns, the I-35 south frontage road will take you to FM 306 anyway. Follow FM 306 approximately 8.8 miles to South Access Road on your left. The parking area and trailhead will be across the spillway on your left.

Maricopa Riverside Lodge, Canyon Lake
29.86456, -98.16477
12381 FM 306, Canyon Lake, TX 78133
(830) 964-3600
maricopariversidelodge.com
52 road miles, 0:54 drive time
Difficulty: Moderate

MARICOPA RIVERSIDE LODGE IS AN OLD-SCHOOL, NINETEEN-room motel remodeled in 2011. Located at the very end of the upper tailwaters (12–18-inch slot limit) and beginning of the "Trophy Zone," where only one fish over 18 inches may be kept (fly or lure only), this is a year-round hotspot for big browns and rainbows. Maricopa's property includes more than 100 yards of stream bank, and a cement sluice next to the FM 306 bridge is a dandy launch for a kayak or canoe. Maricopa charges $10 per vehicle for day-use anglers and paddlers.

What You Will Find
When you get to the motel, check in and pay your $10 at the office. You can back down the cement drainage to drop a paddlecraft off, or simply park in the motel's lot if you plan to wade. Access the water anywhere from the bridge to the end of the Maricopa property, a little more than the length of a football field upstream.

46 Maricopa Wade (Wading or Paddling Upstream from the Bridge)
The water here is still very cold, just a little less than 3 river miles below the spillway. Wading upstream in knee- to waist-deep water is fairly straightforward, though, with the deeper channel along the far bank, river right. A bit more than 400 feet above the bridge, a shallow run with some large rock formations is a likely spot to find trout.

Continue wading river left (your right) to get around the bend and to a rocky run and rapid that has produced some beautiful holdover fish in the past. At about 400 yards above the bridge, the river gets wide and deep and is best paddled if you continue upstream. Horseshoe Falls,

Stocked and holdover rainbow trout are the main attraction on the Guadalupe River. There are plenty of fish in the 15- to 20-inch range, and 20-plus inch fish are not uncommon.

easily portaged river left, is 1.4 miles above the bridge. If you choose to paddle downstream, through the extremely productive Horseshoe, or "Tuber's Loop," the next access point is at **Whitewater Sports** (see below).

You shouldn't be afraid to throw streamers in this (or, really, any) section of the river. Black, beadhead woolly buggers (size 6–12) almost always (eventually) get bitten, and one friend fishes nothing but Lunch Money baitfish imitations here and does well enough.

But the most productive setup for trout on the Guadalupe is usually going to be a nymph rig. On the Guad, this typically is an indicator, an attractor fly (girdle bugs, Pat's Rubber Legs, and aggravators are popular choices, as are egg flies) with a nymph (hare's ears and zebra or sparkle midges in sizes 16–22 are popular choices) dropper tied 12–18 inches below the attractor fly. Check with a local fly shop to see what flies have been working best in recent days. The strike indicator should be adjusted for the water depth, allowing the nymph to bounce along on or just above the bottom.

🗺️ **From downtown**, take I-35 south to Exit 195 and go right on Watson Road, which dead ends at Hunter Road (Farm Road 1102). Go left on Hunter Road and continue to Hoffman Road. Go right on Hoffman Road and then right on Farm Road 306. If you miss any of these turns, the I-35 south frontage road will take you to FM 306. Follow FM 306 approximately 6.9 miles to the motel on your left.

Whitewater Sports, New Braunfels
29.86129, -98.15757
11860 FM 306, New Braunfels, TX 78132
(830) 964-3800
floattheguadalupe.com
51.4 road miles, 0:54 drive time
Difficulty: Easy to Moderate

WHITEWATER SPORTS IS, WITH MARICOPA RIVERSIDE LODGE, one of the bookends of the "Tubers' Loop" or "Horseshoe"—a 1.0 mile-long bend of the river. The lower half of the loop is eminently wadeable, but you'll want to wait until after Labor Day when the tubers thin out. Between September and May, Whitewater offers $10 per vehicle day passes for anglers.

What You Will Find

Park in the lot near the office, pay the day fee, and walk or drag your kayak down to the water; there are paved paths next to the bridge and just upstream from the office. You'll definitely want to drop your boat off if you have to park in the overflow parking area next door.

47 **The Horseshoe** (Wading Upstream from the Bridge)
The Horseshoe holds big trout all year long, and at flows of 350 cfs or less it can easily be waded river right (your left, the inside of the bend) a little more than halfway back around to Maricopa Riverside Lodge, or about 0.6 miles. You'll encounter some waist-deep water along the way, and even deeper pools in the center of the channel, but also some beautiful rock gardens and riffles, particularly near the end of the wadeable section.

Kevin Stubbs guides anglers from his raft near the Ponderosa Crossing. The Guad is one river where hiring a guide—for the first trip, at least—makes sense.

One of the locals here feeds the trout from his residence; he'll probably let you know if he thinks you are mishandling fish.

Remember that setting the hook on a trout can be a bit different than the strip-set we usually use on bass and carp. You can raise the tip of your rod sharply to hook a turning fish (this is a classic "trout set" and works especially well when fishing nymphs under an indicator), but you can also strip set on trout, especially the streamer eaters. Some experts argue that trout sets should be done sideways, sweeping the tip parallel to the water and in the direction of curve in the line. The thought here is that the weight of line and water will do most of the work for you, requiring only a short tug on the line. Dry flies call for a trout set, with the added thrill of watching it happen in front of you.

If you paddle downstream from Whitewater, the next access point is at **Rio Guadalupe Resort** (29.84372, -98.16888), 1.6 miles downstream.

From downtown, take I-35 south to Exit 195 and go right on Watson Road, which dead ends at Hunter Road (Farm Road 1102). Go left on Hunter Road and continue to Hoffman Road. Go right on Hoffman Road and then right on Farm Road 306. If you miss any of these turns, the I-35 south frontage road will take you to FM 306. Follow FM 306 approximately 6.4 miles to Whitewater Sports (you'll also see a sign for Whitewater Amphitheater) on your right.

Top right: Living Waters Fly Fishing Guide Marcus Rodriguez leans out to net a client's fish.

Bottom right: Rodriguez with a client's rainbow trout. The Guad is one river it pays to learn with a guide.

Lazy L&L Campground, New Braunfels
29.81800, -98.17563
11699 River Rd., New Braunfels, TX 78132
(830) 964-3455
lazylandl.com
55.6 road miles, 1:26 drive time
Difficulty: Easy

LAZY L&L IS A SPRAWLING CAMPGROUND ALONG RIVER ROAD
with a boat launch, restrooms, a small camp store, and a shoreside trail
that offers access to two additional properties upstream, all the way to
the Ponderosa Bridge. L&L charges $10 per person for day use, and the
campground's 5 mph speed limit is strictly enforced.

What You Will Find
The Lazy L&L Campground covers fifty-five acres and may be the best
deal going for day users on the Guadalupe. The main campground features about three-quarters of a mile of river frontage, with an additional
0.6 miles between River Road and the water upstream to just above the
Ponderosa Crossing. Day users can cover much of this on foot. (Lot 3,
above the Ponderosa Crossing, is off-limits except to GRTU lease access
program members, but the stream bed is public; see below.)

 The Hog Trough and Bear Creek
(Fishing Lazy L&L—a Large Property/Multiple Access)
In addition to plentiful parking, lots of bank access, and an improved
kayak and raft launch, there is a broad, limestone shelf that follows the
north bank of the river here. That ledge is the key to wading this stretch
of the river at higher flows, up to 450 or 500 cfs, and in any flow provides
shelter for fish and funnels the river current into feeding lanes. In other
words, be sure to drift some flies along the edge of the ledge.

Target seams at the edge of faster water as you wade upstream river
left (your right). About 400 yards above the boat launch (29.81887,
-98.17540), you'll encounter a rock garden, and just above that, the "Hog
Trough," a narrow funnel that usually holds large trout.

The river is not especially fast here, and you should have no problem
paddling up to the Ponderosa Crossing (or farther) if you would like to
go upstream. Downstream, though, is a bit more interesting. At about 0.4
miles below the boat launch, Bear Creek flows out of the Ingram Ranch

Brad Boone wrangles an indicator nymphed trout to the raft while being guided by Living Waters Fly Fishing's Chris Johnson.

The reach below Rocky Beach is broad and deep. Fish hold in the deep, limestone seams in the river bed, which also make wading treacherous.

river right. A short drag across a gravel riffle will bring you to a huge, deep pool that is home to some heart-stopping bass.

This pool, about an acre in size, is deepest near the northwest corner, where there also is some good structure. The shallow water below the mouth of the creek here also holds fish, as does the brushy, undercut bank on the east side of the pool and the shallower, boulder-strewn southern end ... basically, the entire pool is sort of magical. These big fish do see quite a few flies, so bring your A-game, and some meat.

At the bend in the river where the Bear Creek pool joins the Guad, a deep washout beneath several cypress trees almost always holds trout (on my last trip, we also caught a redhorse sucker here). This fast run and the riffle below it are also somewhat accessible from the bank river left, which is still part of L&L.

If you are paddling—and this is a fine reach of river to experience in a kayak—you'll see the private Ingram bridge at just over 1.0 miles below the L&L boat launch. An eddy here collects trash; be a pal and stop and pack some out, would you? Your next access point downstream is **Rocky Beach** (29.80294, -98.17272), 1.6 river miles below L&L.

Getting There

From downtown, take I-35 south to Exit 195 and go right on Watson Road, which dead ends at Hunter Road (Farm Road 1102). Go left on Hunter Road and continue to Hoffman Road. Go right on Hoffman Road and then right on Farm Road 306. If you miss any of these turns, the I-35 south frontage road will take you to FM 306. Follow FM 306 over the first Guadalupe River bridge at Whitewater Sports, and then—before you get to the second bridge and Maricopa Riverside Lodge—go left on Farm Road 2673 (Sattler Road). Just past the Stripes convenience store in Sattler, take a left on River Road. Follow River Road approximately 2.8 miles to the campground on your right.

Action Angler, New Braunfels
29.80374, -98.16235
9751 River Rd., New Braunfels, TX 78132
(830) 708-3474
actionangler.net
55.5 road miles, 1:15 drive time
Difficulty: Easy to moderate

ACTION ANGLER, A FLY SHOP AND GUIDE SERVICE (SEE THE **Appendices**) on the upstream side of the **3rd Crossing bridge**, also offers access to fly anglers for $10 per person. Pay inside if the shop is open, or at the honor box on the trail to the water if it isn't or you can't be bothered to walk up the hill. This also typically is a non-exclusive lease access site for GRTU members.

What You Will Find

Parking at Action Angler is up the hill from River Road, in front of the shop. From the parking area, follow the well-marked trail to the river. If you plan on launching or retrieving a canoe or kayak here, you should do that right next to the bridge; it's still going to be a haul getting it up to Action Angler's driveway.

49 Old Camp Beans (Wading Upstream from the Bridge)

The slack water between bridge pilings and a deeper hole river left, under and just downstream from the bridge, are worth a few casts. I've always found trout here, though they are rarely large.

Wade upstream in ankle- to knee-deep water with a spectacular, honey-colored and honeycombed cliff rising above you river right (your left). This shallow run can sometimes hold smaller trout. Watch for them rising from lies around the scattered rocks in the stream.

At about 0.3 miles above the 3rd Crossing bridge, you'll begin to see deeper runs and pools, particularly river left. This is the reach known as Old Camp Beans, where I caught my first rainbow trout more than forty years ago. The first of the pools you'll encounter is a washout around a cypress stump (it was a tree when I first saw it). There is usually at least one trout hanging out here, at the edge of the fast water. The next pool upstream is chest-deep against the east bank. I recall one day several winters ago when my friend Cory Sorel and I tricked four trout from this one spot.

A bit farther upstream, cross a deep chute over jagged karst to reach the deep, quiet pools against the bank river right. This is an excellent spot to sight-cast to rainbows. The bank upstream from these pools also holds good fish.

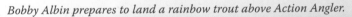

Bobby Albin prepares to land a rainbow trout above Action Angler.

Corey Sorel casts to a rainbow trout lying at the edge of the current near Old Camp Beans.

A gravel beach river left (your right), 0.5 miles above the bridge and just above the narrow chute marks the end of easily wadeable water here. You can go a little farther, and in lower flows, you can wade all the way to Rocky Beach by hugging the east bank, but I've never been able to do it without taking a swim.

The Trophy Trout Zone (only one fish over 18 inches may be harvested, on lure or fly only) continues another 3.2 river miles downstream to the 2nd Crossing bridge. **Camp Huaco Springs** (29.76037, -98.13989), about 5.5 miles below Action Angler, has in previous years served as a free TPWD lease access point and receives wintertime trout stockings. Those fish are not expected to survive through the summer.

From downtown, take I-35 south to Exit 190B in New Braunfels. From the frontage road, go right on Post Road and then right on Gruene

Road and left on Rivercrest Road. This little zigzag will bring you to TX 46 (Loop 337). On TX 46, continue for about 1.3 miles to River Road on your right. Follow River Road for a little more than 8.1 scenic, winding miles to Action Angler on your left. This is the back way in to all of the Guadalupe River trout fishing access points, unless you're coming from points south, in which case it may be the most direct route.

GRTU Lease Access Program
grtu.org

GRTU's popular lease access program is tweaked almost every year. For the 2018–2019 season it was expanded to 850 available spots and came with improved digital maps and orientation materials. It sold out within weeks. For an additional $165, active GRTU members (you can pay for your membership and the lease access program at the same time) are given access to fourteen to eighteen leased properties on the river and a heads-up on GRTU's stocking locations and schedule. That second thing is important, because telemetry studies show that trout don't move very far from the place they are planted. A pair of studies between 2008 and 2010 found that trout moved a median distance of just 245 meters and 420 meters, respectively, from the places they were put in the water. A few of the sites, like Action Angler, also are pay-to-play locations, but lease access program members get in free. Most years slightly fewer than half the leases provide access year-round; the others are available just for the trout "season."

 Lovely Day, Drew Nelson

 The Real Pit BBQ

Open 11–7 Tues.–Sat., 11–5 Sun., and 11–2 Mon.

The barbecue joint next to the Canyon Lake VFW Hall, at the corner of River Road and Ranch Road 2673, is a no-frills, come-as-you-are kind of place. There can be a bit of a line at lunchtime (usually at least one of the patrons is wearing waders), and seating is at picnic tables on a semi-enclosed patio. Order at the window and then wait to be called. Everything is good here, including the house-mixed limeade, but there is no alcohol. Fortunately, ReelFly Fishing Adventures is just across the street, and Donovan will be happy to serve you a complimentary Real Ale while you browse the shop.

Safe and Legal on the Guad

Wading Guidelines

Keep in mind that the water in the ten or twelve miles of river below Canyon Lake Dam stays cold—very cold—year-round. That is, after all, why trout can live here. Wet wading is an option during the warmest months, but waders are welcome all year long here, and mandatory in the wintertime. A wading belt is always a good idea (the purpose is to stop large volumes of water from filling your waders if you slip under), and in higher flows a wading staff and an inflatable PFD are good safety precautions.

Felt-soled or studded wading boots are a good idea as well. In many areas, the limestone bed of the Guadalupe is heavily seamed and slick; in others, jumbled boulders create tripping hazards. Filling your waders on a chilly winter day can be a trip-ending experience, or worse. I speak from teeth-chattering experience.

Current is the other thing to think about. GRTU publishes a guide to safe wading, based on the long, aggregate experience of its members, and recommends the following:

Flows below 100 cubic feet per second (cfs) have slow current and the river is accessible to most anglers. Flows between 200 to 300 cfs can be undertaken by most experienced waders, but inexperienced waders should take extra care. Flows between 300 to 550 cfs should be waded only by those who have experience wading swift water conditions and, preferably, have local knowledge of the river. Flows above 550 cfs are unsafe to wade.

You can find current Guadalupe River flows online at the GRTU website (grtu.org); in a handy at-a-glance map format at the Guadalupe-Blanco River Authority website (waterdata.usgs.gov); or

sidebar continues on page 330

Corey Sorel fights a rainbow trout on a beautiful reach between Rocky Beach and Action Angler.

by searching online for "USGS 08167800 Guadalupe Rv at Sattler, TX." You can also call the USACE office at Canyon Lake Dam, 830-964-3342, for current conditions.

Special regulations

There are two distinct populations of trout anglers on the Guadalupe. The first includes conventional gear anglers and a whole lot of kids. They congregate below the release gates at the dam, on the north bank of the river, and at free leased access sites far downstream. Die-hards follow the stocking trucks (TPWD publishes the state's stocking schedule online). They bait tiny hooks with corn, salmon eggs, or chunks of Velveeta cheese and are probably going to keep the five fish the law allows. And that is perfectly okay. Some of the youngsters—people like me, lo those many years ago—will form memories that will bring them back years or decades later with a fly rod in hand.

The second group includes fly (and some spinning rod) anglers. They are reading water, picking likely seams and lies, and targeting what may be the rainbow or brown trout of a lifetime. These guys and gals probably release every single fish they catch and may swear off trout fishing altogether during the warmer months, when a prolonged fight and handling can be lethal to a trout.

You'll find these trout anglers in two areas of the river: from a point 800 yards below the Canyon Lake Dam to near Whitewater Sports at the easternmost bridge on Farm Road 306, where anglers may keep up to five fish under 12 inches in length and one fish over 18 inches in length, but no more than five fish total. All fish harvested must be caught on artificial lure or fly.

This is the heart of holdover territory; most fly fishers prefer to release all fish caught in this reach of the river.

The reach between the FM 306 bridge and 2nd Crossing on River Road is the Trophy Trout Zone, and anglers may keep just one trout over 18 inches, taken on fly or artificial lure only. Below 2nd Crossing, statewide bag and size limits for rainbow and brown trout apply: five fish, in any combination, with no minimum length.

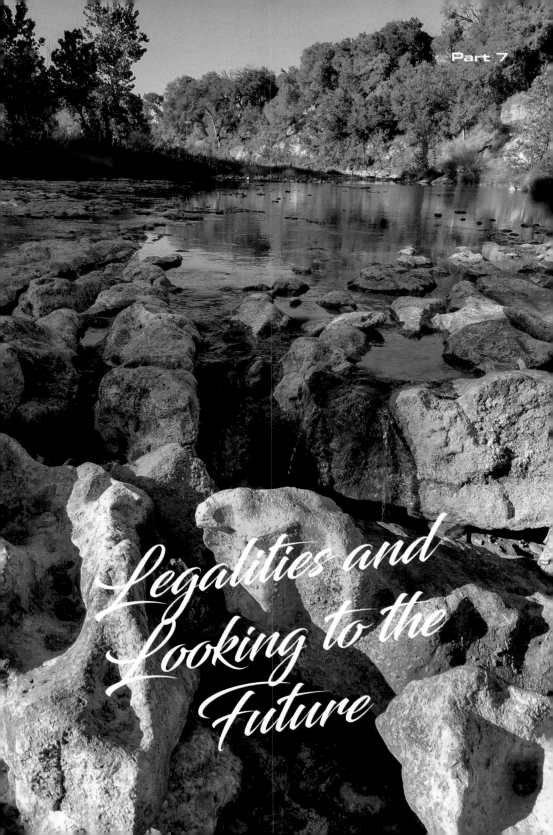

Part 7

Legalities and Looking to the Future

Chapter 22

Texas River Law

Nearly two decades ago I was fishing downstream of a Ranch Road crossing on a Hill Country river. A shot rang out, and I heard the impact of the bullet in the bank ahead of me. Another shot rang out, and another. On the bank to my right, a couple of young men appeared, pacing angrily, beers and rifles in hand.

"You're on private property! We own this river and you need to get off!" Given that I had my oldest son, then 3, with me, I was not happy. Given that the guys on the bank were armed, and possibly inebriated, I left.

That was when I started to pay attention to the issue of public access to the waterways in this state, an interest that carried through to my small role in expanding the Texas Paddling Trails program to inland waters as an employee of the Texas Parks & Wildlife Department (TPWD).

Fish or paddle Texas streams long enough, and it will happen to you, too: you will be hassled, accused of trespassing, run off, or even physically

Above: A common and frustrating problem is when a landowner illegally blocks access to the stream channel as seen here on the San Gabriel River.

Left: An adjacent property owner staked a claim to a gravel bar in the Lampasas River, which is illegal under Texas Law.

threatened by an irate landowner. With the population of Texas projected to double by 2050, and the amount of water to—*at best*—stay the same, such conflicts are bound to become more common.

It's possible that when that happens, it is the landowner who is breaking the law, not you.

The local sheriff's deputy may not know the relevant statutes and may side with the landowner. The county's game wardens should have a better grasp of the underlying law, and more independence, but (as has happened to me and to others) may not immediately be available or able to offer a definitive answer about a particular creek or stretch of river.

In all likelihood, you will be advised to leave, if for no other reason than to defuse the situation at hand. And, snap! Just like that, your right to enjoy the natural resources of the state has been surrendered.

Due to the Lone Star State's unique history—Texas was a sovereign nation that entered the Union by treaty and retained both its public debt and its public lands—the federal laws that govern navigation and public access issues on the waterways of many western states have almost zero relevance to the interior waterways of Texas.

And it is a **right**, enshrined in common law, in the Texas Constitution, and in statutes. It repeatedly has been affirmed by Texas courts and legal opinions of the Texas Attorney General over the past 150-plus years.

It would be terrific if somewhere there existed a master list of streams, or maybe a map, that indicated which rivers and creeks are accessible to the public. It would be almost as good if there were a single state agency you could go to and get a definitive answer to your question—maybe even before you get on the water.

The frustrating truth is this: you will find none of that in Texas. There are approximately 3,700 named streams, fifteen of those major rivers, flowing over 191,000 miles in the state, and at least four state agencies and 254 local jurisdictions with a dog in this hunt.

Here's what you need to know:

Determining Whether a Stream is Public

Streams can be considered public for any of three reasons: The public may use streams that are perennial and are part of a grant made under Spanish or Mexican civil law. The public may use streams that are navigable in fact; that is, they historically have been used to float boats or goods or raw materials (such as logs). And the public may use streams that are navigable by statute, which the Republic of Texas defined in 1837 as those waterways whose beds maintained an average width of 30 feet.

The rights of the public to use these streams (or streambeds) for lawful purposes are, in practice, identical, regardless of whether the waterways are perennial, navigable in fact, navigable by statute, or some combination.

Perennial Streams

Under the civil law prior to December 14, 1837, rights to perennial streams (defined in some places as those that flow all or most of the year) were retained by the sovereign. Those rights were affirmed by the Republic of Texas, and later the State of Texas, which succeeded to ownership of the waters in those early land grants.

> "From its earliest history this State has announced its public policy that lands underlying navigable waters are held in trust by the State for the use and benefit of all the people."
>
> TEXAS SUPREME COURT IN *State* of *Texas v. Bradford*, 50 S.W.2D 1065 (*1932*)

What that means in practice is that the public retains the right to use some streams that are quite small—in some cases much smaller than 30 feet in width. But on some larger rivers (the San Marcos River comes to mind), there is no need to determine whether the stream is navigable in fact or statute. (The San Marcos, by the way, is a trifecta river, passing all three tests.)

Streams that are Navigable in Fact

A stream can be navigable in fact if canoes, steamboats, ships, or even logs have been or are floated down (or up) it; think Buffalo Bayou, the Sabine River, or the Brazos.

In 1917, in *Welder v. State* (196 S.W. 868 (Tex. Civ. App.), the Austin Appeals Court wrote that navigability "in fact" should consider public utility, not commercial use, and that "... hunting and fishing, and even pleasure boating, has been held to be proper public uses."

The state generally owns the beds of streams that are navigable in fact, and public access to larger rivers is rarely contested, but many smaller streams may meet that test as well. Also, streams that are navigable in fact are almost always also navigable by statute.

Streams that are Navigable by Statute

A stream also can be navigable by statute, sometimes referred to as "navigable in law." In 1837, the Republic of Texas passed a law (now codified

in the Texas Natural Resources Code, Section 21.001(3) that said streams
with an *average* width of 30 feet are navigable, and that the state (generally) owns the beds of those streams.

Here's a simplified example: *Little Creek is 45 ft. wide where it joins
Big River. It maintains a width of 45 feet for five miles above the confluence. For the next 10 miles, above that, Little Creek maintains a width of
30 feet. For the next five miles above that, 15 ft. Little Creek is navigable
by statute to mile 20 above Big River.* That is what the letter of the law
says.

When we talk about the width of a stream, we are really talking
about the width of the streambed. It doesn't matter whether the creek is
bank-full, has a trickle in a channel in some portion of the bed, or if the
water has gone underground for some distance. The depth of the water
is utterly unimportant. Appeals court rulings *Texas River Barges v. City
of San Antonio,* 21 S.W.3d 347 (Tex. App.— 2000) and Texas Attorney
General Opinion: S-208 (1956) affirm that the public retains a right to
use dry streambeds.

How the width of a stream is measured is a bit complicated and relies
on a novel legal construct called the "gradient boundary" (or sometimes
referred to as the mean or average gradient boundary). To find the gradient boundary, it's helpful to be a professional surveyor and to know some
math. But there is another, only slightly less precise option.

Robert D. Sweeney Jr., TPWD general counsel, wrote a helpful article,
"Riverbeds and Banks: Title and Regulatory Issues," for the Texas Bar's
Real Estate, Probate, and Trust Law Reporter (Vol. 54, No. 4) in which
he addresses this issue.

With his permission, it is worth quoting at length here:

> *With experience, even non-surveyors can estimate the line with
> some accuracy. A riverbank at near normal flow, or somewhat
> less than normal, generally displays a line of upland vegetation
> along a bank, and a relatively bare, vegetation-free bank below
> it. Vegetation that grows in the water, such as bald cypress trees
> and submerged or emergent vegetation such as cattails, sedges,
> spike rush, and smartweed, must be disregarded. In a multiyear
> drought, moreover, vegetation may creep down the slope (espe-
> cially fast growing species such as sycamore and baccharis), but
> it will be of a different character than the truly "upland" vegeta-
> tion, which will consist of mature trees such as oaks, cedar elm,*

green ash, and perennial bunch grasses. A botanist or an ecologist with knowledge of riparian systems can provide helpful expertise. This line of permanent upland vegetation will in almost all cases closely approximate the gradient boundary line.

Now that you know where to look for the gradient boundary, think back to that hypothetical example of "Little Creek" above. What's missing? Any directive as to the interval at which to measure the width of the streambed. Nowhere in statute or case law is there any sort of standard method of determining the "average." Does one measure the streambed every foot? Every ten feet? Every mile? No one knows.

In practice, on-the-ground surveys are conducted at public road crossings (and for some, relatively short distance upstream and downstream). Sometimes a game warden will look at a contested piece of water and, based on his opinion, a local prosecutor may decline to pursue a trespass citation.

Gravel banks, islands, and sandbars may be and often are found within the streambed, and, generally, are public. Unless the waterway is in flood and out of its banks, in which case ... not so much. However, impoundments that extend beyond the stream's bed also extend the public's right to use the contiguous waters.

Legal Access to the Water

Access to public waters must be through public lands or rights-of-way. Access is most often found at public road crossings and also sometimes from city, county, and state parks or greenbelts. Anyone can seek landowner consent to access public waters from private land. Sometimes it is granted.

Some jurisdictions (Hays County, for instance) have limited the public's access to navigable waters by passing ordinances prohibiting parking on public rights-of-way. This is an issue that seems ripe for further exploration and, possibly, a legal challenge.

In other places, an adjacent landowner may fence across the right-of-way to the abutment of a bridge over a navigable stream. This is a common scenario on Salado Creek, the forks of the San Gabriel River, and the Lampasas River. In 1953, Texas Attorney General Opinion: S-107 addressed fishing rights of the public along a stretch of the Trinity River. That opinion stated that:

The riparian owners cannot prevent the public from gaining access to the river by means of a highway right of way by erection of a fence thereon and cannot prevent the public from going up and down the river in boats and fishing in its waters by the erection of fences across the river.

Other landowners, particularly those who own land beneath or on both sides of a navigable stream (also known as a "Small Bill" stream, see below), erect fences (usually short-lived, due to flooding) across the bed. The Texas Penal Code, the Texas Parks and Wildlife Code, and in some cases the Texas Water Code prohibit such impediments in navigable waterways.

When erected on state-owned streambeds, the State of Texas, through the Office of the Attorney General, can sue a landowner to have these impediments to navigation removed.

Fences across streams, in my view, call for a bit of common sense on

A chain link fence and "No River Access" sign across a farm to market road right of way in Bell County appear to have no legal justification.

NO PUBLIC
ACCESS
TO RIVER
PRIVATE PROPERTY
NO TRESPASSING

the part of the angler. A landowner may have a legitimate need to control the movement of his or her livestock; some forward-thinking ranchers have installed man-gates in those fences to allow the public a safe and easy way through.

"Small Bill" Streams: When Land Ownership Doesn't Matter

If the stream is otherwise navigable, ownership of the streambed is immaterial. Landowners sometimes will insist that they own the streambed and therefore you are trespassing, even if you are in the water. They may, but you probably are not.

Sweeney, in "Riverbeds and Banks," writes that "While all state-owned watercourses are navigable, not all navigable watercourses are state-owned."

Imprecision and carelessness in the late nineteenth and early twentieth centuries resulted in survey lines crossing streambeds in some places, even though the law forbade it. A 1929 law commonly known as "The Small Bill," today found at Tex. Rev. Civ. Stat. Ann. art. 5414a (1962), relinquished the state's title to those streambeds where the submerged lands were required to make up the total acreage in the survey.

The same law asserted that the public would retain its rights to use those streambeds. These are called "Small Bill" streams, and they include reaches of Onion Creek.

The lawful use of a navigable waterway in Texas encompasses all sorts of things—from hiking and camping, to fishing and (sometimes) hunting, to swimming and paddling. As of the passage of amendments to Section 90 of the Parks and Wildlife Code in 2003, lawful use does not include driving a motorized vehicle in a streambed for recreational purposes. Another amendment to Section 90, passed in 2015 as House Bill 3618, prohibits camping or building fires in the much-contested Blanco River streambed. (See the **Blanco River** chapter.)

Determining navigability

Only a court can definitively say whether a stream is navigable. In the absence of such case law (which does exist for some water bodies), or a previous agency opinion, the General Land Office may offer an opinion. In rendering an opinion, the GLO looks at several other factors as well: the date of the original survey or grant (is it a perennial stream?) and whether survey lines cross the streambed (is it a "Small Bill" stream?). If

While S.B. 155 received widespread attention for protecting streambeds from recreational vehicles (or, if you were an off-road enthusiast at that time, taking away part of the playground), it also contains an important reiteration of the public's navigation rights: "The legislature also recognizes that public access to navigable rivers, navigable streams, and the beds, bottoms, and banks of navigable rivers and streams is: (1) a right granted to individuals under the Texas Constitution; and (2) an important economic and recreational resource for the people of this state."

you are in doubt, contact the GLO (**www.glo.texas.gov**) and ask for an opinion.

Very occasionally the GLO will send professional surveyors out to take a look-see in person. Sometimes TPWD will ask game wardens to do the same. Usually this happens at road crossings, casting above and below the access point for some reasonable distance, and typically only in response to a permitting fight, trespass charge, or lawsuit.

While I cannot offer an iron-clad guarantee, I have gone to great lengths to ensure that all of the access points listed in this book are legal and that every reach of water I describe is navigable and you have a right to fish there.

If you explore smaller waters, which are often the best waters, either in Central Texas or farther afield, make sure you have a firm grasp of the patchwork of laws and opinions that govern access and navigability.

When Push Comes to Shove

So what do you do if you are approached by a landowner? First, remain calm and be polite. While you shouldn't have to explain yourself while exercising a legal right, it is understandable that a property owner—especially in a remote area—may be curious about a stranger loitering near his or her home.

Not all landowner interactions are bad; I have had some wonderful and enlightening conversations with ranchers who have seen "seventy years of Texas" and have provided valuable context for my fishing adventures.

There also is the chance that the person protesting your presence sincerely believes you are on his or her lawn, so to speak. If the landowner threatens to call the sheriff's office, offer to call the game warden. TPWD's 24-hour law enforcement communications center (512-389-4848 or 1-800-792-4263) can route you to a game warden in the landowner's county.

As an alternative, you can be proactive and program the local game

warden's mobile number into your phone. As the state agency responsible for "law enforcement off the pavement," TPWD makes its peace officers' phone numbers available to the public. Just go to tpwd.texas.gov/warden/ and select the county where you intend to fish.

The sad truth is that landowners adjacent to public waterways have plenty of legitimate gripes, including an astounding amount of trash at and downstream from some public access points, folks traipsing across their property or cutting fences, and occasional acts of vandalism.

Maybe if they see enough of us acting responsibly—packing other people's trash out with us, practicing catch-and-release fishing, and passing through the neighborhood quietly and respectfully—those negative attitudes will change.

But maybe not. Some people are just hardheaded. For those folks, the State of Texas has provided a statute known as the "Sportsman's Rights Act" (Parks and Wildlife Code Section 62.0125) that makes it a Class B misdemeanor (the same level of offense as criminal trespass, Texas Penal Code Section 30.05) to "intentionally interfere with another person lawfully engaged in the process of hunting or catching wildlife."

Interestingly, the law specifies that the "process" includes "camping or other acts preparatory to hunting or catching of wildlife that occur on land or water on which the affected person has the right or privilege of hunting or catching that wildlife."

There are those of us, the people John Graves called "river-minded folk," who believe the approximately one million acres of public lands submerged beneath the state's inland waters—about the same amount of land found in all of Texas' state parks and wildlife management areas combined—are crucial to our quality of life. For some of us, they may be necessary to life itself.

Exercise your right to enjoy them responsibly.

 Texas River Song, Lyle Lovett

Chapter 23

The Future of Texas Waters

IN THE TWO YEARS IT TOOK ME TO WRITE THIS BOOK, I DROVE more than 2,500 miles and waded and paddled more than 150 miles of water on Central Texas rivers and creeks. Through my research and experiences, I became even more aware of the rise and fall of water levels, the changes to riverbeds after severe flooding, and man's effects on nature. And while I believe that I will always be able to find some beautiful, fishable water in the area, I'm not so sure my children will have the same opportunity. What follows are my biggest concerns about the future of Texas's rivers and streams.

A Rise in Demand Meets a Drop in Supply

The Office of the State Demographer projects that the population of Texas will double to about fifty-four million souls by the year 2050. Much of that population growth—driven mainly by immigration from other U.S. regions, as well as abroad—is already showing up in Central Texas along the I-35 corridor.

Hays (Onion Creek, Blanco River, Pedernales River, San Marcos River), Comal (Comal River, Guadalupe River), and Williamson Counties

(San Gabriel River, Brushy Creek) continue to grow at rates north of 20 percent annually, with Hays posting an astounding 35 percent population increase between 2016 and 2017 and Comal ranking as the nation's second-fastest growing county in 2017. The Austin-Round Rock metro area, meanwhile, was the third fastest-growing city in the nation in 2018.

The Texas Water Development Board estimates that groundwater and surface water together will supply about 15.2 million acre-feet (about half from each source) in 2020, adequate for the state's needs now. But, over the next fifty years, supplies fall to 13.6 million acre-feet while demand increases to 21.6 million acre-feet.

Disparate Management Schemes

It's an unfortunate quirk of Texas history that groundwater and surface water are managed separately, and under different laws. In a 1904

decision (*Houston & Central Texas Railroad Co. v. East*), the Texas Supreme Court chose to uphold "the rule of capture," a doctrine of English common law that basically allows landowners to pump every bit of groundwater below their property, without regard to whether it makes an adjacent landowner's well—or a nearby stream—go dry.

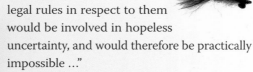

"We have reached the time in the life of the planet, and humanity's demands upon it, when every fisherman will have to be a riverkeeper, a steward of marine shallows, a watchman on the high seas."

THOMAS MCGUANE, *The Longest Silence: A Life in Fishing*

In its ruling, the Court reasoned that "... the existence, origin, movement and course of such waters, and the causes which govern and direct their movements, are so secret, occult and concealed that an attempt to administer any set of legal rules in respect to them would be involved in hopeless uncertainty, and would therefore be practically impossible ..."

More than a century later, Texas is the only Western state that still follows the rule of capture, despite the fact that we now have a good understanding of how groundwater moves and the causes that govern their movements. We know, for instance, that water that disappears into the Dry Blanco streambed re-emerges downstream, and at Jacob's Well on nearby Cypress Creek, but also in Spring Lake (the source of the San Marcos River) and, in drought years, as far north as Barton Springs, in an entirely different river basin.

We know that the sandy Trinity Aquifer recharges more slowly than the limestone karst of the Edwards Aquifer. We know that aquifers produce the springs that fill the streams that feed the estuaries on the Texas Gulf Coast. We know that all water is connected, and that when we degrade or exhaust one source, we inevitably impact the others.

A 1917 state constitutional amendment,

the "Conservation Amendment," explicitly recognized that the conservation and development of all natural resources in the state are public rights and duties, and authorized the Texas legislature to "pass all such laws as may be appropriate." It's an invitation that the state's part-time lawmakers have so far declined to take definitive action on.

There have been steps in the right direction, with groundwater districts and aquifer authorities that rarely encompass sufficient jurisdictions to manage groundwater effectively. Pilot projects are exploring the desalination of marginal groundwater supplies, technologies that also could be used on the Gulf Coast, where there just happens to be a nearby, vast, natural gas reserve to power desal plants, already approaching competitive costs with some other sources of water.

Watershed alliances, springs coalitions, and other conservation groups have had some notable successes in protecting and conserving both ground and surface waters, but there is so much more to do.

Better water conservation practices will certainly have to be part of the mix, as well as better stewardship of the surface water we have. Surface water is allocated by permits issued by the Texas Commission on Environmental Quality under a system known as "prior appropriation," or, to put it simply: first come, first served. More senior water rights (those permits granted earlier) trump junior rights. Some of our creeks and rivers are oversubscribed; that is, if everyone exercised their rights to divert or pump surface water, they would literally drain some streams dry.

Creeks and Rivers Are Already Affected

The direct effects of increased population and the brisk pace of development in Central Texas are more immediately noticeable on area streams. They include increased, untreated runoff that cannot recharge the aquifers through new roads and parking lots and roofs (what the experts call "impervious cover"); new (and old) wastewater treatment plants that sometimes have accidents and other times simply don't give a crap about the (literal) crap they are dumping into the rivers; and neighborhoods and golf courses and resorts and vineyards that may or may not have thought about establishing an adequate riparian buffer or a system to capture or filter fertilizers and pesticides in runoff.

These challenges show up in algal blooms in reaches of river adjacent to new vineyards and below golf courses, in degraded water quality below wastewater outfalls, and in increased turbidity (dirty water) after even relatively short-lived rain events.

Algae occurs naturally in Texas' streams, but mats of "pond snot" are unnatural and signal a water quality problem—most likely high levels of nutrients from fertilizer runoff or faulty wastewater treatment.

The worst-case scenario, if the present trajectory does not change, is that the beautiful spring creeks and fast, clear rivers I have enjoyed my entire life will be reduced to lifeless trickles of effluent. Not this year, or next year, but almost certainly by the time my children's children are old enough to pick up a fly rod or paddle a kayak.

Even now, you can pretty much count on at least one of the streams I describe in these pages being degraded in some way, some time. It will not be every time you visit, but if you get on the water enough, at some point you will wrinkle your nose and think, "Ugh. Not good." Sadly, that's just part of being an angler in a fast-growing urban area (though it shouldn't be). For the present, you'll have plenty of other options nearby and the next big rain will flush the stream clean. Again.

Fighting for Healthy Waterways

As anglers, we demand very little of the rivers and creeks we love. We treasure streams for what they are, not for what they add to the tax base or for how much we can take from them. We have a profound interest in all of the things that go into sustaining a healthy waterway—environmental flows, water quality, flora, and fauna.

Texas does not have a longstanding tradition of riverkeepers, of men and women who dedicate their lives to a particular stream and speak for it. Maybe it's time—past time, really—we all take on that responsibility. After all it is *our* water, held in trust for us by the State of Texas.

Here are some easy ways to make a difference:

- Take along a mesh trash bag and pack out someone else's garbage the next time you go fishing.

- Volunteer at one of the big river cleanup events, like the LoCo Trash Bash or the Brushy Creek Cleanup.

- Take some pictures, log the coordinates, and call the Texas Commission on Environmental Quality (888-777-3186) and TPWD's Spills and Kills Team (512-389-4848) when you run into a suspicious algae bloom or some nasty water.

Litter at river access points is an indication of a serious lack of give a damn. It's also illegal.

- Attend your local planning and zoning commissions' meetings.

- Get involved with a friends of the parks group or similar organization.

Make no mistake: the challenges facing Texas waters now and in the coming years are daunting. Access points and reaches of rivers can be cleaned of litter in a day or a weekend, local zoning requirements can be changed in a year or in an election cycle, but the issue that will determine the future viability of not just our streams but of this entire region—where we get our water and how we use it—is a generational challenge.

There are smart people of good will who already are working to address some of these challenges; organizations like Texas Rivers Protection Association, Texas Streams Coalition, the Save Our Springs Alliance, the Wimberley Valley Watershed Association, and the Llano River Watershed Alliance, just to name a few. The Texas Living Waters Project's website offers an extensive rundown of the challenges facing Texas water—it's a great one-stop education. These organizations could use our help. If enough of us transform our caring into action, maybe—just maybe—our children and their children will get to experience the tug of a native fish in a clean, clear Central Texas stream, too.

 The Clearwater, Matt the Electrician

SHOPS, CLUBS, GUIDES, LIVERIES

CENTRAL TEXAS HAS A ROBUST FLY FISHING INFRASTRUCTURE, WITH AN embarrassment of riches when it comes to fly shops, guides, and fly fishing clubs.

The area has both a Cabela's and a Bass Pro Shop; both have respectable fly fishing departments and—if you visit at the right time—knowledgeable staff. Fly fishing is just a tiny fraction of the big-box retailers' sales, though, while for the dedicated fly shops in the area it is everything.

Fly shops typically meet or beat the big-box prices and have a larger selection of fly tying materials and flies than the big-box stores, and the pros that staff the shops have both a deep knowledge of the sport and the time to introduce you to it. Fly shops typically host fly tying nights, free introductory casting lessons, and other events. They are likely to welcome you with a hot cup of coffee or a cold beer and invite you to stay for a while. Fly shops are cultural centers as much as retailers, and you should take advantage of everything they have to offer.

This book is designed to make do-it-yourself fly fishing trips easy. That said, there is no better way to quickly learn a river or improve your abilities than to book a professional guide. You should do it at least once. Fly fishing guides, like men and women in all professions, vary in quality; the ones listed here are people I know and trust and are guaranteed to work hard to put you on fish and to teach you some stuff along the way—they are not the only guides in Central Texas.

Fly Shops

Living Waters Fly Fishing

103 N Brown St., Round Rock, TX 78664

(512) 828-3474

livingwatersflyfishing.com

Living Waters Fly Fishing celebrated its tenth anniversary in 2018, and is a full-service shop with an expansive fly tying inventory, outstanding in-house fishing guides, and friendly, knowledgeable staff. The shop carries TFO, ECHO, and Scott rods, as well as a full range of Tenkara USA rods, and is a member of the Tenkara USA Guide Network. Chris Johnson, who owns the business, is an FFI-certified casting instructor and offers lessons by appointment. The shop hosts free special events every month—topics range from fly fishing locally to Rio Grande Cutthroat trout conservation. Be sure to sign up for the mailing list and attend one of their free, regularly scheduled "Introduction to Fly Fishing" classes. Complimentary coffee and, at events, world-famous Round Rock donuts.

Orvis Austin

10000 Research Blvd. Ste B04-B, Austin, TX 78759

(512) 795-8004

stores.orvis.com/us/texas/austin

The Austin Orvis store in the Arboretum is the second incarnation of Orvis in Austin. Managed and staffed by actual fly anglers, the store's fly fishing section is right up front and includes an expansive selection of flies (from the looks of it, everything in the Orvis catalogue plus lots of local favorites). Rods and reels are limited to the Orvis brand, but then Orvis makes some great gear. Check the schedule for the free Fly Fishing 101 and women's-only fly fishing classes in the summer, and drop by for the monthly Fly Fishing Trivia Night. Complimentary beer by Austin Beerworks.

Sportsman's Finest

12434 Bee Caves Rd., Austin, TX 78738

(512) 263-1888

sportsmansfinest.com

Sportsman's Finest has been a southwest Austin fixture since 2004. Offering a full range of fly tying supplies and fly fishing equipment (rods by R.L. Winston, Thomas & Thomas, G. Loomis, Scott, Sage, Hardy, TFO, and ECHO), the store also caters to shooting sports enthusiasts, with both a casting pond and an archery lane. Sportsman's Finest has a certified casting instructor on staff and recently began offering fly fishing travel services. Free Tuesday night fly tying always draws a crowd, including a gratifying number of young people. Complimentary beer by Twisted X Brewing Co.

ReelFly Fishing Adventures
1642 FM 2673, Canyon Lake, TX 78133
(830) 964-4823
reelfly.com

First opened in 2013, ReelFly was purchased in the fall of 2017 by Donovan Kypke and carries a full line of fly rods (C. Barclay Fly Rod Co., Sage, Redington, ECHO) and fly tying materials, as well as apparel from Howler Brothers and Free Fly, among others. In 2018, ReelFly became an Orvis-authorized dealer. Guided trips have always been central to this shop's mission and today include the Canyon Lake tailwaters, just across the street, as well other Hill Country rivers and the Texas Gulf Coast (owner Kypke is a Port Aransas native and redfish finnatic). Complimentary beer by Real Ale Brewing Co.

Action Angler
9751 River Rd., New Braunfels, TX 78132
(830) 708-3474
actionangler.net

Action Angler is all about the fishing. Established in 2001, it's the only stream-side fly shop in Texas, and for a day fee of $10 it offers fly fishing-only wading access to a premier reach of Canyon Lake tailwater centered on the 3rd Crossing bridge. Action Angler offers guided trips on the Guadalupe, the San Marcos, the Colorado, and other area rivers, as well as trips in the state of Colorado (Roaring Fork, Frying Pan, Colorado, Gunnison Rivers) during the summer months. The shop is usually closed during the summer but can be opened, and guides booked, by appointment. Brands include ECHO, Redington, Galvan, Rio, Airflo, Korkers, and more. This is the only shop in the area that offers wader and boot rentals ($20/day). In late fall and early winter, as the Guadalupe River trout season kicks off, look for affordable, 2- and 4-hour fishing clinics offered by the shop to prepare anglers for the season.

Gruene Outfitters

1629 Hunter Rd., New Braunfels, TX 78130
(830) 625-4440
grueneoutfitters.com

Gruene Outfitters was founded in 1989, and, from the start, fly fishing was an integral part of the business. Located just a short stroll from the historic Gruene Hall, the fly shop (at the back of the store—see if you can make it past the cool t-shirts and the Free Fly and Howler Brothers racks) is still staffed by experienced anglers and carries brands such as TFO, R. L. Winston, Scott, Abel, Tibor, and more. Gruene Outfitters carries a wide range of fly fishing accessories and a modest selection of flies.

Bass Pro Shops

200 Bass Pro Dr., Round Rock, TX 78665
(512) 876-2700
basspro.com

Bass Pro is not a fly shop, per se, but there is a fly fishing department inside the giant outdoor retailer's Round Rock location. The primary advantage to shopping at Bass Pro is the extended hours; if you find you've run out of extra-small dumbbell eyes at 8 p.m., it's pretty much your only option. The store does have a good selection of budget-friendly fly rods and accessories, as well as an expansive reel selection.

Cabela's

15570 S. I-35 Frontage Rd., Buda, TX 78610
(512) 295-1100
cabelas.com

Outdoor retailer Cabela's offers quite a respectable rod and reel selection, including the CGR fiberglass rods I've mentioned. Along with a wide range of tackle accessories, some fly tying materials, and frequent sales, it's worth a visit. Several long-time employees in the fly fishing department can offer expert advice on tackle selection and local waters. And no, they can't give you permission to fish for the trout in the faux stream that runs through the middle of the store.

Guides

In addition to the guide services listed below, please note that the Living Waters Fly Fishing, ReelFly Fishing Adventures, and Action Angler fly shops all employ full-time, professional guides, and trips booked through these shops are a substantial portion of their business.

All Water Guides

(512) 571-3073

allwaterguides.com

Alvin and Lenée Dedeaux operate All Water Guides, the premier fly fishing guide service in Central Texas. You may have seen Alvin, who before he began guiding full time two decades ago was the longtime manager of Texas's first fly shop, in YETI's Devils River video. Lenée is currently the only full-time female fly fishing guide working in Central Texas. She may be the only full-time guide anywhere in the state with an M.S. in Aquatic

Resources. All Water Guides maintains a roster of talented and friendly local guides and with their fleet of jet boats and rafts offers trips on the Colorado River, the San Marcos River, the Guadalupe River, and the Llano River, as well as the middle Texas Gulf coast. All Water Guides is the only Orvis-endorsed guide service in the area; in 2015 it was honored as a finalist for Orvis Guide Service of the Year, and in 2016 Alvin was a finalist for Orvis Guide of the Year.

Expedition Outfitters

(210) 602-9284

expedition-outfitters.net

Longtime guide Kevin Stubbs offers trips on the Llano, San Marcos, and Guadalupe rivers, and his streamside private and group fly fishing lessons are a terrific value that include casting instruction and tips on reading water and finding access. Farther afield, Kevin guides raft "safaris" on the Devils River, where arrangements with large ranches there enable him to offer clients cabins with air conditioning and fireplaces, as well as miles of riverfront access. Alone among Texas fly fishing guides, Kevin also guides a little-fished reach of the Rio Grande below Lake Amistad, with access through private land.

Texas Hill Country Fly Fishers

(512) 589-3474

hillcountryflyfishers.com

Kevin Hutchison has guided Central Texas waters for more than two decades and is an Orvis-endorsed guide. He's also the guy who took on the Herculean task of updating and revising Bud Priddy's classic *Fly Fishing the Texas Hill Country*. Kevin is an FFI-certified casting instructor and expert fly tyer and guides the Llano, San Marcos, Guadalupe, and Blanco rivers. He has negotiated access to that latter, closely-guarded river through private ranches, which provides anglers an opportunity to experience the area's best smallmouth bass fishery.

Upstream on the Fly
(512) 348-8359
upstreamonthefly.com

Since 2012, Greg Welander (the former longtime fly fishing manager at Sportsman's Finest) has been guiding the Llano, Colorado, San Marcos, and San Gabriel rivers. In 2017, he added the Highland Lakes. Whether you book a walk-wade trip on the Gabe, a float trip on the Llano, or a ride in Greg's Hog Island skiff on Lake Travis, you are certain to enjoy the day and learn a thing or two. Greg especially enjoys introducing new anglers to the sport, and his cheerful, outgoing personality makes him well-suited to family trips.

Whiskey River Expeditions
(435) 225-6636
whiskeyriverchronicle.com

Davin Topel is an amiable Midwesterner by birth and upbringing, a Utah whitewater rafting guide by training, and a masterful distiller of fine spirits by trade. When he is not making whiskey, you can find him guiding fly anglers on the Guadalupe, San Marcos, Lower Colorado and Devils rivers. It's sort of like fishing with a younger, more stable Hemingway; you can be part of the story, and chances are a wee dram and a fine cigar will figure as well.

Getting the Most Out of a Guided Trip

Some anglers book a guide with the notion that the professional will guarantee fish, or at least a shot at a trophy fish. News flash: no one can guarantee fish. Smart anglers book a guide to learn new water and to improve their skills. But you'll probably catch more fish than you would have on your own, too.

For a great guided trip experience, communication is key. Don't be afraid to ask lots of questions and to let a prospective guide know what your expectations are *before* you book the trip. If your focus is on improving your casting, or if you really just want to hunt that once-in-a-lifetime fish, be sure to say so up front. Some people like lots of feedback. Others just want a ride to good water. Don't make your guide guess which one you are.

Be honest about your experience and abilities. You are unlikely to be the absolute worst caster the guide has seen, and even if you are, he or she is unlikely to tell you that. Be sure to confirm with the guide what gear you are expected to bring with you and what he or she will provide (usually, guides provide rods, reels, leaders, flies, and non-alcoholic beverages; waders, polarized sunglasses, and the like are on you). If you have any dietary preferences or restrictions (shore lunches are a treasured tradition on full-day trips), be sure to let your guide know that.

By the time you've concluded this conversation, you'll probably have a good idea of whether you'll enjoy being in close proximity to this person for four to eight hours. If that prospect does not excite you, it's okay to say, "You know, I'm going to have to rethink this," and move on down the list.

Note that in Texas, anyone who charges for a fishing trip must hold a guide license from the Texas Parks & Wildlife Department (TPWD); saltwater guides must also be licensed by the U.S. Coast Guard (or if guiding kayak trips, hold a Paddle Craft All-Water Guide license from TPWD). If your guide isn't licensed, he or she is not really a guide. Find someone else.

It is customary to tip your guide at the end of the trip; 10–20 percent of the trip cost (or $50–$100) is the usual range and, as with any service, the amount should reflect your satisfaction with the experience.

Fly Fishing Clubs

Fly fishing clubs provide social, angling, and educational opportunities for members and their guests through monthly meetings, outings, and other special events. Many have formal relationships with Scouts or other youth organizations to teach young people about fly fishing and fly tying. Most, but not all, are affiliated with Fly Fishers International. Most clubs meet in rented, donated, or borrowed spaces; the best way to get in touch or to join is usually through their websites (or just show up at a meeting and introduce yourself!). Show up early (usually an hour before the scheduled program starts) for fly tying and casting practice.

Waco Fly Fishing Club
wacoflyfishingclub.org

Club meetings are held on the second Tuesday of each month at 7:00 p.m. at the Lake Waco Wetlands (1752 Eichelberger Crossing Rd., China Spring, TX 76633) unless otherwise stated.

San Gabriel Fly Fishers
sgflyfishers.com

An FFI-affiliated club, SGFF meets the third Tuesday of every month at 7 p.m. (arrive at 6 p.m. for casting and fly tying) at the Boy Scout Hut in San Gabriel Park (441 East Morrow St., Georgetown, TX, 78626). The club is active in local conservation efforts.

Austin Fly Fishers
austinflyfishers.com

An FFI-affiliated club, AFF meets at the Northwest Recreation Center (2913 Northland Dr., Austin, TX 78757) on the third Thursday of every month at 7:00 p.m. Notable AFF outreach programs include Casting for Recovery and SKIFF (Soldiers' Kids Involved in Fishing Fun).

Central Texas Fly Fishers
ctff.org

Central Texas Fly Fishers is the FFI-affiliated club in San Marcos and meets the second Tuesday of each month at 7 p.m. at the Dunbar Recreation Center (801 Martin Luther King Dr., San Marcos, TX 78681). CTFF is heavily involved in supporting and expanding Project Healing Waters Fly Fishing programs for veterans. CTFF also hosts a free, monthly fly tying night (open to the public) at the Old Fish Hatchery in San Marcos.

New Braunfels Fly Fishers
newbraunfelsflyfishers.com

The New Braunfels Fly Fishers is an FFI-affiliated club and meets at 7 p.m. the fourth Tuesday of each month. Meetings are held at the New Braunfels Public Library (700 E Common St., New Braunfels, TX 78130).

Fly Fishers International
flyfishersinternational.org

FFI is a terrific resource for new and seasoned anglers; find local clubs and councils and educational resources related to casting, fly tying, and conservation on the organization's website.

Guadalupe River Trout Unlimited
grtu.org

With 5,500 members, GRTU is the largest chapter of Trout Unlimited, one of the leading conservation organizations concerned with rivers and native fishes in North America. In Texas, GRTU is responsible for stocking trophy trout in the Guadalupe River and for the historic agreement with the Guadalupe-Blanco River Authority that guarantees the minimum flows required to keep them alive. The organization's annual spring "Troutfest" expo draws more than 3,000 participants, and the January youth trout camp (for young people ages 12–17) is a comprehensive, hands-on introduction to trout fishing.

Paddlecraft Rentals and Shuttles

There are a number of paddlecraft liveries on the Colorado, Guadalupe and San Marcos Rivers. Most offer hourly, half-day, and daily rentals of canoes, kayaks, and stand-up paddleboards (SUP), as well as shuttle services for those paddling their own boats. Most also offer river access, and some require reservations in advance of rental. Check websites for directions, current hours and inventories, and rates.

ACK
austinkayak.com/rentals

Locations in Austin, San Marcos, San Antonio, and Spring. Canoe and kayak rentals for 24-hour periods; not on the water, but ACK will provide soft racks and straps so you can take your paddlecraft wherever you like.

Bastrop River Co.
bastropriverco.com

The Bastrop River Co. is located on the Lower Colorado and offers canoe, kayak, and SUP rentals as well as guided tours and shuttle services.

Congress Avenue Kayaks
congresskayaks.com

Kayak and SUP rentals with a boathouse and restroom facilities on Lady Bird Lake close to the Congress Avenue bridge. (Pro tip for bat watching: bring an umbrella!)

Cook's Canoes
cookscanoes.com

Cook's Canoes rents canoes and kayaks and provides shuttle services for those with their own boats in the heart of the best fishing on the Lower Colorado River, downstream of Austin in Webberville.

Gruene River Company
gruenerivercompany.com

Gruene River Company offers inflatable and rotomolded sit-on-top kayak rentals and shuttle services on the Guadalupe River.

Guadalupe Canoe Livery
guadalupecanoelivery.com

Located in Spring Branch, offers raft and kayak rentals and shuttle services.

Guadalupe River Whitewater Sports
lazylandl.com

Owned by and located at Lazy L&L Campground, offering rentals of rafts and kayaks as well as shuttle services.

Olympic Outdoor Center
kayakinstruction.org

Olympic Outdoor Center offers sit-on-top kayaks, whitewater boats, and SUP on the San Marcos River right at I-35.

Paddle with Style
paddlewithstyle.com

Paddle with Style, located in Martindale, offers canoe and kayak rentals and shuttle services on the San Marcos River.

Rowing Dock
rowingdock.com

Kayak, paddleboat, and SUP rentals on Lady Bird Lake.

Texas River School
texasriverschool.org

Texas River School is a nonprofit organization that offers youth programs, a fleet of fifty rental canoes, shuttle services, and a one-acre day use area and overnight campground on the Lower Colorado River. The day use area and campground are part of TPWD's River Access and Conservation Area lease program and require reservations and a small fee for their use.

Texas Rowing Center
texasrowingcenter.com

Canoe, kayak, and SUP (more than four hundred paddleboards in stock!) rentals on Lady Bird Lake, restrooms on-site.

Zilker Park Boat Rentals

Canoe, kayak, and SUP rental located on Barton Creek in Zilker Park.

STREAM ACCESS

Chapter 4: Lampasas River
FM 1690 near Adamsville (31.242261, -98.117366)
FM 2527 bridge (31.23618, -98.11897)
FM 580 crossing (31.17184, -98.07101)
FM 2313 crossing (31.11895, -98.05533)
Old Maxdale Bridge, Killeen (30.98992, -97.82894)
TX 195 crossing (30.973171, -97.777378)

Chapter 5: Salado Creek
I-35 at the Stagecoach Inn, Salado (30.94413, -97.53913)
Sherrill Park, Salado (30.95186, -97.52477)
East Amity Road (30.963306, -97.488692)

Chapter 6: San Gabriel River, North Fork and Mainstem
North Fork, US 183, Liberty Hill (30.70043, -97.87758)
San Gabriel River Brewery, (500 Chaparral Dr., Liberty Hill)
North Fork, Tejas Camp, Liberty Hill (30.69583, -97.82797)
Ronald Reagan Blvd. (30.69776, -97.84944)
Russel Park (30.67226, -97.75468)
North Fork, Chandler Park, Georgetown (30.65334, -97.69754)
San Gabriel River Trail crossing (30.662813, -97.706521)
Mainstem, San Gabriel Park, Georgetown (30.64740, -97.67207)
Granger Lake (30.65307, -97.41277)
Mankin's Crossing (30.64584, -97.58418)
Katy Crossing Trail Park (30.656225, -97.658162)

Chapter 7: South Fork San Gabriel
US 183, Leander (30.61982, -97.86022)
RM 1869 (30.65991, -97.93843)
Ronald Reagan Blvd. (30.61165, -97.81882)
Garey Park (30.61165, -97.81882)
River Down Rd., Georgetown (30.61761, -97.70785)
Wolf Ranch Town Center, Georgetown (30.62789, -97.69278)
Blue Hole Park (30.643151, -97.679865)

Chapter 13: Brushy Creek
Champion Park and Hairy Man Rd., Cedar Park (30.51152, -97.75847)
Great Oaks Dr. (30.52149, -97.735876)
Brushy Creek Regional Trail (30.52547, -97.72351)
CR 137, Hutto (30.506854, -97.548799)
Old County Rd. 137 (30.51807, -97.54644)
Riverwalk Pedestrian Bridge (30.52310, -97.56038)
Chris Kelley Blvd. (30.52594, -97.56660)
Chisholm Trail Park (30.512064, -97.689527)
Memorial Park (30.512303, -97.685592)
Veterans Park (30.514766, -97.675553)
CR 123 Crossing (30.53093, -97.589405)
Red Bud Lane (30.53074, -97.61401)
Norman's Crossing, Taylor (30.489056, -97.499279)
FM 973 Crossing (30.469034, -97.463487)

Chapter 14: Colorado River
Colorado Bend State Park (2236 Park Hill Dr., Bend, TX 76824)
Inks Lake State Park (3630 Park Rd. 4 W., Burnet, TX 78611)
Hippie Hollow Park (7000 Comanche Trail, Austin, TX 78732)
Lady Bird Lake, Austin (30.26181, -97.74877)
Red Bud Isle Park, Austin (30.291732, -97.787492)
Barton Creek (Zilker Park) (30.264236, -97.768109)
Town Lake Metropolitan Park at Auditorium Shores (30.26181, -97.74877)
Congress Ave. Kayaks (30.26060, -97.74178)
East Avenue at I-35 (30.25199, -97.73664)
Festival Beach (30.248630, -97.727783)
Lakeshore at Lady Bird Lake (30.244095, -97.724670)
Montopolis Bridge, Austin (30.24702, -97.69033)

Lost Pines Nature Trail Park (30.07365, -97.30961)
Texas River School campground (30.25675, -97.63392)
FM 973, Austin (30.20850, -97.63853)
TX 130 crossing (30.20917, -97.62244)
Austin's Colony HOA Park (30.22543, -97.59165)
Little Webberville Park, Webberville (30.22966, -97.51812)
("Big") Webberville Park, Webberville (30.209488, -97.498906)
FM 969 near Utley (30.16779, -97.40324)
Barton Creek at South MoPac Expressway (30.24408, -97.80987)
Barton Creek at Trail's End Access, Camp Craft Road (30.27512, -97.82522)
Bull Creek at Bull Creek Park (30.37088, -97.78528)
Bull Creek at St. Edward's Park (30.40663, -97.79035)
Walnut Creek at Big Walnut Creek Nature Preserve (30.32851, -97.64740)

Chapter 15: Onion Creek
Garison Rd., Buda (30.09429, -97.83894)
Twin Creeks Rd. (30.12665, -97.82162)
Old San Antonio Rd., Manchaca (30.13274, -97.81070)
Brandt Rd. (30.15876, -97.77584)
Onion Creek Greenbelt Park, Austin (30.17179, -97.74355)
First Trail Crossing (30.16481, -97.75131)
Second Trail Crossing (30.16691, -97.75493)
McKinney Falls State Park, Austin (30.180834, -97.721986)
Upper Falls (30.18472, -97.72582)
Richard Moya Park (30.16991, -97.66507)
Barkley Meadows Park, Del Valle (30.18653, -97.62625)
TX 71 (30.18857, -97.61829)
Spur Trail (30.18932, -97.62120)
TX 130 (30.18845, -97.62710)
Southeast Metropolitan Park (30.19440, -97.60990)

Chapter 18: Pedernales River
RM 1320 Near Hye (30.27176, -98.54561)
Pedernales Falls State Park, Johnson City (30.308043, -98.257662)
Milton Reimers Ranch Park, Dripping Springs (30.33370, -98.12231)

Chapter 19: Blanco River
Wayne Smith Lake Dam (30.10032, -98.44307)
Blanco State Park (101 Park Rd 23, Blanco, TX 78606)
G. W. Haschke Lane, Wimberley (29.990545, -98.199831)
Slime Bridge (29.96750, -98.18949)
7A Ranch, Wimberley (29.98636, -98.11048)
Old Martindale Road Crossing, San Marcos (29.871882, -97.916842)
Five Mile Dam Park Complex, San Marcos (4440 Old Stagecoach Road, Kyle, TX 78640)

Chapter 20: San Marcos River
City Park (29.88603, -97.93512)
Rio Vista Park (29.87845, -97.93393)
FM 1979 Crossing, Martindale (29.83240, -97.84235)
Allen Bates River Park (29.83717, -97.84265)
Spencer Canoes & Shady Grove Campground, Martindale (29.83019, -97.84275)
Staples Dam (29.78272, -97.83104)

Chapter 21: Guadalupe River
Guadalupe Park, Canyon Lake (29.869756, -98.196098)
Maricopa Riverside Lodge, Canyon Lake (29.86456, -98.16477)
Whitewater Sports, New Braunfels (29.86129, -98.15757)
Rio Guadalupe Resort (29.84372, -98.16888)
Lazy L&L Campground, New Braunfels (29.81800, -98.17563)
Rocky Beach (29.80294, -98.17272)
Action Angler, New Braunfels (29.80374, -98.16235)
Camp Huaco Springs (29.76037, -98.13989)

ACKNOWLEDGMENTS

ANYONE WHO WRITES ANYTHING ABOUT TEXAS RIVERS DOES SO IN THE shadow of the late John Graves and his remarkable book, *Goodbye to a River*. Published in 1960, it has never gone out of print. I first read Graves's account of that three-week canoe trip as a college student three decades ago, and it has shaped the way I think about Texas and rivers ever since.

This book would not have been possible without regular fishing partners and members of my tribe (in no particular order): Randy Easterly, Mike Barker, Cory Sorel, Matt Bennett, Merrill Robinson, Davin Topel, Edgar Diaz, Dustin Scott, Jess Alford, Brent Ormand, James Reese, Bobby Albin, Brad Boone, Hunter Barcroft, Don Walden, Ryan Gold, Mike Schlimgen, Eric Bourquin, Kevin Olivier, Ian Reddy, Blake Smith, Chris Leslie, Alana Lyons, and Jake Lyons. I'm blessed to have a lot of fishy friends; if I have missed someone, please forgive me. Thanks for going fishing with me and teaching me stuff.

John Henry Boatright not only went fishing with me and taught me stuff, he was particularly generous with his knowledge of the San Marcos and Guadalupe Rivers, which he grew up on. Likewise, John Erskine, of All Water Guides, waded, rowed, and jetted three rivers with me; he graciously shared some key insights about the Lower Colorado River that I otherwise would have missed. Chris Johnson, of Living Waters Fly Fishing, has been a font of enthusiasm and knowledge, particularly regarding Brushy Creek and the Guadalupe River and the fish that live in both streams. He's also a lot of fun on the river. My friend Donovan Kypke of ReelFly Fishing Adventures has been an enthusiastic supporter, and near the end of my work on the book saved me from making a grave error, for which I owe him another fishing trip.

My old friend, Danny Paschall, has been a companion on (sometimes instigator of) most of my significant adventures since our Army days a quarter century ago. He offered useful, early feedback on the manuscript and also accompanied me on some of my peregrinations along area streams.

Thanks to Jud Cherry for his insights on teaching kids to fly fish, and to Colin Hall for helpful information about Walnut Creek.

The good people at G&H Towing Co. (looking at you, Elaine and Bret), my employers at the tugboat day job, graciously allowed me time off to complete this manuscript (also, I may have done a little writing on the boat).

Former colleagues at TPWD, notably Tim Birdsong, Dijar Lutz-Castillo, Marcos de Jesus, Steve Magnelia, Melissa Parker, and Kelly Conrad Simon patiently answered my queries, and their knowledge informs the fish and wildlife chapters, among others. Adam E. Cohen, Melissa Casarez, Dr. Gary Garrett, and Dr. F. Douglas Martin at the University of Texas Natural History Collections were patient and helpful as I worked out my understanding of native and introduced fishes. I am grateful to T. Mark Blakemore for his helpful comments on the Texas River Law chapter.

Please assume any errors are mine, not theirs.

Stephen Garmon, a park ranger at Pedernales Falls State Park, was especially helpful in providing unpublished information about that park and the Pedernales River. Tim Speyrer and Michael Brewster at Travis County Parks likewise were patient in answering my questions about units in their system, and Chief Park Ranger Dan Chapman, also of Travis County Parks, answered my questions about paddling access on Onion Creek.

My good friend Chris Barclay gave me early, useful feedback on the manuscript. Chris also designs and builds the world's finest fiberglass fly rods, and scarcely a week goes by when I don't have one or another of his fishing poles in my hand.

Howler Brothers and Rajeff Sports (ECHO Fly Rods) offered early support, and I thank them.

Jeff Troutman, host of the *Remote. No Pressure.* podcast has been an enthusiastic supporter, and I have benefited from our continued conversations. Mike Duecy at *The Tejas Angler* podcast is a kindred spirit, and his support is deeply appreciated.

My relationship with my publisher, Mark Sedenquist, dates back well over a decade, and his exacting standards have made me a better writer and researcher. I'm grateful beyond words for the opportunity, and for the work of his outstanding team of editors, cartographers, and designers.

Thanks to my uncles: Bob Albin, for boats; Dick Hoese, for fish and science; and Elmer Joe Stacy for fishing trips, fishing tackle, and stories. Thanks to Frank and Diane (and Steven) Sbrusch for that first trip down the Guadalupe River.

My father, Bob Reed, was the first person to take me fishing, to help me turn over rocks and logs to see what lived underneath, to put a camera in my hands, and to show me that books could show me the world. My mother, Judy Reed, has been incredibly gracious in her support of this project by helping me carve out time to scout and write, picking up the slack for two busy parents, and more. I am eternally grateful to them for all of that and so much more.

My three sons—Patrick, Conor, and Aidan—have waded creeks and rivers with me, patiently endured my absences, and have, at every turn, reaffirmed the sense of wonder and beauty I first experienced as a child in the outdoors. This book and all that went into it is for them.

Finally, I literally could not have done this without the support of my wife, Carrie. A busy professional herself, she took care of the children, attended sports, school, and Scouts events on my behalf, made excuses for me when I missed gatherings of family and friends, and kept the house running. When I was ready to throw in the towel, she made me keep going. Thanks, babe. Your turn, now.

 The Cape, Guy Clark

Photo Credits

INTERIOR PHOTOS BY THE AUTHOR, EXCEPT ON THESE PAGES AS NOTED:
Jud Cherry (232, 237), Lenée Dedeaux (147, 194, 197, 302, 306), John Erskine (159, 191), Edgar Diaz (41), Randy Easterly (270), Joe Esparza (48), Chris Johnson (131,135, 154, 158, 244, 247, 252), Scott Kerrigan (193, 199), Jake Lyons (213, 214), Brendan McKirahan (292), James Reese (24), Merrill Robinson (40, 66, 68, 75, 157), Erich Schlegel (1/2 title, 23, 124), Mike Schlimgen (249, 250, 297,298, 300, 303, 304), Cory Sorel (12, 141, 142), Odum Wu (187, 189)

SOURCES AND FURTHER READING

THE BOOKS LISTED BELOW INFORMED MY OWN WORK IN ONE WAY OR another. They are all worth your time. Kevin Hutchison's expansive listing of Hill Country river access points, *Fly-Fishing the Texas Hill Country*, will guide you to even more access on an even greater number of streams, especially rivers south and west of Austin that are outside the scope of this volume. Be sure to pick up a copy at your local fly shop or order one online.

Much of my research was conducted online. I relied on the University of Texas Fishes of Texas project for authoritative information about freshwater fish species; the Texas State Historical Association's Handbook of Texas Online for background on the origin of river names and their early history; and the copious information published on the Texas Parks & Wildlife Department (TPWD) website for everything from Texas river law to fishing regulations, and more.

Books

Behnke, Robert J. *Trout and Salmon of North America.* New York: The Free Press, 2002.

Burnett, Jonathon. *Flash Floods in Texas.* College Station: Texas A&M University Press, 2008.

Crisp, Margie. *River of Contrasts: The Texas Colorado.* College Station: Texas A&M University Press, 2012.

Ferguson, Wes. *The Blanco River.* College Station: Texas A&M University Press, 2017.

Graves, John. *Goodbye to a River, a Narrative.* New York: Vintage, 2002.

Hutchison, Kevin. *Fly-Fishing the Texas Hill Country*. Smithville: Fishhead Press, 2008.

Sansom, Andrew. *Water in Texas: An Introduction*. Austin: University of Texas Press, 2008.

Shook, Phil. *Fly Fishers Guide to Texas*. Belgrade: Wilderness Adventures Press, 2008.

Sibley, David. *The Sibley Guide to Birds*. 2nd ed. New York: Alfred A. Knopf, 2014.

Online Sources

Hendrickson, Dean A., & Cohen, Adam E. (2015). Fishes of Texas Project Database (version 2.0). Texas Advanced Computing Center, University of Texas at Austin, accessed March 20, 2019, **http://www.fishesoftexas.org (http://doi.org/10.17603/C3WC70)**.

Texas Agricultural Extension Service, Texas A&M University System. "An Analysis of Texas Waterways," accessed March 20, 2019, https://tpwd.texas.gov/publications/pwdpubs/pwd_rp_t3200_1047/index.phtml.

Texas Parks and Wildlife Department, "Texas Paddling Trails," accessed March 5, 2019, **https://tpwd.texas.gov/fishboat/boat/paddlingtrails/**.

Texas Parks and Wildlife Department, "Texas River Guide," accessed April 4, 2019, **https://tpwd.texas.gov/landwater/water/habitats/rivers/**.

Texas Parks and Wildlife Department, "Outdoor Annual," accessed April 4, 2019, **https://tpwd.texas.gov/regulations/outdoor-annual/fishing/**.

Texas State Historical Association, multiple authors. "Handbook of Texas Online," accessed December 12, 2015, **http://www.tshaonline.org/handbook/online/**.

INDEX

M